Scarecrow Film Score Guides
Series Editor: Kate Daubney

D1282284

Nino Rota's
The Godfather Trilogy

A Film Score Guide

Franco Sciannameo

Scarecrow Film Score Guides, No. 9

The Scarecrow Press, Inc.
Lanham, Maryland • Toronto • Plymouth, UK
2010

SCARECROW PRESS, INC.

Published in the United States of America
by Scarecrow Press, Inc.
A wholly owned subsidiary of
The Rowman & Littlefield Publishing Group, Inc.
4501 Forbes Boulevard, Suite 200, Lanham, Maryland 20706
www.scarecrowpress.com

Estover Road
Plymouth PL6 7PY
United Kingdom

British Library Cataloguing in Publication Information Available

Library of Congress Cataloging-in-Publication Data
Sciannameo, Franco.
 Nino Rota's the Godfather trilogy : a film score guide / Franco Sciannameo.
  p. cm. — (Scarecrow film score guides ; v. no. 9)
 Includes bibliographical references and index.
 ISBN 978-0-8108-7711-5 (pbk. : alk. paper)
 1. Rota, Nino, 1911–1979. Motion picture music. 2. Motion picture music–
History and criticism. 3. Godfather (Motion picture) 4. Godfather, part II
(Motion picture) 5. Godfather, part III (Motion picture) I. Title. II. Title:
Godfather trilogy.
 ML410.R82S355 2010
 781.5'42–dc22   2010018177

In loving memory of my sister
Luciana Sciannameo

Contents

Musical Examples

Editor's Foreword

Since I established the concept of the film score guides in 1999 and wrote the first volume on Max Steiner's *Now, Voyager* score (in the series' initial incarnation with Greenwood Press), film musicology has continued to undergo rapid expansion and change. While ten years ago, the notion of score-focussed scholarship seemed an obvious way to consolidate just one area in a rapidly diverging field, such is the diversity of film music composition practice now that the focus on the score as a textual origin is at times anachronistic and outdated, as perhaps is the implication that techniques of film scoring are distinct from techniques used for composing soundscapes for other multi-media forms, such as computer games and other web-based creativity. The prevalence of the temp track, the influence of computer and electronic composition techniques, and the trend towards director's cuts in DVD release will all need to be reflected in the way this series evolves and the high level of analysis and reading its authors bring to bear on the music they reveal to us. These are the challenges for any academic discipline, to chart and understand the dynamic leading edge of a field while ensuring that its foundations have been soundly explored. Film musicology has, in most respects, managed to achieve this balance very well through the appearance of new journals, a significant increase in conference activity, and a broader recognition by mainstream musicology and film studies of areas of mutual interest.

The contribution of the Scarecrow series of Film Score Guides is to draw together the variety of analytical practices and ideological approaches in film musicology for the purpose of studying individual scores. Much value has been drawn from case studies of film scoring practice in other film music texts, but these guides offer a substantial, wide-ranging, and comprehensive study of a single score. Subjects are chosen for the series on the basis that they have become and are widely recognized as a benchmark for the way in which film music is composed and experienced, or because they represent a significant stage in the compositional development of an individual film composer. A guide explores the context of a score's composition through its place in the career of the composer and its relationship to the techniques of the composer. The context of the score in narrative and production terms is also considered, and readings of the film as a whole are discussed in order to situate in their filmic context the musical analyses which conclude the guide. Furthermore, although these guides focus on the score as written text, bringing forward often previously unknown details about the process of composition as they are manifested in the manuscript, analysis also includes exploration of the music as an aural text, for this is the first and, for most audiences, the only way in which they will experience the music of the film. The scores of *The Godfather Trilogy* are paramount examples of this latter principle, offering as they do the aural equivalent of iconic visual moments for which the first film in particular is so renowned.

This volume on *The Godfather Trilogy* shows another significant development in film musicology, the drawing together in analysis of more than one film in a non-linear, cross-textual approach. The opportunity to analyze trilogies is both enthralling and overwhelming to the film musicologist, for while there is generally unprecedented scope for seeing how a composer works and reworks limited material over a far larger scale than a single film permits, it can be a logistical and conceptual problem to impose scholarly uniformity over material that might have been composed over many years. Where no uniformity exists, where personalities and circumstances, even additional composers, have disrupted the homogeneity, what can we learn about how context imposes itself on the score?

These are just a few of the challenges facing Dr. Sciannameo in his analysis of the music for these most famous of films, for the other great burden is to impose any kind of reading at all on a soundtrack which is so distinctive in the film music repertoire, not to mention the global soundscape. The substantial proportion of previously composed music which emerges during the films, in addition to the culturally distinctive original material, brings multiple frames of reference to both audience and scholar, while the films' other narrative components draw on complex models which are both finite in their specificity and universal in their appeal. Professor Sciannameo has endeavored to unpack these distinct functions of Italianness and Italianicity in such a way that they can inform our reading of the music too, thus indicating how the soundtrack can be both separated and inextricably repackaged within the film for our understanding. Nonetheless, however intricate and multiple the possible readings are, the soundtrack speaks so directly to the films' content that readers of this volume, whatever their level of musical knowledge, should find much that will illuminate their enjoyment of this extraordinary trilogy.

Dr. Kate Daubney
Series Editor

Acknowledgements

This work could not have been completed without the assistance of many. I wish to thank Kate Daubney, series editor of the Scarecrow Film Score Guides for her continuous support throughout this project's evolution, her acute vigilance upon contextual matters, and her love for making everything fit right. I express thanks to Jeannie Pool, colleague, musicologist, and composer who has been extremely helpful in providing me with access to the Paramount music archives, now sealed and stored off-site, and introducing me to the office of Marty Olinick, director of Paramount Music. I salute Nina Rota, the composer's daughter, who over the years has offered me a benevolent nod to several Rota projects I have been engaged with, and Francesco Lombardi, a member of the Rota family and curator of the Archivio Nino Rota (ANR) at the Fondazione Giorgio Cini in Venice. Dr. Lombardi has given generously of his time in Venice and in other parts of the world where we have had a chance to meet. I thank Tegan Kossowicz and Larissa Caschera at Famous Music Corporation for expediting the process of securing permission to quote Rota's musical examples. A heartfelt thank-you goes to my wife, Louise Cavanaugh Sciannameo, for a first reading of this manuscript. Likewise, I thank our son Nicholas Sciannameo for his support and ever-present technical expertise. I thank my film music students at Carnegie Mellon for many animated discussions about the trilogy and Nathan Hall in particular for expertly setting the musical examples and formatting this book. Ultimately, I thank my late sister Luciana Sciannameo, who did not live to see this book in print but who heard so much about it over hours of transatlantic telephone conversations. To her memory this book is dedicated.

Introduction

The music is used for imaginative reminiscences,
and almost always in some climactic context.

—Joseph Kerman[1]

The scope of this volume reflects my desire to re-introduce critics, film musicologists, cinemagoers, and fans of Francis Ford Coppola's cinema and Nino Rota's music to the events that led to the realization of the three films that comprise *The Godfather Trilogy*, and to comment on their musical and cultural significance. Released in 1972, 1974, and 1990, respectively, Coppola's three-part saga constitutes one of the greatest artistic accomplishments and financial successes in the history of Hollywood cinema.

Coppola's trilogy provides a sensitive, as well as a detailed look at an entire segment of American life vis-à-vis the Italian Diaspora by portraying two concurrent cultures over the course of most of the twentieth century.

Through analytical observations about the form and significance of Coppola and Rota's achievements, this book discusses how a filmmaker and a composer worked to revise the conventions of the American crime film in light of the Vietnam era while offering a critique of capitalism as represented by the criminal underworld, its inherent violence, and the struggle occurring among Hollywood's power brokers over the making of the film. Ultimately, elements of opera add considerably to the impact and cinematic style of Coppola's epic vision of an Italian-American criminal dynasty.

The Godfather Trilogy is a 545-minute film consisting of 76 tales spanning the gamut of the literary genre from classical to modern mythologies that revisit a great many familiar cinematic typologies, such as early gangster pictures, film noir, and spectacular epic. This trilogy is lushly enhanced by a music soundtrack that stretches over three hours: 77:70 minutes of music composed by Nino Rota; 52:43 minutes composed by Carmine Coppola; and 50:19 minutes of source music specifically arranged for the film. The latter category incorporates a large portion drawn from Mascagni's opera *Cavalleria rusticana* used in the conclusion of Part III.

Rota composed the original scores for Parts I and II, while Carmine Coppola wrote the music for all the incidental cues and the original score to Part III, which includes the re-use of some of Rota's newly recorded cues. Although Rota and Carmine Coppola shared an Oscar for Part II (Best Original Score, 1974), I do not consider them as the co-authors of the trilogy's music soundtrack insomuch as stylistic and qualitative differences marking the two composers' works are too disparate to warrant a comparison. Each man's *raison d'ècrire* was to "underscore" the concepts of *Italianness* (Rota) and *Italianicity* (Coppola), a quasi-leitmotiv whose significance I stress and explain throughout this volume. This said, I want to reiterate that this book is about Nino Rota's music and his interpretation in musical and psychological terms of the layers of narrative present in Parts I and II. Therefore, a detailed analysis of Carmine Coppola's contribution to *The Godfather Trilogy* may be the topic for another study.

A major undertaking in writing this book consisted in devising a strategy that enabled me to integrate 212 music cues into a compact format suitable for scholarly analysis while keeping alive the essence of what Joseph Kerman termed "imaginative reminiscences." Having discarded a detailed genetic analysis of each cue, I opted for presenting the reader with an anthology of selected tales in the guise of scenes from a hypothetical operatic palimpsest entitled "The Sound of *The Godfather Trilogy*" while the appendix that follows constitutes a comprehensive cue-by-cue musical guide designed to help the reader navigate the musical text of this complex cinematic œuvre.

I conducted research at two archives: (1) Cosby Music Building at Paramount Studios in Hollywood, which preserves the original scores and parts used to record the trilogy's music soundtrack, and (2) Fondazione Giorgio Cini in Venice where the Archivio Nino Rota (ANR) is housed. Rota's manuscripts and notebooks pertaining to the music written for Parts I and II offered me the opportunity to establish genetic itineraries traceable in the composer's first impressions upon viewing the film, his spotting notes, musical sketches (avant-texts) and finally the complete cues (Urtexts) which often differ substantially from what one hears on the actual soundtrack. Fortunately, some of these Urtext cues were recorded and commercially released on disc, so reconstructions can be executed if only for analytical purposes. In this book I offer several examples of genetic criticism applied to some of Rota's cues composed for Part I and II.

Chapter 1 probes Rota's formation as a musician amidst the cultural climate established by Italian Fascism. In this chapter I examine the composer's initial stylistic adherence to the Mussolini-dictated or inspired concept of *Italianness*, and I then focus on Rota's return to a more congenial nineteenth-century formulaic vocabulary. The composer regarded modernistic attempts to reform the musical language not so much as an evolutionary process but as a series of aesthetical and technical problems in need of solutions. Therefore, for Rota, composing for motion pictures became the practice of an ongoing laboratory dedicated to solving particular musical problems applied to the cinematic text. As a consequence, Rota stressed by example the notion that there was no difference between high- and lowbrow music. Problem-solving implied that music was at liberty to morph from one genre to another without encountering aesthetical barriers. I invite scholars interested in Rota's aesthetical yet practical views to compare the scores of his works listed in two essential volumes—*La filmografia di Nino Rota*, a cura di Fabrizio Borin (Archivio Nino Rota, Studi I–Firenze: Olschki, 1999) and *Catalogo critico delle composizioni da concerto, da camera e delle musiche per il teatro*, a cura di Francesco Lombardi (Archivio Nino Rota, Studi IV–Firenze: Olschki, 2009)—in order to appreciate the protean itinerary of Rota's music.

Chapter 2 is dedicated to Rota's involvement with cinema and his collaboration with many celebrated directors. As a master at problem solving, Rota showed a tremendous sense of adaptability in conforming to the musical visions of personalities as diverse as those of Visconti, Fellini, De Filippo, Zeffirelli, and Coppola among others. Rota's name is now indelibly engraved in the film music pantheon, and the scores he wrote for *Il gattopardo*, *La dolce vita*, *Otto e mezzo*, *Napoli milionaria*, *Romeo and Juliet*, and *The Godfather* have become "exemplars" for any composer wishing to enter the highly competitive field of composing for the movies. Rota wrote no treatises on the subject, he had no direct pupils, and he offered laconic statements about his art in sparse interviews. His ability resided in pure intuition supported by an enormous amount of practice gained through the creation of more than 145 film scores. In Visconti and De Filippo, Rota found two intellectuals gifted with a formidable sense of theater that blended unique musical sensibility and knowledge. In Fellini he found a "magical" friend whose relationship went far beyond professionalism as they traveled into the realm of occult studies, a great passion of Rota's. Zeffirelli offered him the diversion to compose at the whims of a capricious yet genius-like artist for whom Rota had a great deal of affection. Finally, the celebrated composer detected in the young Coppola extraordinary creative gifts, which he deemed worth cultivating despite the web of political intrigues which dominated Paramount Pictures in the late 1960s.

Chapter 3 deals with the sensitive issues of cultural analysis vis-à-vis the Mafia as a concept embedded within the Italian-American community and the perception, by most American people, that every Italian-American was tainted by. It is my hope that I have been able to convey to the reader the urgencies pervading this chapter's overtones; immigration, integrated citizenship, and the defense mechanisms Italian-Americans had to put into place to protect their atavistic culture. I believe that these are fundamental notions necessary for a proper understanding of the chapters to follow.

"The Sound of *The Godfather Trilogy*" (Chapters 4 and 5) constitutes the core of this book. In it I research the film's musical subtexts underscoring a group of pivotal scenes. This lengthy section is divided into three subchapters dealing with what I call "choral family scenes and tales of love and death." In describing and analyzing these scenes, I rely substantially on the notes Rota jotted down in the course of various spotting sessions. Discussed here for the first time, Rota's notes reveal the composer's interpretation of Coppola's cinematic narrative and the scoring methodologies he employed—or intended to employ—in order to enrich such narrative. An appendix, a cue-by-cue reconstruction of the entire trilogy's music soundtrack, supports these two chapters. This appendix is not only a vital instrument that sustains the whole nomenclature of Chapters 4 and 5 but it will serve as the essential platform for launching further studies on the music in *The Godfather Trilogy*.

NB: Translations from the Italian set in italics are by the author.

Chapter 1

Nino Rota at the Heart of the *Novecento*: A Problem Solved

*I saw that defenseless, kind, smiling little man, always trying to make
an exit through doors that did not exist; he could have made an exit
through a window like a butterfly wrapped up in a
magical, unreal cloud.*

—Federico Fellini

It should not surprise anyone that a book about Nino Rota's film music
begins with a quote by Federico Fellini. Rota is known as the musician
who wrote those wonderful, life-as-a-circus, heartbreaking tunes for *La
strada* (1954), *La dolce vita* (1959), *Otto e mezzo* (1963), and *Amarcord* (1973). I am even tempted to think of Rota as a character belonging to Fellini's imagination—a little man with a big head and short legs
playing the piano or waving a baton in front of an invisible orchestra
from a podium too large for his small figure. Fellini's prodigious
sketch-books, authentic (pre)texts to his surreal characters and stories,
contain several caricature drawings of Nino Rota resembling Schroeder
in the "Peanuts" comic strip.[1] Fellini had genuine affection for Rota
and his music; he thought of him as a magical friend. However,
Fellini's omnivorous personality dwarfed that of the excessively timid
Rota who, ironically, to this day continues to receive individual attention by virtue of having played a secondary role in the great director's
life and career. Rota was a composer, who while holding his ground
solidly in the Italian musical establishment, was regarded as inconse-
quential by the exponents of the avant-garde. In this chapter I will
demonstrate how Rota turned his traditionally organic musical roots
into creative originality and how he considered composing as a series
of problems in need of resolutions. A review of Rota's upbringing in
the sociopolitical climate that characterized Italy between the wars of
1915–1918 and 1942–1945 will serve as a palimpsest to my narrative.
　　Giovanni (Nino) Rota was born in Milan in 1911 to a musical, af-
fluent family. Ernesta, Nino's mother, was a pianist pupil of her father
Giovanni Rinaldi, a noted piano teacher/composer who wrote exclusively for his instrument in styles inspired by the works of Chopin, De-
bussy, and early Scriabin.[2] The Rinaldis and the Rotas did not cultivate

1

Italian operatic music, perhaps revealing their elitist yet provincial stance toward what they perceived as "common" musical taste. Young Nino's music instruction then took place at the Rotas' Milanese home and in Arturo Toscanini's house where Giovanni Perlasca imparted bi-weekly theory and *solfège* lessons to a group of privileged youngsters, including Wanda Toscanini (Arturo's daughter and future wife of pianist Vladimir Horowitz). Perlasca had invented a mechanical, interactive, game-like system for teaching successfully the rudiments of music to children. It seemed that his method had met with Toscanini's approval.

In the aftermath of the Great War, Milan had become the political and cultural heart of Italy; institutions like the Conservatorio, Teatro alla Scala, Casa Ricordi, the Futurist movement, the rise of Fascism, and the development of *Novecento* made the northern Italian metropolis the place where things happened. *Novecento*, literally meaning 900, was an elegant euphemism addressing a 20th-century art movement characterized by severity, formal asceticism, and neo-*Renaissance* qualities. It was the brainchild of Margherita Sarfatti, a formidable art critic, collector, connoisseur, and Benito Mussolini's mistress and cultural mentor.[3] Thus, I would say that Sarfatti's *Novecento* and Mussolini's *Fascismo* arose simultaneously to conjoin as one movement, aspiring to become complementary to each other if similarity of ideologies between art and politics were ever possible. The *Novecento*'s principal exponents included painters Mario Sironi and Achille Funi[4] who, spurred by Sarfatti, sought throughout the 1920s and early 1930s to revitalize Western art's classical traditions with modernist pictorial inventions. They invited Italian artists of diverse schools into the movement with the purpose of establishing a united front aligned with Mussolini's political quest for combining tradition and modernity. However, the debate over the *Novecento*'s validity raged on for almost a decade as Fascists, whose views became increasingly divided between progressive and conservative, argued endlessly about the merits of traditional versus modern styles in the fine arts, architecture, music, and literature as well as political ideologies. Mussolini, no doubt influenced by Sarfatti and by other strong personalities like the poets Gabriele D'Annunzio and Filippo Tommaso Marinetti,[5] often championed modernism by getting personally involved in the realization of the "Exhibition of the Fascist Revolution's Decennial" in 1932, Giovanni Michelucci's designs for the *Santa Maria Novella* railroad station in Florence, and the Florence and Venice International Festivals of Contemporary Music among other important artistic events.

Although Mussolini offered the *Novecento* movement his personal prestige by inaugurating its initial exhibitions in 1923 and in 1926, he never recognized it as the regime's official artistic expression though Sarfatti had wished him to do so. Thus, throughout the Fascist period (1922–1944), currents and styles as diverse as *Pittura Metafisica* (Giorgio De Chirico), *Novecento* (Mario Sironi and Achille Funi), *Scuola Romana* (Giacomo Balla and Renato Guttuso), *Aeropittura* (Marinetti, Balla, and Enrico Prampolini), and the abstract sculptures of Lucio Fontana were allowed to co-exist in open competition for Il Duce's approval and financial support.

Italian music during the 1920s and 1930s has been examined at various levels reaching conclusions similar to those concerning the plastic and figurative arts, architecture, and literature with the difference that musicians are the bearers of a universal language that allows them to pitch their tent wherever the pasture is greener. Hence, nationalistic side taking, proclaimed artistic creeds, and other creative restrictions are often overlooked by the genuine artist. During Fascism, some musicians moved away for racial reasons like the Jews Mario Castelnuovo-Tedesco, Vittorio Rieti, Renzo Massarani, and the great Arturo Toscanini,[6] who, although not a Jew and maybe because of his own dictatorial character, never approved of Mussolini in the first place. Others remained in Italy playing by the rules of the game. They included Ildebrando Pizzetti, Gian Francesco Malipiero, Alfredo Casella, and Ottorino Respighi—a group known as *La generazione dell'ottanta* (members of the generation born around 1880).[7]

Highly intellectual Pizzetti and Malipiero gave dignity to the new political ideology. By contrast, Pietro Mascagni, the celebrated composer of *Cavalleria rusticana*,[8] behaved like a petulant Fascist who blatantly sided with Mussolini while asking for privileges as though he were the only Italian composer deserving attention. Other musical celebrities, like Giacomo Puccini—during the last two years of his life[9]— and Respighi, surfed the new sociopolitical wave, accepting honors and enjoying the privileges.

The Fascist period provided also a great opportunity for the so-called *compositori di regime*, utilitarian musicians who sought career advancement through political maneuvers. Chronicles of the time report hundreds of names of composers, practitioners, and impresarios who embraced the regime's rules as their artistic creed, swimming in a sea of intrigue, subterfuge, and ambiguity. Many composers wrote hundreds of forgettable works hailing Mussolini's utterances.[10]

In sum, Respighi, Casella, Pizzetti, and Malipiero's polyphonic so-
lidity, clarity of forms, simplicity for melodic lines, rhythmic vivacity,
architectural balance, plasticity, and objectivity contributed to restore a
balance between tradition and modernity in the name of a newly found
Latin and Mediterranean spirit encapsulated in the words *Italianità*
(Italianness) and *Romanità* (Romanness). These musicians became the
pillars of what I would call the Italian musical *Novecento*, and their
activities as composers, critics, performers, and world ambassadors of
Italian music and culture counterbalanced the popular vogue of operatic
verismo reflected mainly in the works of Pietro Mascagni, Ruggero
Leoncavallo, Giacomo Puccini, and Umberto Giordano.[11] Such a musical potboiler stirred at will by the puppeteers of Benito Mussolini's
cultural and political nationalistic ideologies generated a complex maze
of styles, currents, and counter-currents through which young composers like Rota, Goffredo Petrassi, and Luigi Dallapiccola had to find
their own voice.

Given such a landscape I want to explore the formation of a teenaged musician like Nino Rota as well as to single out some of the people who strongly influenced the process, including Margherita Sarfatti
accompanied by her vast coterie of artists, writers, intellectuals, and
even Benito Mussolini who showed pleasure in meeting the young man
in a rare one-on-one encounter.[12]

Deeply anchored in the 19th-century's musical tradition, a pupil of
Pizzetti and Casella, Rota absorbed the 1930s fashionable concept of
Italianness as his way to embrace modernity. The works he composed
during the 1920s and 1930s express the feeling of Italianness filtered
through the tenets established by the Pizzetti–Malipiero–Casella–
Respighi Quadrunvirate and Sarfatti's interdisciplinary *Novecento*
movement. Therefore, the severity, formal asceticism, and neo-
Renaissance qualities associated with the *Novecento* were transformed
by Rota into clarity of melodic, harmonic, and rhythmic language displayed within rigorous formal structures that distinguished his works
from those of *La generazione dell'ottanta* and from the dense neo-
baroque and neo-classical works of his contemporaries Petrassi and
Dallapiccola as well. They, like the majority of Italian composers, writers, artists, and architects of the period strove to achieve an acceptable
stylistic representation of Mussolini's nationalistic cultic game.[13]

At the age of eight Rota composed several songs for voice and piano dedicated to noted vocalist Anna Maria Rota,[14] and *Il mago doppio*,
a suite for piano four-hands written as a commentary to a fable of his

own invention, a piece which prognosticated Rota's propensity to explore the narrative potential of music.

Shortly after Rota completed the score of the oratorio *L'infanzia di San Giovanni Battista* for vocal soloists, chorus, and orchestra, it was performed first in Milan on April 22, 1923, and then in Turcoing, France, to great acclaim. He was hailed by the local press as the "new Mozart," and news of the event accompanied by a photo of the wunderkind even reached the pages of the *New York Times* (October 21, 1923).

From 1924 to 1926, Rota studied composition privately with Ildebrando Pizzetti, who was then director of the Milan Conservatory. During this period, Rota composed his first opera, *Il principe porcaro* (*The Swineherd Prince*), after Hans Christian Andersen, and a *Concerto* for cello and orchestra (1925).[15] Following a disagreement with Pizzetti, who wished his pupil, and probably Signora Rota, to refrain from having Nino's student works publicly performed and, above all, published, the Rotas sought new teachers. At first they thought of Charles Koechlin, but then the choice became Maurice Ravel who, at that time, was on a concert tour of Italy.[16] However, after having examined Nino's works, Ravel decided not to take him on as a pupil.[17] In the meantime, Rota kept his pen moving under the tutelage of Mario Castelnuovo-Tedesco, another Pizzetti pupil who, having emigrated to the United States in 1938, established himself in Hollywood as a sought-after film composer and teacher; Henry Mancini, Jerry Goldsmith, Nelson Riddle, André Previn, and John Williams were among his pupils.[18]

In 1927, Rota moved to Rome to study with Alfredo Casella. The most open-minded and cosmopolitan Italian musician of the period, Casella made sure Rota was exposed to new musical trends. From Rome, Casella maintained contact with the most important musicians in the world, allowing Rota many opportunities to meet the finest composers, from Manuel De Falla to Igor Stravinsky. With the latter, Rota began a friendship which lasted a lifetime.[19]

In 1930, after three years of intense study, Rota took the Diploma in Composition examination at the "Santa Cecilia" Conservatory in Rome: Casella insisted that the young composer have his "papers" in order.[20] Thereafter, Arturo Toscanini, a longtime friend of the Rinaldi and Rota families, arranged for Rota to study at the Curtis Institute of Music in Philadelphia[21]; 1931 and 1932 were spent at Curtis. Rota studied composition with Rosario Scalero[22] and conducting with Fritz Reiner. It seems that Toscanini disliked the fact that, in Rome, Rota was under what he described as Casella's "arid and cerebral" influence.[23] At Curtis, Rota had among his classmates Samuel Barber and

Milanese childhood friend Gian Carlo Menotti; Rota, Barber, and
Menotti were invited to contribute some short works for the Curtis Carillon Series published by Schirmer in 1934. Rota's contributing pieces
were entitled *Campane a sera* and *Campane a festa*.[24]

When Rota returned to Italy from Philadelphia, he was already a
mature composer equipped with an eclectic musical background. In
Italy he probed the fields of popular music, commercial song, and operetta, absorbing styles and idioms, which soon were put to practical use.
In 1933, he had the opportunity to write his first soundtrack for *Treno
popolare*, a film by debutante director Raffaello Matarazzo.[25] This film,
whose title could be translated as "A Train for the People or Popular
Trains" presented a series of entertaining vignettes aboard a train carrying members of the Italian working class on a short, state-sponsored
summer vacation trip from Rome to Orvieto in the countryside. The
film, inspired by the social realism of earlier Russian filmmakers' "direct cinema," reflected a key element in Mussolini's proletarian new
plan to gain consensus among the masses. In fact, *Il Duce* wished to
promote a kind of lowbrow culture based on standardized forms of lei-
sure and diversion through the novel propagandistic means of cinema.[26]

The music track of Rota's first film consisted of very simple songs
and little marches written in a style very much in tune with the political
and social climate portrayed in the film. *Treno popolare* was not a success, however Rota's songs were subsequently published "in folio,"
recorded, and radio broadcast, thus contributing to Rota's sudden popularity.

It must be pointed out at this juncture that with the increasing
availability of radio receivers in lower- to middle-class households,
Italian music preferences shifted considerably from opera to popular
music. This trend offered national notoriety to musicians who would
have been otherwise relegated to the localized fame of live performances. The musical intelligentsia, though, regarded writing a song and
profiting monetarily from it as something beneath the mission of an
academically trained composer. Therefore, Rota's early successes in
the burgeoning field of radio songs lowered his standard in the eyes of
many among his colleagues who began to question his artistic integrity
or their own inability to write a good tune.

Beginning with *Treno popolare*, Rota, instead of leading the "double life" typical of the film composer with concert and/or operatic music aspirations, carried on his workload with tenacious professionalism.
In fact, he entered a new phase of activity: teaching. In 1937 Rota was
appointed to teach just about everything at the *Liceo Musicale* in Tar-

anto, the ancient city of Tarentum on the Ionian Sea in Apulia, perhaps once historically important but certainly not in the mainstream of musical events. According to Rota himself, the two Taranto years (1937–1938) were a miserable experience during which he almost ceased composing.[27] Soon, however, Rota was in Bari, an important city on the Southern Adriatic shore of Apulia, as professor of harmony and counterpoint at the local Liceo Musicale. The year was 1939. Ten years later, he became the much loved director of that institution which, in 1959, was elevated to the rank of State Conservatory, the Conservatorio "Niccolò Piccinni." Rota kept both his position and residence in Bari until retirement in 1977.[28]

Cinema made a call to Rota again in 1942, with a new film by Matarazzo, *Giorno di nozze* (Wedding Day), a sentimental comedy of mistaken identities stitched together by Rota's lighthearted songs which, in those days, were welcome as a much needed panacea for a brewing war closing in on the lives of the Italian and indeed European people. *Giorno di nozze* was a decent box office success that solidified the composer's presence in film music for a lifetime. I will return to Rota's career as a film composer in Chapter 2.

Rota and his mother Ernesta spent the 1940–1950 decade in Torre a Mare, a fishing village eleven kilometers south of Bari along the Adriatic Sea. This village, now a thriving seaside resort, is also my hometown. It was there that many families sheltered themselves from the calamities of the war while anxiously awaiting for its cessation. Torre a Mare became a sort of communal fairyland where meals were shared, stories were told, and many movies were watched while music and war bulletins were heard through the static of radio speakers. As a young boy, I remember Signora Rota-Rinaldi crossing Torre a Mare's piazza like an exiled queen followed by young maestro Nino. They lived in a house not far from ours and in the summer months I could hear Rota playing his (perennially out-of-tune, I was told) upright piano. It was in Torre a Mare, during the war years, that Nino Rota composed *Il cappello di paglia di Firenze*, a sentimental/comic opera that was represented ten years later in April 1955 at the *Teatro Massimo* in Palermo. The immediate appeal of this opera upon a libretto by Ernesta Rota-Rinaldi based on Eugene Labiche's play was reconfirmed by a memorable production at the *Piccola Scala* in Milan under the direction of Giorgio Strehler.[29] The year was 1958. The opera made the rounds of the major opera houses and the success of Rota's music was something of a shock to some Italian critics who wished to relegate Rota to film scoring. They viewed *Il cappello di paglia di Firenze* as a scornful gesture to any form of musical progressivism. See, for instance, the opening measures of the Overture:

Ex. 1.1. Overture from *Il cappello di paglia di Firenze.*

Instead, the musician proved to be organic and faithful to his artistic *credo* by fusing much of his pre-existing film music into an opera which is a masterpiece of musical nostalgia filled with refreshing arias, *concertati*, and recitatives woven in a pleasant, graceful, and vivaciously comic musical context echoing or parodying 18th-century *opera buffa*, Viennese operetta, and Parisian *vaudeville*. On the other hand, *Il cappello di paglia di Firenze* can be viewed as a *pasticcio*, a *Divertissement*, or even a private musical game Ernesta and Nino Rota engaged themselves with during the war years, a time when looking back at Rossini and Offenbach offered them relief from a precarious present and an uncertain future. But, how does one justify Strehler's revival of the opera at La Scala in 1958, a time when conservatism, a prerogative of the political Right, was viewed by the Left as a euphemism for dilettantism? One wonders what the significance of representing a contemporary opera "in C major" could have been when a composer like Luigi Nono was asserting himself as a strong cultural exponent of the Italian Communist Party while Luciano Berio and Bruno Maderna were creating a thriving electronic music studio in Milan.[30] Having said this, I believe that it is unfair to politicize Rota's music and make the composer appear indifferent to the problems of the time. The fact is that Rota did not need to search for "new" musical languages; his was a music "without a crisis" which he nourished with optimism, thus *Il cappello di paglia di Firenze* was, according to Rota, a problem solved, a successful manifestation of musical happiness. Prior to *Il cappello di paglia di Firenze* Rota had written two operas of large proportions, *Ariodante* (1938–1941) and *Torquemada* (1943), both strange dramatic works composed in 19th-century Italian operatic style—the very style that was "not cultivated" in his grandfather's and parents' households. Before a cheerful audience and dismayed critics, *Ariodante* was premiered in Parma on November 22, 1942, as part of the festival Teatro delle Novitá di Bergamo. *Torquemada* was never performed. Of these two operas, Dinko Fabris wrote, "Rota reacted to the tragic war years ravaging Italy by following two antithetical paths; escaping into Ariosto's dream world with *Ariodante* and plunging into the suffocating oppression of the Inquisition with *Torquemada.*"[31]

During this period, Rota composed several other works, including a *Concerto* for harp and orchestra (1943), another *Sonata* for viola (or clarinet) and piano (1945) *Sinfonia sopra una canzone d'amore* (1947), the radio opera *I due timidi* (1950), and *Variazioni sopra un tema gioviale* for orchestra (1953).[32]

I due timidi (The Two Shy People) is a chamber one-act opera for radio created by Suso Cecchi D'Amico and Nino Rota in 1949–1950. Although Rota had no direct experience with radio drama productions like Bernard Herrmann for example,[33] he did participate successfully in the 1932 competition for Radio Music promoted by the Second International Festival of Contemporary Music in Venice. This idea of music to be "heard" through the sound waves and not seen performed in concert aimed to introduce sound technology as a necessary element in a new way to listen to music and to perform it. Rota's entry entitled *Balli* for small orchestra did not win the competition, however it received an honorable mention and has remained the only surviving work of the group.[34]

In 1950 RAI (Radio Audizioni Italiane), the state-controlled radio broadcast system, counted 4.5 million listeners, the equivalent of 101 per 1000 residents.[35] Programs were broadcast by three networks each catering to a social/cultural stratum of the population. Terzo Programma (RAI's third network) was devoted to classical music, literary and artistic debates, and theatre, and it served the needs of approximately 20 percent of radio users. A relatively small audience then appreciated radio dramas as well as operas expressly conceived for the medium. On the other hand, the more popular networks 1 and 2 emanated traditional opera broadcast. Therefore, the opportunity to compose an opera for radio presented Rota with another problem in search of solution: writing music for an opera to be solely heard and imagined by employing a familiar musical vocabulary.[36] Notwithstanding the numerous reminiscences from Puccini's *La bohème* and *Gianni Schicchi*,[37] *I due timidi* is a delightful example of a soundtrack for cinema of the mind, a radio phonic success, a problem solved. It was unfortunately obliterated in 1952 by re-proposing the opera in a theatrical version, thus defeating the purpose of its very conception.

During the period 1973–1977, Rota composed his last opera, *Napoli milionaria*, upon a libretto written by Eduardo De Filippo (1900–

1984) after the homonymous play and film by the same author. This opera, still unpublished, was performed only once on June 22, 1977, at the Spoleto XX Festival dei Due Mondi and broadcast "live" by the Eurovision television network. Like *Il cappello di paglia di Firenze* (1944–1956) twenty years earlier, Rota looked at *Napoli milionaria* as an opportunity to take stock of his most memorable works to date. This opera contains an avalanche of quotations derived from the music tracks of the films *Napoli milionaria, Le notti di Cabiria, Toby Dammit, Plein Soleil, Le tentazioni del dottor Antonio, La dolce vita, Rocco e i suoi fratelli,* and *Waterloo.* Following the opera's première, critics from both sides of the Italian cultural–political debate remained deeply perplexed about its artistic values. Favorably inclined critic Paolo Isotta, for instance, after prefacing his critique with admiration for the composer, wrote that the opera was indeed a monumental failure, unable to reflect De Filippo's Neapolitan spirit for the simple reason that the great actor/playwright was not starring in it and therefore, in *Napoli milionaria* the opera, mere words crammed together in a libretto set to music aimed mostly at being functional were a big disappointment.[38] Furthermore, critic Luigi Pestalozza did not hesitate to classify Nino Rota and Gian Carlo Menotti's entire operatic Spoleto entourage as a bunch of mercenaries who had reduced De Filippo's populist theatre to a sort of musical comic book in which a heavy dose of Puccini's and Mascagni's music was dished out to the audience by an astute "illustrator" [Rota] well-versed in the art of exploiting the commonplace and the banal.[39] Aside from Pestalozza's evident disdain for the art of film music as practiced by Rota, it should not come as a surprise that this critic's Marxist critique was adamantly positioned against the Menotti's Spoleto Festival viewed as just another dreaded American capitalist cultural invasion. In my opinion, Pestalozza failed to appreciate Rota's uniquely populist approach to a form of opera theatre which, through De Filippo and perhaps Dario Fo, wished to pay homage to the Brecht–Weill theatre so akin to Pestalozza's thinking. *Napoli milionaria* should be viewed as an Italian-Neapolitan folk-opera in the Gramscian sense, that is to say a work whose music identifies its characters as a people and as an abstract representation of their social organization through familiar sounds and melodies embedded with communal values. From such a point of view Rota's *Napoli milionaria* was not a failure but a problem solved!

    In conclusion, it is worth considering a few of Rota's statements about contemporary music he cared to make public in the course of an interview granted to Leonardo Pinzauti in 1971.[40] Rota said that modern music had become too cerebral, that it no longer communicated something that people could understand. Karlheinz Stockhausen's declaration that the interest of music rested in discovery and invention, that the musician had become a biologist considering music as a new science . . . gave him the impression that Stockhausen was indeed referring to phenomena caused by lack of philosophical preparation, by improper use of concepts or wrong concepts all together. However, Rota acknowledged that Stockhausen's world was an important reality deserving an analysis of the cultural context in which it thrived. Similarly, Rota discussed Arnold Schoenberg, whose *Pierrot Lunaire* he considered "an experiment in coloration, a problem solved," adding that although he admired Schoenberg the man he found him uninteresting as a composer. The latter statement is intriguing in light of fact that Alfredo Casella, Rota's most influential teacher, was responsible for bringing Schoenberg and his "Pierrot Ensemble" on a tour of Italy's major musical centers in 1924.[41] Casella, always a staunch supporter of the Second Viennese School, passed along to his students an appreciation for the music of Schoenberg, Berg, and Webern. Regarding *Pierrot Lunaire* Casella stated,

> It is indeed a masterwork and not an experiment that generates more or less happy results. The work possesses all the characteristics of a masterpiece: perfect eurhythmic relations between the means employed and the obtained final result. Further, it possesses other characteristics typical of the masterpiece: full and homogeneous style. Schoenberg's style is in fact unique and unmistakable like Bach's, Mozart's, Rossini's or Chopin's.[42]

Obviously, Rota did not agree with Casella's enthusiastic statements as he only appreciated *Pierrot* for its experimental values upon which he did not elaborate. It is remarkable, though, that Rota was not afraid of making public such strong opinions about the most iconic figure in musical modernism. Regarding Alban Berg, many a student of Rota recall their teacher illustrating at the piano from memory large portions of *Wozzeck*.[43] Furthermore, when in 1960 RAI–Radio Televisione Italiana commissioned a group of noted composers, including Roman Vlad and Vladimir Vogel, to write a work based on a 12-note series that Darius Milhaud had discovered in the final scene of Mozart's *Don Giovanni*, Rota contributed a *Fantasia* for Piano and Orchestra. In this remarkable work he showed familiarity with the 12-tone technique, which he treated in a parodist fashion. Rota probably viewed

Mozart's incidental use of a series of 12 tones as a problem solved in terms of representing the metaphysical symbolism of *Don Giovanni*.[44]

Rota died on April 10, 1979. He was a musician for whom there existed no barriers of genres, categories, or qualifications. For Rota, music was just music or, as Fellini would have put it, Nino was music. Rota's life was dedicated to his music, the Conservatorio in Bari,[45] and an unusual group of friends. Rota's companion and confidante had always been his mother Ernesta. Upon her death, the composer, who never married but fathered a daughter, lived alone in a large apartment in central Rome's Piazza delle Coppelle and in a one-room studio at the Conservatorio "Niccolò Piccinni" in Bari. He also had a major interest in hermeticism, a passion he shared with Vinci Verginelli, the author of many texts, which he set to music.[46] Rota and Verginelli researched and collected a priceless library of rare hermetic texts dating from the 15th, 16th, 17th, and 18th centuries. This collection, comparable in size and quality to the Paul and Mary Mellon Collection (Alchemy and the Occult) at Yale University, filled the rooms of Rota's house in Rome. Upon Verginelli's death in 1987 the collection was bequeathed to the Accademia dei Lincei in Rome.[47]

Rota's interest in hermetic matters is revelatory for future studies concerning this musician's thinking, personality, his world views, and the people around him. Even Federico Fellini, despite 30 years of collaboration, was not fully part of Rota's inner circle, although he too was interested in the occult (see note 20). Professional life was, then, rigorously separated from personal goals. In fact, in writing Rota's eulogy entitled *L'amico magico*, Fellini revealed that at times he felt puzzled by certain aspects of Rota's behavior; Fellini's exquisite sensitivity detected something extraordinary in Rota but could not quite put a finger on it, or perhaps he did not wish to write about it![48]

Nino Rota was a successful composer who made a good living with his art and craft. At no time was he ever drawn into the intricate politics infesting the Italian cultural spectrum. He sailed through the maelstroms of Italian Fascism, the horrors of World War II, and the growing pains of the Italian Republic followed by its scandalous plunge into corruption while presiding over the development of an important State Conservatory. During the 1960s and '70s it was easy for Italian intellectuals to accuse one another of becoming opportunistic crowd pleasers paying occasional homage to modernity. Rota was often regarded as a sold-out tunesmith serving the capitalistic international film industry, a remark I may add that is too commonly launched against film music composers.

Chapter 2

Musical Styles In and Out of Diegesis

Dear Masetti,
I have reflected at length about ways to satisfy your request for
a contribution. But my reflections led to the conclusion, certainly
very personal, that does not allow me to find a proper angle to say
or write something about the relationships between music and
cinema: or, at least, to say something valid in general terms
that could remain as such in the time ahead.

—Nino Rota[1]

As noted in the previous chapter, solving musical problems was one of Rota's professional and artistic goals that, while displaying the highest degree of craftsmanship, remained deeply rooted into the music of the past. Professionalism was expressed not only through a rigid work ethic but also in composing for the cinema, an activity that became his most challenging and rewarding professional outlet. In this chapter I trace Rota's flexibility in working with some of the most influential directors of the 20th century. I also attempt to demonstrate how the composer solved myriad problems that arose from such eclectic collaborations. Rota's involvement with film music began early in his career thanks to the efforts of Enzo Masetti,[2] a pupil of Franco Alfano and a pioneer in Italian film music. Since the early 1930s Masetti promoted a national debate on the artistic merits of composing for motion pictures and radio thus encouraging several established composers, like Pizzetti, Malipiero, and Riccardo Zandonai,[3] to embrace film music as a legitimate art form.[4] Needless to say, young, versatile composers like Nino Rota found themselves in advantageous positions as work in cinema became available to them. I have already remarked in Chapter 1 on Rota's early film experience in 1933 beginning with the collaboration to Matarazzo's *Treno popolare*, so when the same director called on the composer again in 1942 to score *Giorno di nozze*, a Lux Film Production, Rota began a working arrangement with this studio that continued until 1960.

Lux Film was an important multifaceted cinematic enterprise, somewhat modeled after the classical Hollywood studio system. Financed by industrialist Riccardo Gualino, Lux was administered by Guido M. Gatti and directed by Fedele (Lele) D'Amico, both committed champions of the modernist movement in Italian music.[5]

It was certainly by no mere chance that Gatti and D'Amico engaged Rota as Lux's chief staff composer since they were determined to elevate the quality of Italian film music to the highest artistic degree possible in accordance with Masetti's advice and practices and their own refined sense of aesthetics. Thus, Gatti and D'Amico were successful in luring to the studio—besides Rota—composers like Ildebrando Pizzetti, Goffredo Petrassi, Luigi Dallapiccola, Roman Vlad, Carlo Rustichelli, Giovanni Fusco, Mario Nascimbene, and Vincenzo Tommasini to score some of Lux' full-length features and short documentaries. However it was Rota who showed the kind of enduring professionalism necessary to score virtually any picture by any director at any time. Though this situation was financially rewarding, it clearly vexed Rota from time to time as shown through private correspondence with his cousin Titina or with interviewers. Such consternation is reflected in comments like the following:

> It is true that cinema made me waste a lot of time; I am too agreeable, I cannot say no, consequently I got involved in the making of too many uninteresting things.[6]

> If it was not for my usual fear that by rejecting a film offer it won't come back when needed, I'd throw the whole business out the window.[7]

Nonetheless, following *Giorno di nozze*, Rota's assignments at Lux continued with a film directed by Renato Castellani, *Zazá* (1942), a story about a *fin-de-siècle* truculent love affair between a family man and a cabaret singer who ultimately sacrificed her love for the man so that his child could regain a father. For this picture Rota composed a *verismo*-drenched non-diegetic score and several diegetically performed cabaret songs that evoked the nostalgic, decadent world of *La Belle époque*.[8]

Rota's collaboration with Lux films included 26 films. In addition he worked for other studios with important directors whose taste in music demanded his ability and willingness to devise new collaborative working methods. In the following pages I propose a panoramic view of Rota's collaborations with some famous moviemakers beginning with Luchino Visconti who was undoubtedly one of the most musically knowledgeable and demanding directors in world cinema.[9]

Setting aside *La terra trema* (1948), Visconti's *neorealismo* masterpiece, the great director conceived the structure of the music destined for his films as a Romantic symphony articulated in the traditional structure of four contrasting movements: Allegro–Adagio–Scherzo–Finale (Rondo). Therefore, Visconti's hypothetical symphony functioned like a blueprint upon which the film's narrative and its subtexts were consequently developed. For *Senso* (1954), a Lux Film production based upon a novel by Camillo Boito,[10] Visconti exploited the socially and politically unacceptable love affair that erupted between an Italian Countess, Livia Serpieri (Alida Valli), and an Austrian officer, Franz Mahler (Farley Granger). The story, taking place in 1860 during the Austrian occupation of the Veneto region, was drenched in melodramatic pathos as the protagonists' love sparked during a performance of Verdi's *Il trovatore* when the opera's famous aria "Di quella pira" was sung on stage. It literally ignited a riot in the theatre pitting Venetian patriots against their Austrian occupiers. By using Verdi's music diegetically, Visconti wished to reflect Countess Serpieri's truly patriotic colors, while by underscoring the film with a Germanic symphonic work of large proportions he planned to align the audience's feelings with Franz Mahler's in order to justify Serpieri's passion for him. The complexity of this task is typical of what a composer could expect from Luchino Visconti who, having discarded a repertoire symphonic work by either Beethoven or Brahms, chose instead Anton Bruckner's *Seventh Symphony* which Rota had to cut and paste to accommodate the film's narrative in every detail. Ultimately, the melodramatic quality of Bruckner's music, so well tailored by Rota, runs parallel to the images forming not only the film's scenic soundscape but its historical, sentimental, and moral definition as well.[11] I wish to add here that Rota was not new to the adaptation of pre-existing music to films. For instance, another Lux Film production, entitled *Melodie immortali* (1952), was a biographical fantasy on the life of Pietro Mascagni which compelled Rota to glue together scenes taken from Mascagni's operas, including large portions of *Cavalleria rusticana.*

Another Visconti–Rota success was the 1957 film *Le notti bianche* (*White Nights*, 1957), a story inspired by Fyodor Dostoyevsky. According to Visconti scholar Geoffrey Nowell-Smith, this film, produced by CIAS/Vides (Rome) and Intermondia Films (Paris), established the opposition of two levels of reality, the actual and the ideal. As he put it: "The actual is characterized by transience, modernity, social dissociation: the pop music, the youths on motorbikes, the prostitute and her client, the passer-by. The ideal, by its nature, is less readily concretized in particular images. It is the product of the transforming power of the imagination."[12] For the "actual" phase of the film narrative, Rota assembled an array of commercial songs fashionable in the 1950s which were heard diegetically, while for the "ideal" level of reality he composed a lyrically beautiful (under) score which Visconti demanded be written in the spirit of German Romanticism, including direct Wagnerian quotations which foreshadowed his 1973 film *Ludwig*.

Rocco e i suoi fratelli (Rocco and His Brothers) is considered the gem of the Visconti–Rota partnership. In this 1960 film, co-produced by Titanus and Les Films Marceau, Visconti returned, albeit partially, to *neorealismo*, therefore the use of diegetic or diegetically implied music employed by Rota resulted in a more decisive and efficient score than his own non-diegetic one. In all, *Rocco* was a score inspired by southern Italian folk tunes that enabled the composer to express the nostalgic mood of hordes of southern people emigrating to northern Italy, a socioeconomic phenomenon that occurred during the years after World War II. His successful evocation in this score of the nostalgia emigrants felt toward their country of origin will be mentioned later in my discussion of Rota's adaptation of certain instrumental characteristics of *Rocco*'s score to music cues in *The Godfather Trilogy*'s Part I and Part II.

As was the case with *Senso* and the use of Bruckner's *Seventh Symphony*, Visconti longed for an original symphonic fresco of Verdian proportion for *Il Gattopardo* (1963), a spectacular *Risorgimento* saga after the homonymous novel of Giuseppe Tomasi di Lampedusa.[13] This time, Rota preempted the director's musical vagaries by using a work in four movements he had composed in 1947, *Sinfonia sopra un tema d'amore* (Symphony on a Love Theme). This piece, written in a style oscillating between Brahms and Dvorak yet pervaded with Rota's Italianate melodic flair proved ideal for Visconti's Romantic symphonic vision. Ultimately, three movements of this symphony became the backbone of *Il Gattopardo*'s music track. *Sinfonia sopra un tema d'amore* was not completely unknown though; Rota had used portions of it in the film *The Glass Mountain*, a 1949 British production directed by Henry Cass. Furthermore, the "love theme" upon which the symphony was based had been taken from the score written for *La donna della montagna*, a 1943 Lux Film production directed by Renato Castellani.

Rota collaborated with Visconti one last time on *Il lavoro* [The Job], an episode of the compilation film *Boccaccio '70*. Other episodes in the film were directed by Mario Monicelli (*Renzo e Luciana*), Federico Fellini (*Le tentazioni del dottor Antonio*), and Vittorio De Sica (*La Riffa* [The Raffle]). In *Il lavoro*, Rota juxtaposed the strains of a sophisticated jazz score to fragments of a quasi-atonal chamber symphony reminiscent of early Schoenberg. From an analytical standpoint, *Boccaccio '70* offers the scholar the unique opportunity to observe Rota's chameleon-like musical transformations as he deals with two directors as diverse as Fellini and Visconti.

In 1950, the composer began an important collaboration with Eduardo De Filippo, the Neapolitan actor, playwright, screenwriter, author, and poet who dominated the Italian theatrical scene for most of the 20th century.[14] The warm and picturesque flow of humanity emanating from his plays has drawn appreciation from all over the world, and Eduardo—as such was his stage name—became the best-known Italian playwright since Luigi Pirandello.[15] As in the Venetian 18th century of Carlo Goldoni, Eduardo wrote plays for his company and thus, by extension, for his family, so his works tended to be about Neapolitan family relations pervaded by the omnipresent spirit of the *Commedia dell'Arte*. Rota was immensely attracted by Eduardo's artistry and quintessential Italianness and he scored the film *Napoli milionaria* (1949) after the 1945 play by the same title. This film, also known to the Anglophone world as *Side Street Story*, combined satire and comedy about ordinary Neapolitan people during World War II. Eduardo and Rota followed it with *Filumena Marturano* (1951); *Marito e Moglie* (1952); *Ragazze da marito* (1952); *Quei figuri di tanti anni fa* (1965 tv); *Fortunella* (1957); *L'ora di punta* [second episode of *Oggi, domani, dopodomani*] (1965); and *Spara forte, più forte, non capisco . . .* (1967).

Of the films listed above, *Fortunella*, a Lux Film produced by Dino De Laurentiis starring Giulietta Masina in the title role, deserves particular attention. The film was partially directed by Federico Fellini whose collaboration with the production team must have, perhaps unintentionally, somewhat irritated the very susceptible Eduardo. Proof of such friction transpired in a note Rota addressed to his cousin Titina on January 28, 1958. He wrote:

Then I'll return to Rome to record Fortunella whose music I have written with Fellini's collaboration without De Filippo knowing about it (he goes into fits of jealousy and hysterics about this film which De Laurentiis wished Fellini to shoot half of; however, De Filippo himself is re-shooting some scenes as we speak).[16]

This reveals something of Rota's working methods and how he sought when necessary the collaboration of more amenable partners in order to bring a work to completion.[17]

But, the troubles with the unfortunate *Fortunella* were not over. Fifteen years later a theme taken from this film's music track became a source of great discontent for Rota because upon release of *The Godfather* and the enormous commercial success of its "Love Theme," Rota was accused of plagiarism. The maestro paid no attention to such a fracas because he was well aware of the tune's origin and if anything, it would have been a case of self-plagiarism. The situation, however, became aggravated by the intervention of *Fortunella*'s producer De Laurentiis who demanded his rights to the tune, although, it was discovered, he had never paid Rota any money at all for the work done on the film in the first place. The case, although officially closed, provoked a number of Italian film music composers, siding with De Laurentiis, to send a collective telegram of protest to the American Academy Awards Committee upon learning about Rota's nomination for an Oscar. The committee withdrew the nomination and Rota had to wait for *The Godfather Part II* to collect his long due award, which he shared with Carmine Coppola, Francis Ford's father.[18]

Over the span of a 30-year collaboration, Federico Fellini's films and Nino Rota's music have become part of a global currency of cultural meaning which have prompted a body of writings mostly centered on a common denominator. In general, many critics have concluded that Rota's contribution to Fellini's films reflected the composer's subjugation to the omnivorous director to the point that in order to have a function, his music had to remain simple. To put it another way, Rota's main task was to "Fellininize" the pre-existing music already selected by the director or to validate certain co-protagonist symbioses between characters and instruments, which inherently developed in the course of the filmmaking process. I am referring here to Gelsomina (Giulietta Masina) playing the trumpet and The Fool (Richard Basehart) playing a *violino piccolo* in *La strada*,[19] Cantarel playing his accordion in *Amarcord* (1974), or even the grotesque love-making rituals of Giacomo Casanova (Donald Sutherland) interacting with a mechanical musical bird in *Casanova* (1976), to give some well-known examples.[20]

A famous-turned-infamous instance of musical "Fellinization" was a theme used in *La dolce vita* whose origin generated an uproar on the part of Universal Edition, publishers of Kurt Weill's *Die Dreigroschenoper* because of the similarity between *Die Moritat von Mackie Messer* and Rota's thematic rendition of it.[21] In the course of an interview granted to American film critic Gideon Bachman,[22] Rota reacted to the accusation of having plagiarized Kurt Weill by saying that Fellini used several pieces as temporary tracks during the film's shooting including Kurt Weill's celebrated *Die Moritat von Mackie Messer*. In the process of replacing some of those tracks, and since permission to use Weill's ballade was denied by the publisher, he (Rota) was compelled to compose a theme that by coincidence sounded like Weill's[23]:

mf

Ex. 2.1. Theme from *La dolce vita*.

Ultimately, at least as far as Fellini's visual conceptions were concerned, Rota's "simplicity," as well as the thematic quotations and the reformatting of others' music became functional elements of Fellini's cinematic narratives as they blended to the point of becoming one indivisible entity.

On separate occasions, Fellini and Rota were asked to expand on their collaborative methods. Their replies were more often than not ambiguous and careless. Here is, for instance, a quote taken from an address Fellini delivered to the students of the Centro Sperimentale di Cinematografia in Rome:

> I prefer to work with maestro Rota because I think he is congenial enough to my purposes, my kind of stories, therefore we work together in a very jovial atmosphere. I never make musical suggestions because I don't know about music. At any rate, because my ideas about the film are very clear, my work with Rota proceeds along the film script. I sit next to him at the piano telling him exactly what I have in mind. I must say that Nino Rota is the most humble among film composers, because, I think, he writes extremely functional music. He has no desire to make his music "heard." He is aware that music in a film must assume a secondary supporting role, with sporadic exceptions naturally.[24]

Interestingly, Fellini's assertion that he never made musical suggestions to Rota is contradicted by the composer, who told Gideon Bachman[25] that often Fellini's input to his composition process brought concrete results. For instance, Rota's original theme for the little march in *Otto e mezzo* consisted of the following phrase:

Ex. 2.2. Theme A from *Otto e mezzo*.

which Fellini completed as follows:

Ex. 2.3. Theme B from *Otto e mezzo*.

Rota's serpentine, chromatic motif could have been repeated in circle many times, if not brought to its conclusion by Fellini in a positivistic diatonic fashion. Rota and Fellini worked sitting side-by-side at the piano bench when selecting tunes for their films. So, there was indeed a collaborative process in place between the two artists, a process that often reached full fruition during the final recording session of a film's soundtrack when changes to the score were made until the very last minute.[26]

Customarily, Nino Rota spotted every film he scored at a studio equipped with a moviola and a piano as documented by his numerous notes jotted in several notebooks preserved at the Archivio Nino Rota in Venice. Then, the composing process began, followed by various phases of adaptation. For some of Fellini's films, both composer and director spent time searching for special sounds they wished to infuse the picture with. Consider for instance the tonal mix of *La dolce vita*'s title music as well as the "Ecclesiastic Fashion Show" in *Roma*.

Both episodes evoke the decrepit yet mysteriously luxuriant world hidden behind the Vatican walls with its blend of corrupt Roman aristocracy and forced pageantry, which Fellini so ably and cruelly exposed for the world to see. Musically, Rota created a cold, detached, morbid music track at odds with his personal brand of religious mysticism so effectively expressed in his oratorio *Mysterium* of 1962.[27]

Regarding *Satyricon*, Fellini and Rota looked for an African-Oriental-Asian type of music in order to underscore images that were remote in time and space. Rather than evoking a precise historical time, the aim in this film was to create a musical color by employing a large apparatus of electronic effects, Tibetan-like chants, and Gamelan techniques revealing Rota as a very attentive connoisseur of the avant-garde music of the 1960s. However, the score to *Satyricon* is also rich in melodic fragments such as the following tune heard played by an unaccompanied flute during the *Trimalchio's Banquet* episode, and later as a Greek song performed by the effeminate boy Giton accompanying himself on the lyre followed by another version sung in Swahili by a slave girl.

Ex. 2.4. Theme from *Satyricon*.

Therefore, one may conclude that Rota took the idea of *Klangfarben-melodie* very much into consideration and applied it properly. Something similar occurred when composing the score for *Casanova*. There the idea was not to create a music track even remotely evoking the 18th century, but to infuse the film with something ritualistically mechanical aimed at de-humanizing the figure of the protagonist by reducing him to the level of a puppet.[28]

A fragment of documentary evidence of Fellini and Rota's collaborative relationship can be seen in two documentary films entitled *Zwischen Kino und Konzert–Der Komponist Nino Rota* (1993), directed by Vassili Silovic,[29] and Mario Monicelli's *Un amico magico: Il Maestro Nino Rota* (Istituto Luce, 1999). Both documentaries show a film clip portraying Fellini and Rota working at the piano as they selected the musical themes for *Amarcord*. After various unsuccessful trials, Rota finally played what became the title theme, much to Fellini's joy, who emphatically declared: "Great! With this theme we can do the entire film!" Whether the two artists were playing for the camera or not is irrelevant in this instance, because such was in reality the nature of their working method.[30]

Rota's professional relationship with Lina Wertmüller (b. 1926) was born on the fringes of the Fellini–Rota partnership as the female director followed in Fellini's footsteps at the beginning of her career. Wertmüller was the first woman ever to be nominated for an Academy Award for Best Direction (*Pasqualino Settebellezze* [Seven Beauties], 1975). In addition to their strong professional ties, Rota and Wertmüller developed a close friendship that lasted until the composer's death in 1979. The collaboration between the two artists reached a peak in 1965 with the popular television eight-part series *Gian Burrasca*.[31] For this production Rota composed dozens of songs, some of which, like *La pappa col pomodoro* (see the following example) became extremely popular jingles among youngsters and adults alike.

Ex. 2.5. Theme from *La pappa col pomodoro*.

The silliness of this tune, silly because such it needed to be, provoked Rota's critics to launch a ferocious attack against the composer who, according to them, had fallen to the lowest degree of any artistic and ethical decency, especially in light of his position as the director of a major musical institution. In reality, those critics failed to understand that the composer's creativity had, in effect, reached new levels of popularity by writing tunes for the most popular and infamous medium of the turbulent 1960s—television—while harvesting success after success in cinema, opera, and concert hall without ever changing his stylistic personality.[32] Interestingly, *Gian Burrasca* was revived in 2002 by Italian television, showcasing a new cast and state-of-the-art technologies while preserving Nino Rota's original music.[33]

Another highlight of the Wertmüller–Rota collaboration was the 1973 *Film d'amore e d'anarchia* (Love and Anarchy) for which Rota re-elaborated a number of street songs fashionable in the Fascist era.

Rota's other key working relationship was with Franco Zeffirelli, a director whose influence is still felt across all fields of artistic endeavor. Zeffirelli, born in Florence in 1923, became an icon of Italian contemporary culture molded in the cast of Luchino Visconti. Although Rota and Zeffirelli collaborated on only three Shakespearean projects, the 1968 Paramount film *Romeo and Juliet* became a blockbuster that made Rota's a household name in the United States.

Their relationship began when Zeffirelli took on the production of *Much Ado About Nothing* requested by Sir Laurence Olivier for his new National Theatre Company at London's Old Vic in 1965. Rota composed the incidental music to the play, notwithstanding a dose of skepticism almost as an antidote to Zeffirelli's customary boisterous enthusiasm as shown in a letter to his cousin Titina dated December 27, 1964:

> . . . *I saw Zeffirelli [in London] only for part of an afternoon and I think that we have established the music for Much Ado About Nothing with a superficiality typical of a descended of Michelangelo and, for that matter, of Paolo Emilio Tosti. Who knows, perhaps something good may even come up . . . let's hope.*[34]

Zeffirelli's success with *Much Ado About Nothing* paved the way for one of the most exciting cinematic collaborations of the 1960s, *The Taming of the Shrew* which combined the talents, tempers, and antics of Richard Burton, Elizabeth Taylor, and Franco Zeffirelli. This celebrated production was filmed in Rome in 1966 at the new Dino De Laurentiis studios. Rota's contribution consisted of pseudo Elizabethan music. According to Zeffirelli's accounts, it was during the shooting of *The Taming of the Shrew* that the idea of filming *Romeo and Juliet* came to fruition.[35] He wrote:

> *That May [1967] I moved my entire company including the principals of Romeo and Juliet. There we all were, during the hot summer, living as if in a cheerful, busy commune; Olivia [Hussey] and Leonard [Whiting] rehearsing on the lawn; Nino Rota writing the music in the salon; Robert Stephens and Natasha Parry learning their lines or swimming in the pool—it was a dream world.*[36]

So, Rota composed a score whose love theme, constructed in an archaic harmonic language using the Aeolian mode, became one of the most popular tunes of the decade.[37]

Needless to say, in Hollywood's financial worldview, Nino Rota's *Romeo and Juliet* score gained the composer considerable currency. So, when Francis Ford Coppola advanced his name as his choice for composing *The Godfather*'s soundtrack, the Rota name was not entirely new to Paramount's executives.

Chapter 3

Ethnicity and Literary Adaptation in *The Godfather Trilogy*

I feel that the Mafia is an incredible metaphor for this country. Both are totally capitalistic phenomena and basically have a profit motive.
—Francis Ford Coppola[1]

I Believe in the Mafia

In November 1971, producer Al Ruddy and other Paramount executives attended the screening of the director's cut of *The Godfather*. As the film commenced, character Amerigo Bonasera, instead of speaking the scripted line "I believe in America," proclaimed in a Stentorian tone: "I BELIEVE IN THE MAFIA, THE MAFIA HAS MADE MY FORTUNE AND I RAISED MY DAUGHTER IN THE MAFIA FASHION."

"What the fuck is *this!*" was the most polite of the many expressions to erupt from a very upset Al Ruddy. The revengeful joke, thrown at the producer by the film's crew, had indeed hit its intended target![2] Although Francis Ford Coppola said that he considered the Mafia a metaphor for capitalist America, and Mario Puzo had no problems in mentioning the word Mafia copiously in his best-selling novel,[3] the Italian American Civil Rights League was adamant about the use of the word, and it made the issue forcefully clear to the film's producer Al Ruddy in the course of much protracted negotiations. Finally, Ruddy and the League reached the agreement that the word Mafia would never be mentioned in the film. The League, on the other hand, was allowed to "plant" some of its members on location at various New York shooting sites, just to keep "running things smoothly," and . . . to lend a touch of "authenticity" to the story.[4]

Are the *Godfather* films really about the Mafia though? Have they contributed to the stereotyping of all Italian Americans as Mafia-tainted immigrants? Has Nino Rota's iconic music become the "spinal soundtrack" for the instant evocation and gratification of such feelings?[5] As I respond affirmatively to all three questions, I discuss, in the course of

25

the following pages, the impact that Coppola's *Godfather* films have had on the Italian American community over the past 25 years, and I illustrate how some key elements of Italianicity placed opposite to the concept of Italianness have permeated Puzo and Coppola's works. Therefore, I begin by quoting a portion of an article by William V. Shannon which appeared in the *New York Times* of August 1, 1972, strongly denouncing the film *The Godfather*:

> No one denies that a few Italian-Americans are gangsters. To that extent, "The Godfather" rests on a substratum of fact. But for the millions of Italian-Americans who are not gangsters, the success of this film raises an enormous cultural obstacle. It retards their efforts to overcome this dark legacy from the past and to establish positive heroes for their children to emulate.[6]

The above remarks show how the Italian American Civil Rights League's concerns were somewhat justified—albeit for all the wrong reasons—in wanting the word Mafia out of the film's script. But, what does the word Mafia represent? Here is a succinct review of the general perception of the dreaded word and its attribute *mafioso(i)* which identifies its practioners.

Although the words Mafia and its euphemism *La Cosa Nostra* (Our Way or Our Thing) are not part of the film's explicit vocabulary, their implicit presence excite our curiosity even more compellingly for the reason that the etymological origin of the word Mafia is, according to a recent study,[7] as complex as the concept it signifies. In fact, its roots can be traced all over the Mediterranean Sea's Arabic, Iberian, Sicilian, and Semitic shores where, *mutatis mutandis*, "olives and bullets" are still a valid currency.

The Mafia is a contagious mental state that fascinates, seduces, and infiltrates everything involving history and politics. Its adoption is a linguistic synonym for all confederated crime and has the psychological effect of conditioning people to believe that organized crime is an Italian-American invention based on the culture of their ancestors, and an Italian-American monopoly.[8] Or, as Alessandro Camon put it, "The Mafia is a society so secret that it denies its own existence. Therefore, the Mafioso is compelled to categorically deny any association with or knowledge of the organization, to the extent of dismissing the very notion of Mafia as 'a myth.'"[9]

Rather than a criminal though, the *mafioso* is often addressed as a "Man of Honor"[10] in a quasi reference to Miguel de Cervantes' ancestral *hombre honrado*, thus giving the attribute a positive endorsement from 16th-century Spanish literature. Similarly, in 18th-century southern Italy (for centuries under Spanish domination) the early bands of *mafiosi*, commonly known as *briganti*—an attribute meaning "troublemakers" derived from *Brigantaggio* (brigandage)—were in effect protectors of the southern Italian people against villains. Therefore, brigandage was equated with heroism, as the peasants manifested their state of oppression while murder and theft were easily excused for the sake of expediency.

Often, though some historical accounts vary, their essence remains unaltered. For instance, Italian American novelist Gay Talese describes the origin of the Mafia in his best-selling family saga *Unto the Sons* as follows:

> . . . Many of the noble families of Sicily and southern Italy supported the cause of the mob, which had meanwhile organized itself into a secret group led by underground chieftains who, according to my father, were the first "godfathers" of the Mafia. This, my father insisted, is how the Mafia began—as a revolutionary resistance dedicated to the overthrow of such tyrannical foreign despots as Charles d'Anjou. And while these goals were later corrupted and replaced by ones that were entirely self-serving, the Mafia's underground network, which was first operational in the anti-French massacre of 1281 (which became popularly known as the Sicilian Vespers and inspired the Verdi opera that I often heard played on my father's Victrola during my boyhood in Ocean City), continued to exist as a vengeful force in Sicily and southern Italy for years eternal.[11]

As one would have expected, Talese's tale about the Mafia's origin possesses some of those same undertones found in Puzo and Coppola's narratives that consider the Mafia as a place of refuge and comfort, a symbolic return to the maternal womb. So, the *mafioso*, a man indeed honored with power, was also a man endowed with a physical fat belly: a pregnant man. A *uomo di panza*, literally meaning a man of belly who knew how to keep things for himself—in his guts as it were. Remember that Vito Corleone's ultimate vindictive gesture toward Don Ciccio (*The Godfather Part II*) consisted of slicing open the old *mafioso*'s fat belly, killing him while symbolically deflating his power.

Why and when did the Mafia and *mafiosi* arrive in the United States? A time-honored answer to the question tells that many of the criminals who came to this country were southern Italians trying to escape punishment. In reality though, from 1895 to 1908, during the period of increasing industrialization and capitalist development, unrest among the mass of people became more marked; the ideas of socialism and anarchism were taking root, and in the absence of a "strong" central government (plus the need for cheap labor in America) the encouragement of emigration was the best way out of a serious national dilemma. As statistics point out, between 1901 and 1913, some 1.1 million Sicilians emigrated—a little less than a quarter of the island's entire population. Of those, roughly 800,000 made the United States their destination. Inevitably, some were "men of honor" (*mafiosi*), smart and ruthless criminals who sought to establish protection regimes and other criminal activities among their fellow immigrants and along the trade routes connecting the two shores of the Atlantic.[12]

Economist Francis A. Walker, president of the Massachusetts Institute of Technology and former superintendent of the 1891 federal census, blamed the "vast hordes of foreign immigrants" for a reduction of America's native stock, emphasizing that these new immigrants were incapable of adapting to American political institutions and social life.[13] Regarding the southern Italians, Walker added that the figure of the *padrone* (owner, master, boss), so pervasive among southern Italian immigrants, was "an a-historic personification of greed and primitive cruelty," and in the eyes of many nativist Americans, virtually every middle-class immigrant was tainted by the suspicion of being a *padrone*. Thus, if the *padroni* were seen as rapacious masters, then the workers were stereotyped as the "*padrone's* slaves" who had no aptitude for American Freedom. Unfortunately, southern Italians themselves promoted this image of Italian workers as helpless, childlike "slaves."

The reader may recall Vito Corleone's flashback scenes in *The Godfather Part II* when the character Don Fanucci not only impersonated a typical neighborhood *padrone* but was a representative of the *Mano nera* [Black Hand] *mafioso* organization as well. Vito Corleone ultimately murdered Don Fanucci, thus liberating the neighborhood of the *mafioso-padrone's* predatory presence and establishing his own paternalistic, Godfather-like influence.[14]

Another keen observer of New York City's early 20th century socioeconomic landscape was photojournalist Jacob August Riis, who became directly acquainted with the Italian immigrants in New York City, the majority of whom were destitute and disorderly. They occupied areas of the city deemed somewhat unsafe. Nevertheless, Riis remarked that perhaps for that very reason, their picturesqueness, while still quaint, exotic, and seductive, became both a menace and a rebuke to American character and American progress. Italian immigrants thus constituted a subject for the illustrators and sentimental travel writers who ventured into New York's Lower East Side to produce colorful sketches and articles for magazines such as *Harper's New Monthly Magazine* and *The Cosmopolitan*.

At this juncture, I classify the preceding observations about the Italian (mostly southern) immigrants as manifestations of Italianicity, viewed as exotic spectacle at the expense of an ethnic group whose skin color was considered less than white.

Aside from widely read magazine articles, Riis' depiction of the Italians was more scientifically documented in his classic sociological and photographic book *How the Other Half Lives* (1890), a volume still in circulation. This book was, in my view, a source of inspiration not only for Puzo's novel but also for set designer Dean Tavoularis and Francis Coppola in their reconstruction of the many familiar New York City sets shown in the flashback episodes of *The Godfather Part II*.[15] Riis' book constitutes the most detailed, eloquent, and firsthand set of observations about a social phenomenon that, once revived by Puzo's words and Coppola's cinematic narrative, continues to hold its value and sense of shocking outrage. Therefore, viewers cheer when Vito Corleone kills Don Fanucci, they understand Vito's rationale when the up-and-coming Godfather slices Don Ciccio's belly, and in general they develop a sympathy for the Godfather figure portrayed in the flashback scenes of *The Godfather Part II* comparing him to a Robin Hood of sorts in his quest to squelch corruption and restore dignity among his people.

In another celebrated book, *On the Trail of the Immigrant*, written in 1906, Edward A. Steiner pointed out that becoming an American involved much more than changing one's clothes, learning some English, and erasing what he called "external racial characteristics." In fact, he prided himself on his ability to distinguish groups through their racial features.

"Give me the immigrant on board of ship, and I will distinguish without hesitation the Bulgarian from the Serbian, the Slovak from the Russian, and *Northern Italian* from the *Sicilian*" [emphasis mine], Steiner wrote, thus presenting the American public with the first clear distinction between Alpine and Mediterranean Italian immigrants.[16]

The distinction between northern and southern Italy/Italians was one that many bourgeois and intellectual Americans would make as they tried to balance long-held notions of romantic, heroic Italy (Italianness) with the negative images of the Italian immigrants written about in the press (Italianicity). Eventually, this distinction was racially codified in official American immigration documents, allowing ordinary Americans to continue to admire Italy in its ordered, virtuous, heroic incarnation in the north, while recoiling from the supposedly disordered, dirty, morally lax southern Italy represented by southern Italian immigrants.[17] American-British/expatriate novelist Henry James (1843–1916) offered one of the most compelling descriptions in the literature about the phenomenon of immigrating to America. In 1907, James wrote an article for *The American Scene* depicting an episode he experienced at Ellis Island, a place that Italians called the "Island of Tears." He wrote:

> On a day of dense raw fog and ice-masses in New York Harbor, an appropriate atmosphere for witnessing a scene that ultimately put a chill in his heart, I saw the immigrants marshaled, herded, divided, subdivided, sorted, sifted, searched, fumigated. Such was an intently "scientific" feeding of the mill, one that gives the earnest observers a thousand more things to think about that he can retell.[18]

As James' article was discussed by the American intelligentsia, eleven-year-old Edward Corsi and his family arrived at Ellis Island, not as derelict southern Italian immigrants but as intellectuals looking for a better life.[19] In 1935, Corsi, author and political leader, published *In the Shadow of Liberty: The Chronicle of Ellis Island*, a widely appreciated study of the immigrant and his problems as the result of his experience at Ellis Island.[20] James and Corsi's vivid accounts, and even Arthur Miller's 1955 play *A View from the Bridge*, eminently fit Coppola's rendition of the Ellis Island ordeal in *The Godfather Part II*.

As I previously noted, in the minds of some Americans, Italians and other new immigrants were seen as less than white, thus they were mixed up with blacks in social relations, in the political maneuverings of the American North and South, and in the public imagination. For instance, the most graphic of the similarities between blacks and Italians was that Italians, like blacks, were considered as a group worthy of lynching. In fact, the 1890s saw repeated lynching of both Italians and blacks.[21] In New York City, hostility toward the Italians peaked in the years leading up to World War I as Americans increasingly saw the [southern] Italian immigrants as ignorant, dirty, dishonest, violent, and criminal people who refused to assimilate. Sicilians were specially singled out for scorn as swarthy *mafiosi*, as transients who came and went at the beck and call of agents and *padroni*.[22]

The immigrants had a tradition of violence born of their resistance to the rural landlords who had exploited them back in Sicily. "When these *mafiosi* moved to United States they were forced to learn a new language, dilute their symbolic integrity, and produce a new criminal esperanto that was open to the influence of other organizations, cultural trends, and the media at large."[23] They formed gangs and secret societies, just as they had done in the old country. As Belgian-born historian Luc Sante stated in the ABC television documentary *Uncovering the Real Gangs of New York*, crime became a necessary means of survival in the lawless slums, which were, consequently, fertile ground for the growth of gangs in the United States.[24]

The Sicilian Mafia in America also faced the problem of trademark control. It was America that turned the word "Mafia" into the best-known brand name in organized crime, beginning with the so-called *Mano nera* (Black Hand), a neighborhood organization that prospered by "protecting" scores of New York businesses in exchange for a percentage of their income. *The Godfather Part II* offers an eloquent example of such practices. I discuss in Chapters 4 and 5 how composer Carmine Coppola underscored these episodes with picturesque imagination, thus giving the scenes an unmistakable feeling of Italianicity reflecting traditions, nostalgia, and the quasi-cult for *La Via Vecchia* [the old-fashioned way]. "My heart was really in the Little Italy sequences," Francis Coppola remembered, "in the old streets of New York, the music, all that turn-of-the-century atmosphere."[25]

To that extent, Coppola the auteur saw the flashbacks in *The Godfather Part II* as a personal film in which he addressed his own ancestry and ethnic heritage.[26] Following the success of Coppola's films, the public expected then, as it does now, that crime have a look, a feel, and a sound—both of its own and through the appropriate media coverage. Crime is not conceivable outside this gestalt: it is a spectacle endemic to the media-controlled world we live in with cinema as the main agent that gives shape to this aesthetic dimension. In fact, cinematic artistic choices in terms of crime representation have become now more conscious and sophisticated than ever. *The Godfather Trilogy* marks a seminal moment in American cultural history because it embraces the responsibility of these choices and does not simplify them to the point where Mafia would be either "condemned" or "glorified." The film's ultimate achievement is a double movement as ambiguous as the Mafia itself, of critique and reaffirmation of the Mafia myth.[27] This is the main reason way I have chosen to focus on the significance of this film from an Italian-American perspective because that seems to me to be the most eloquent—positive or negative—Hollywood cinematic representation of Italian-American ethnicity.

It was not until the 1950s that American public opinion would again begin to confuse the Mafia with organized crime *per se*. In 1951, 1957, and 1959, Americans saw a gallery of gangsters with Italian names parading across their television screens as the Kefauver and McClellan Committee hearings unfolded and the Apalachin conclave was discovered.[28] Then, in 1963, the public absorbed the horrendous tales of *La Cosa Nostra* as narrated by soldier-turned-informant Joseph Valachi.[29] From then on, the Mafia, *La Cosa Nostra*, or whatever it was called was constantly in the news and on film, the process reaching its apogee with the publication of Mario Puzo's *The Godfather* in 1969. Puzo's best-selling book set in concrete the mistaken public perception that American syndicates were entirely a Sicilian import. Therefore, a tiny minority of the Italian-American population, less than one one-hundredth of 1 percent, had besmirched the good name of millions of honest, hardworking men and women bearing Italian names.[30] Even the underworld statistics reported by the press corroborated the fact that since the prohibition era in the New York metropolitan area alone, 50 percent of bootleggers were Jewish, compared to about 25 percent who were Italians.

Italianness, Italianicity, and "Made in Italy"

Italianness is an elusive concept aimed at capturing, in a word, the essence of the Italian people. The concept acquired urgency beginning in 1870, after Italy's political unification process was accomplished and Rome was proclaimed the country's capital. Then, diverse ethnic groups populating Alpine (north of Rome) and Mediterranean (south of Rome) Italy struggled to find ancestral, linguistic, and cultural commonalities. Following the so-called "mutilated victory" at the conclusion of World War I[31] and the consequent rise of Fascism, Mussolini's nationalistic ideologies placed a premium on the concept of Italianness (*Italianità*) and its derivative, Romanness (*Romanità*), as pointed out in Chapter 1. Furthermore, with the rise of German National Socialism in 1932, and its ultra nationalistic *Blut und Boden* (Germanness) doctrine, the idea of Italianness reached paroxysmal levels especially on the eve of the ill-fated Rome–Berlin Axis allegiance proclaimed by Mussolini in 1936.

The turn-of-the-century's great Italian migratory waves toward the Americas, and the United States in particular, reemphasized the fundamental ethnic division between the Italian nationals emigrating from the northern and those emigrating from the southern provinces of the country. Thus, reflecting upon the perception that some preeminent American writers, sociologists, journalists, and reporters made public about the newly arrived Italian immigrants, I find it appropriate to classify the burgeoning Italian diaspora as a manifestation of Italianicity;

patterns of life style, that is, resembling or reevoking those of the Italian towns and villages the immigrants had left behind and the perpetuation of their cultural codes. In sum, Italianicity can be viewed as the migratory variant, or to put it more bluntly, the veneer of Italianness. Having said this, I would add that during the 1920s and 1930s, Italian Fascism fostered the coalescence of the Italian migratory colonies that had settled in various parts of the world. The main objective for organizing and mobilizing these colonies was to restore in their constituencies a genuine concept of Italianness before it turned into Italianicity, thus preserving the Italian spirit and culture from their inevitable absorption, in whole or in part, into the process of Americanization.

Periodicals like *Il Carroccio*, for example, were very efficient in promulgating Mussolini's ideas, particularly in the New York City area, from 1921 through 1935.[32] Fascism's sponsorship of visiting Italian artists, scientists, aviators, men and women of letters, and politicians served to boost the hope that Italian immigrants would one day return to a much more prosperous (under Mussolini's paternalistic rules, of course) motherland—a country they had been compelled to abandon. While many Italian immigrants did return to Italy, millions opted for Americanization, and others remained entrapped, following Italy's declaration of war against the United States in World War II, as enemy aliens facing internment.[33] In some tragic cases, Italian immigrants, having become American citizens, had children who enlisted in the American Army and who found themselves at war with their own relatives. An extreme circumstance was reported of two brothers shooting at each other from opposite camps.

After World War II, the concept of Italianness was relegated to the realm of nostalgia supplanted by the 1950s postwar "economic miracle," which propelled the very fashionable "Made in Italy"—a socioeconomic conglomerate of consumerism, cinema, advertising, fashion design, slick automobiles, and anything Federico Fellini cared to epitomize in *La dolce vita*.[34] As a reactionary phenomenon, the Italian-American diaspora's response to the aggressive, new Italianness typified by the "Made in Italy" provoked a tightening of the old traditions (*La Via Vecchia*) by restoring and encouraging the overusage of arcane dialects and the picturesque adoption of gestures and mores which have, thanks primarily to Puzo and Coppola, become part of a peculiar Italian-American cultural lexicon that transformed itself into a postmodern version of Italianicity.

Strikingly, the reflection of Italian-American culture as found in the first *Godfather* film is balanced by a scholarly investigation of that same culture through Richard Gambino's groundbreaking volume *Blood of My Blood: The Dilemma of the Italian-Americans.*[35] In this book published in 1974 just five years after Puzo's book and two years following the release of Coppola's *The Godfather*, Gambino traces and discusses the problems of identification and integration that Italians, southerners particularly, faced on their struggling road to acceptance as fully white, firstly, and non-hyphenated Americans, secondly. What is significant is that Gambino connects a strong scholarly, sociological, and anthropological study with the firsthand cultural experience of Puzo and Coppola's fictional creations by infusing his book with auto-biographical vignettes, and as a consequence his work provides a key to comprehending the subtleties of novel and film, as well as establishing a foundation for what has become a legitimate academic study of Italian-American identity.[36]

Following Gambino's academic foray into Italian-American Studies, Fred L. Gardaphe has voiced, through his many publications, the effects of Puzo's novel and Coppola's *The Godfather Trilogy* in the Italian-American community by pointing out that since Mario Puzo's *The Godfather* came along in 1969, "Godfather clubs" were being formed by young Italian-Americans who sought an ethnically unified sense of belonging.[37] In fact, cinematic representations of Italian-American ethnicity can be traced back to Frank Capra's films in which the director displayed his Sicilian sense of the world viewed or savored through the American culture that served him to cast those images much more so than many later films that claim to have Italian American themes but miss the mark.[38] Those films perhaps diluted the sense of Italianicity which pervaded them.

In the late 1940s and early 1950s, television played a formidable role in familiarizing American audiences with the lives and mores of the Italian Americans. Government investigations into organized crime (1950–1951) led by Senator Estes Kefauver brought, as noted before, Italian-Americans—hyphenated again for the occasion—to the attention of millions of Americans through the new and pervasive medium of television. Intriguing Senate hearings on live television in everybody's living room was a phenomenon that Puzo and Coppola had to emphasize. In fact, a substantial portion of *The Godfather Part II* is dedicated to a fictitious replica of the 1950–1951 hearings involving Mafia boss Frank Costello by substituting him with Michael Corleone. But radio, television, and cinema gave the lighter fare a good share as well, like the sitcom shows *The Goldbergs* (1949–1956), the radio comedy *Life with Luigi* (1948), turned into a film in 1952, and *I Remember Mama*, another successful radio comedy of 1948. They all tended to show ways (southern) Italian immigrants were assimilated into American culture. However, the only major Italian presence on American television, beyond performers such as Louis Prima, Perry Como, Frank Sinatra, Dean Martin, Connie Francis, and the Kefauver Committee's televised U.S. Senate hearings on crime, was the popular program *The Untouchables*, an ABC television series that ran from 1959 to 1963, sparking great controversy in those days both for its violent content and its portrayal of Italian-Americans.[39] The impact of this series fashioned a mythology about the Italian-American population that would become the foundation of the visual explorations of its ways of life in Francis Ford Coppola's *Godfather* films (1972–1974) and Martin Scorsese's *Mean Streets* (1973). These films, remarked Gardaphe,

> . . . contributed several character types to postwar American culture including the gangster and the uneducated urban blue-collar worker. Prior to the 1960s very few American writers of Italian descent had been educated through college. As a group, Italian Americans would not surpass the national average of the college educated until the 1990s.[40]

On the topic of education, Gambino dedicates a chapter of his book to analyzing the dilemma afflicting the first generation of (southern) Italian immigrants who were reluctant to let their children abandon *La Via Vecchia*, the old way as they called it, to embrace through a college education a new way of life, thus becoming *Americani*.[41] Puzo and Coppola conceived the character of Michael Corleone as the result of such a parental dilemma. In fact, Michael attended Dartmouth College, became a captain in the Army, and was a decorated war hero—a status which, although much appreciated by his father, was not so positively viewed by his brother Sonny, who preferred to remain anchored to *La Via Vecchia* and its old traditions.

While this contrast between the brothers makes for a dynamic fictional narrative, it also presents the very complex exploration of Italianness and Italianicity within the community and its broader context that Gambino and later scholars have considered. Though simplistic, a reading of the cultural system involved shows how life extended into art and on into academic scholarship—from Ellis Island, to Puzo and Coppola, and on to Gambino—and how the tension between Italianness and Italianicity are as dramatically demanding in real life as they are in cultural representations of that life. At the center of the drama as it oscillates mesmerizingly between fact and fiction is the Mafia, and though there has been much deconstruction of the way in which characters and stories emerged and disappeared in the evolution from Puzo's book to Coppola's film, what the two texts and their relationship demonstrates is the primacy of the issue of Italian-American identity in contemporary American culture and the precise reality of the power of the Mafia.

The Literary Adaptation

In a succinct yet eloquent essay entitled "The Literary Adaptation: An Introduction,"[42] British literary critic John Ellis ignited a debate about the differences between story and discourse that must be taken into consideration when discussing the validity of a work's transposition from novel to film.[43] Questioning whether the adaptation traded upon the memory of the novel as it derived from actual reading, or, more likely with a classic of literature from a generally circulated cultural memory, Ellis advised that "the successful adaptation is one that is able to replace the memory of the novel with the process of a filmic or televisual representation . . . the faithfulness of the adaptation is the degree to which it can rework and replace a memory."

Clearly, *The Godfather Trilogy* presents itself as a *sui generis* case since the adapters are author Mario Puzo and film director Francis Ford Coppola who, aside from sharing the same cultural context, assumed full responsibility for transferring the text from one medium to another. Such transference abated the most commonplace arguments against adaptation—that films derived from novels lack originality, foster imaginative laziness, and discredit the autonomy of the medium. Indeed, Puzo and Coppola executed the literary transference from book to film without the intervening movements of induction and deduction which usually produce an appropriate cinematic "re-writing."

Puzo and Coppola worked in tandem while adapting the novel for the screen, so the amount of re-writing in the screenplay was consentient to the highest degree. Ironically though, a reading of Puzo's original novel *The Godfather* is difficult to imagine after having seen the film(s), except perhaps for those episodes and characters present in the book which have been excluded from the screenplay.

Prior to *The Godfather*, Mario Puzo, a writer of Italian ancestry born in New York City in 1920, had published two excellent novels: *The Dark Arena* (1953) and *The Fortunate Pilgrim* (1964). The literary and critical acclaim of these works, however, produced their author little monetary gain. At age 45, Puzo needed a best-seller, a Mafia book, as his publisher suggested. So, in 1968, *The Godfather* was created. Puzo's royalties were topped by a $410,000 fee for paperback rights in addition to the film rights acquired by Paramount Pictures and a lucrative honorarium for writing the film's screenplay.[44] The novel *The Godfather*, comprising "Nine Books" divided into 32 chapters, constituted a palimpsest for *The Godfather Trilogy*'s screenplays and further literary exploits.[45]

At the time of his engagement to direct *The Godfather* (1971), Francis Ford Coppola (born in Detroit in 1939 to Carmine and Italia Coppola) had a handful of minor films to his credit. In contrast to Puzo and Coppola's struggling career stories, Italian composer Nino Rota enjoyed by 1971 an enviable popularity as a film, concert, and stage composer. Therefore, his acceptance to collaborate on a film directed by a young, little-known filmmaker was a unique event that connoted Rota's intuitive recognition of one's talent and Coppola's refined musical taste. Such chemistry of talents produced the masterpiece of film music literature I examine in the following chapters.

Chapter 4

The Sound of *The Godfather Trilogy*: Family Choral Scenes

*Nino Rota was one of those rare composers who wrote only
music they believed in. As an Italian, he was a true melodist,
unabashed to write inspired melodies at a time when his
contemporaries were tempering with experimentations and noises.
Rota's film music will be remembered as the best of its kind.*

—Miklós Rósza[1]

Introduction

As a reflection on Coppola's declaration that "the Mafia is an incredible metaphor for this country because both are totally capitalistic phenomena and basically have a profit motive," I question whether the music used in the trilogy underscores the director's feelings expressed above, and if so, how? Sicilian Mafia as well as Calabrian *'Ndrangheta* and Neapolitan *Camorra* have a long tradition of songs, ballads, and dances praising the lives of those who live outside the rules of law. The style of these songs of blood, honor, and vengeance, much influenced by Mediterranean folk traditions like *tarantella*, *pizzica*, and guttural chants, is a sonic manifestation of the ancient Mafia culture I described in Chapter 3.[2]

However, despite the initial perplexity one may experience upon listening to these songs claiming innocence for crimes committed in the name of an unlawful brand of justice, it is important to remember that these are the same chants ordinary people would sing during long laborious shifts in the olive groves or in the fields, as well as at celebrations and festivals. Thus, this phenomenon accounts for the Mafia's alleged "invisibility" or the *mafiosi*'s ability to blend with the dense fabric of the southern Italian rural population and—by extension—with that of their American "cousins."

39

The music one hears in the trilogy, though, is not based on ethno-musicological scholarship. It is the product of Coppola's vivid musical intuition supported by Rota's well-known professional expertise and Carmine Coppola's *métier* particularly relevant in the choice of source music aimed at representing the sound of everyday life in "capitalistic" America, albeit filtered through the lenses of the Italian-American experience (Italianicity).

Ironically though, in today's media-savvy culture, infested by buzzwords and sound bites, "The Sound of *The Godfather Trilogy*" remains encapsulated in the first 12 notes of Rota's *Love Theme* from Part I (see Mus. Ex. 5.7) were it emanating from an automobile horn, a cellular phone ringtone, a snippet from a television commercial, or, the music background of a video game. There is enough cultural capital charged in these 12 notes that a comparison with the opening four notes of Beethoven's *Fifth Symphony* can be entertained without the risk of blasphemy. The Romantics associated the meaning of Beethoven's musical statement with destiny, foreboding, and death. Nowadays, popular imagination has come to signify Rota's *Apollonia's Theme* (Love Theme from Part I) with something hardly signifiable: the concept of Mafia as the sonic DNA of the trilogy. Despite film producer Al Ruddy and the Italian American Civil Rights League's arm wrestling to keep out any apparent connection between the film's content and the Mafia, Rota's *Love Theme* from Part I did become its motto, albeit for all the wrong reasons, as I demonstrate in the pages ahead.

Rota composed the original scores to Part I (1972) and Part II (1974). Carmine Coppola (1910–1991), Francis' father, wrote a great deal of incidental music and selected/arranged the source music inserted in the film. In addition, Carmine Coppola composed the original score to Part III and reorganized several of the cues composed by Rota for Parts I and II. Nino Rota had died in 1979. Carmine conducted the Hollywood recording studio sessions for the music destined for Part II, sessions which Rota attended, and Part III, as well as for the music recorded on-location throughout the trilogy.[3] Carlo Savina conducted the recording sessions for the music of Part I.[4]

In the course of negotiations, Rota demanded that the finished music track be recorded in Rome. Francis Coppola accepted Rota's conditions and traveled to Italy to work with the composer as necessary. At their first meeting in Rome in August 1971, Coppola brought along a five-hour cut of the film. He and Rota viewed it at the moviola and discussed the outline of the future music track. It seems that Coppola left a copy of the film's rough cut with the composer who, according to his lifelong friend and collaborator Suso Cecchi D'Amico, was able to rescreen it as needed.[5] Coppola returned to Rome a second time in late September with an edited version of the film; at that time, Rota was ready to play for him a vast number of cues he had composed[6]; thereafter, the entire music track was planned except for *Apollonia's Theme*. Rota said the following about his experience with Francis Coppola:

> *In truth, regarding the music to* The Godfather, *Coppola gave me a great idea! On my part though, I have to say, I had developed great admiration for Coppola. He belongs, in fact, to that category of directors who, aside from possessing a true knowledge of music, feels it with profound and rapid intuition. Therefore, I listened to him attentively. He told me to adapt myself to the film's various situations and to compose a music which could constantly recall the origins of the protagonists who came mostly from Southern Italy and Sicily in particular. Coppola insisted that such music had to be embedded with Mediterranean, almost Arabic melodies evoking a feeling of nostalgia for the ancient origins of these people who later migrated to America. Therefore, I composed a music which could appear to go against the film's narrative, but cinematographically speaking it was a good thing because such a contrasting procedure offered more relevance which would not have been possible with a music destined to comment or describe the situation.[7]*

Space does not permit a full identification of the Mediterranean/Arabic qualities present in the music Rota composed for this film. It should suffice to point out, though, that the island of Pantelleria (Italy's southernmost territory) is closer to Tunisia than Sicily. Hence, cultural intercourses between the people inhabiting the shores of the Mediterranean Basin have flourished since time immemorial. Rota's uncanny musical formulaic abilities captured immediately the "Mediterranean, almost Arabic melodies" Coppola alluded to. Consider, for instance, the theme played by the unaccompanied trumpet at the beginning of each part of the trilogy. In this thematic "call" one can hear and "feel" an atavistic sound coming out of the Maghreb. The effect of this melody on the listener can be compared to that of the North African sirocco wind when it surfs across the Mediterranean before blanketing the southern Italian regions of Sicily, Calabria, and Apulia. I imagine that Rota, a longtime resident of Apulia, repeatedly experienced this unique amalgam of hot wind, sand, sea mist, and environmental sounds.[8] Furthermore, Coppola wished the composer to underscore the continuous string of murders occurring in the film with a waltz, a leitmotiv signifying a recurring cycle devoid of closure. So, *The Godfather Waltz* (see

Mus. Ex. 4.2) was born, a tune that slowly turned into a ritualistic Sicilian waltz of vengeance. I will discuss the symbolic applications of this theme in Chapter 5.

Upon Coppola's third trip to Italy in late December 1971, Rota's entire music track was recorded in Rome at the composer's expense with Carlo Savina conducting. In January 1972 Savina traveled to Hollywood to record the definitive version of Rota's cues with an American Federation of Musicians unionized studio orchestra assembled by Paramount.

While it would be speculative to assume that Rota had read Mario Puzo's novel either in English or in Italian,[9] it is plausible that he had familiarized himself with the film script[10] before viewing and "spotting" the picture. Ultimately, Rota checked all cues he had composed against a 22-page musical suggestions typescript dated December 17, 1971, furnished to him by Paramount's music editors John C. Hammell, Bill Reynolds, and Walter Murch.[11] Rota returned the typescript, now in the Paramount Music Archives, accompanied by the following note: "I have seen the film and changed the programming and moved all the changes made in the music carefully. I understand all the trouble and the care you and all your collaborators had in giving to each one [cue] his [sic] right place."

"Choral" Scenes

In his *Philosophy of Music*, a little-known pamphlet published in 1836, Italian political thinker Giuseppe Mazzini launched a diatribe against the theatrical practice of his day of using operatic choral scenes only for spectacular, ephemeral effects rather than sociopolitical pursuits. Mazzini was convinced that great moral and pedagogical lessons could be taught and learned from the choral scenes of operas if they were molded to represent the democratization and the will of the masses.[12] Indeed, Mazzini's plea was heard, and Italian opera houses became the incubators of ardent political sentiments that gained popular strength and spread across the Italian peninsula like wildfire. Thus, the Italian wars for the country's independence and unification, a period known as *Risorgimento*, erupted while the great choral frescoes of Bellini, Donizetti, and Verdi's operas blasted forth as if they had become the *Risorgimento*'s musical background. I only need to mention the opera *Nabucco* and its "*Vá pensiero*," the first of Verdi's great choruses in which one hears the collective voice of a people, a nation, and a community singing in unison to express a feeling of total unity; "a choral texture that becomes a musical metaphor of the democratic ideal."[13] In fact, by 1859 *Vá pensiero* had become the unofficial Italian national anthem so much so that people used the slogan VIVA VERDI (Long Live Verdi) as an acronym for the subversive VIVA Vittorio Emanuele R(E) D'Italia (Long Live Victor Emanuel King of Italy). Over a century later, Luigi Dallapiccola declared: "The Verdi phenomenon is inconceivable without the *Risorgimento* as he absorbed its atmosphere and tone."[14] Verdi composed several great operatic choral settings spanning *Ernani*'s fiery "Si ridesti il Leon di Castiglia" to *I vespri siciliani*, the 1855 opera heavy with *Risorgimento* allusions, whose plot, according to some, gave birth to the Mafia.[15]

My analysis of "The Sound of *The Godfather Trilogy*" is based on my reading of Rota's commentaries and spotting notes of the film's Parts I and II and on the assumption that the trilogy can be viewed as a trans-medial, operatic palimpsest comprising a series of scenes about family (Chapter 4) and the mythologies of love and death (Chapter 5). These scenes are the highlights of the 130 minutes of music that constitute the film's music track.[16] Also, in the appendix I provide the reader with cue-by-cue concordances for the whole trilogy's music track.

Many of the film's episodes involve multitudes of people similar to operatic choral scenes designed to showcase the production's full cast of characters including many extras (Mazzini and Verdi's masses) ably choreographed by the film's director.

Now, before lifting the curtain of my hypothetical operatic stage, I analyze the very brief *Prelude*; that is, the Main Title music as it is heard at the beginning of each part of the trilogy. As Marcia J. Citron noticed, "The internal structure of this motive has a formality resembling a curtain-raiser in the opera—something akin to the formality of the curse at the start of *Rigoletto* or the D-minor chords that begin *Don Giovanni*."[17]

PART I (A-I-1).[18]

The music starts on black screen and is heard until the Paramount logo is shown over a black background flashing the following words in white lettering:

MARIO PUZO'S THE GODFATHER

Solo Trumpet

Ex. 4.1. Title Theme from *The Godfather.* Composer: Nino Rota. Copyright © 1972 (renewed 2000) by Famous Music LLC. International Copyright Secured. All Rights Reserved.

PART II (A-II-1).

Part II uses the same trumpet solo music heard in Part I followed by *Michael's Theme* (see Mus. Ex. 5.2), which underscores Michael's role as the new Godfather. In fact, the screen shows a close-up of Michael with his bodyguard Rocco Lampone kissing his hand, a symbolic gesture of acceptance.

The superimposed title reads:

MARIO PUZO'S THE GODFATHER PART II

PART III (A-III-1).

The title sequence of Part III is substantially longer than the others lasting 2:50 minutes. It showcases the familiar trumpet solo as the title reads:

MARIO PUZO'S THE GODFATHER
MARIO PUZO'S THE GODFATHER PART III

In this version, the trumpet motif is repeated a second time superimposed to a sinister drone underscoring the appearance of the abandoned Lake Tahoe's Corleone Estate as a symbol of the Corleone nuclear family's disintegration.[19] Then, *The Godfather Waltz* is heard in counterpoint to Michael's voice-over reading a letter addressed to his children. The camera pans through family photographs and the view of New York City Harbor. A caption informs the viewer that the scene is set in New York City in the year 1979. This title scene follows directly into Michael's induction ceremony described later in this chapter. An alternate opening, filmed, scored but not used in the film (see A-III-1(b)), would have featured the familiar trumpet solo preceding Archbishop Gilday's monologue.

Thus, this theme is not heard in such monody-like fashion too often. It appears harmonized in various ways according to underscoring circumstances or integrated with the remaining of the cue as in the case of *The Godfather Waltz* at the conclusion of the following choral scene. (See Mus. Ex. 4.2.)

CONNIE'S WEDDING (PART I)
Long Island, New York, 1945

The elaborate Italian-American garden party given in honor of the wedding between Costanza (Connie) Corleone (Talia Shire) and Carlo Rizzi (Gianni Russo) takes place in Long Island, New York, on the last Saturday of August 1945.

Following the film's prologue in Don Corleone's shrouded-in-darkness study, instruments are heard as they tune up [00:06:39-A-I-2], then a sudden blast of sound and light brings the viewer via a very long down shot to the wedding party where guests dance to the diegetically implied sound of a "live" orchestra.

In contrast to the Mafia business attended to in the secret penumbra of Don Corleone's study, the wedding of Connie and Carlo is a family event to be celebrated "under the sun" in as flashy and opulent fashion as possible, albeit within the protection of walled gates and armed gatekeepers surrounding the Corleone's Long Island family compound. The orchestra plays *The Godfather Tarantella* [00:07:00-A-I-3],[20] a spirited score enhanced by the participants' rhythmic clapping of hands to induce all present, young and old, to "prove" on the dance floor the veracity of their Italian blood. The sentimental *Godfather Mazurka* [00:09:19-A-I-4], danced by the older first generation of immigrants, follows the exhausting tarantella. As the camera pans outside the compound's gates where cars are parked, one hears in the distance the sound of *The Godfather Fox Trot* [00:10:58-A-I-5], a clear indication that the second generation of Italian-Americans among the guests has taken over the dance floor, showing their parents how they had indeed become unhyphenated, "white," and bourgeois *Americani*. In fact, at this point Michael Corleone (Al Pacino), wearing a decorated U.S. Army uniform, escorts to a table his all-American girlfriend, Kay Adams (Diane Keaton), introducing her around to the sound of the swingy American tune *Ev'ry Time I Look in Your Eyes* [00:12:03-A-I-6] composed by Carmine Coppola. After a brief return to the fox-trot music [00:15:14-A-I-7], the scene switches to a performance of the interactive bawdy Italian wedding song *La Luna ammenzu 'o mari* [00:15:58-A-I-8]. This folk-like tune and its verses heavy with sexual overtones was attributed to a Sicilian sailor named Paolo Citorello or Citarella. It became very popular among Italian-Americans through the recorded versions of Rudy Vallee in the late 1930s and Dean Martin in the early 1940s.[21] After its choreographed performance in Part I, *La Luna ammenzu 'o mari* and its "flexible" text reached iconic status with blockbuster Mafia movies like Martin Scorsese's *Casino* (1995) and Harold Ramis' *Analyze This* (1999) starring Robert De Niro and Billy Crystal. The nostalgic enthusiasm pervading this musical homage to *La Via Vecchia* (The Old Way) changes suddenly to "bobby socks" hysteria[22] caused by the arrival of Johnny Fontane (Al Martino), a character based on Frank Sinatra, who sings diegetically for Connie her favorite song as a wedding present. The tune is *I Have But One Heart* [00:18:40-A-I-9] by Symes and Farrow.[23]

While Fontane sings, Michael tells Kay the story about the singer/actor's contract being released by a celebrated bandleader through the forceful intervention of Don Corleone (Marlon Brando) who made the bandleader an offer he could not refuse. Kay is appalled upon learning the graphic details of the deal.[24]

This wedding family/choral scene continues with a reprise of *The Godfather Mazurka* [00:21:17-A-I-10] and *The Godfather Tarantella* [00:24:43-A-I-12], interrupted by a curious 11-second snippet of Mozart's "Non so più cosa son cosa faccio" [00:23:04-A-I-11] from *Le nozze di Figaro* showing, perhaps, that opera is indeed a vivid component of Italian-American culture and therefore part of the program.[25]

The scene concludes with Don Corleone dancing with the bride, his daughter Connie, as the guests applaud. The orchestra, consisting of clarinet, saxophone, trumpet, guitar, mandolin, double bass, piano, and drum set, is now in full view playing *The Godfather Waltz* [00:25:51-A-I-13] by Nino Rota.[26] A photographer taking the classic wedding family photo portrait brings this family/choral scene to an end.

This is perhaps the most compelling operatic scene of the trilogy if one excludes the Finale of Part III in which a real opera is used to bring the saga to its conclusion. Connie's wedding has the entire splendor found in the first scene of Verdi's *La traviata*, including the introduction of the full cast of characters and the psychological portraits of single individuals both in the open—the wedding party proper—and behind closed doors in Don Corleone's study.

By contrast, the next choral scene takes the viewer to the Old World to witness Michael's Sicilian rustic wedding ceremony to Apollonia.

Ex. 4.2. *The Godfather Waltz*. Composer: Nino Rota. Copyright © 1972 (renewed 2000) Famous Music LLC. International Copyright Secured. All Rights Reserved.

APOLLONIA'S WEDDING (PART I)
Corleone, Sicily, 1947

Following the failed assassination attempt on Don Corleone's life and Michael's personal vendetta against rival Mafia boss Virgil Sollozzo (Al Lettieri) and the corrupt cop McCluskey (Sterling Hayden), Michael goes into hiding in Sicily for an indefinite period of time under the protection of Don Tommasino (Corrado Gaipa). Mario Puzo and Francis Coppola show the viewer for the first time in the film the land where the Godfather/Mafia saga originated, while placing Michael, ironically the most Americanized member of the Corleone family, in direct touch with his Sicilian roots. I discuss Nino Rota's underscoring of this entire Sicilian episode in Chapter 5. Now, I focus on another familial choral scene, the wedding ceremony and party celebrating the marriage of Michael Corleone and Apollonia Vitelli (Simonetta Stefanelli). The sound of this scene evokes a blend of rural Italianness underscoring the Vitelli family's way of life and elements of Italianicity emanating from Michael. They are especially detectable when Michael's idiosyncratic Sicilian dialect turns into educated American English every time he searches for vernacular words to express himself. Rota and Carmine Coppola underscore these two aspects of the soundtrack by using an old Sicilian folk tune identified as *Antico Canto Siciliano* [01:49:02-A-I-42].[27] This tune is played by a local small brass band when the priest finishes his wedding benediction. It continues to be heard diegetically as the band and the bridal procession move along the streets of the village.

The wedding party then dances a waltz at the sound of "Libiamo" from Verdi's *La traviata* [01:50:05-A-I-43]. Verdi's celebrated choral champagne drinking song, which could have been sumptuously executed at Connie's wedding, is here presented in a skeletal instrumental version poorly rendered by an amateurish village brass band. However, Verdi's music is particularly meaningful at this point in the film's narrative. It serves to remind the viewer that Sicilians used Verdi's toasting song to celebrate the 1860–1870 Italian Unification, the political event that, while liberating their land from the Bourbons' yoke, ushered in the formation of *mafioso* clans. Ironically, in 1947 when this wedding scene takes place, the Sicilian people were still using Verdi's toasting song to celebrate Sicily's liberation from the Nazis that occurred in 1943 through the efforts of Anglo-American troops, who, many historians argue, employed the collaboration of the Sicilian Mafia to achieve major strategic goals.[28]

This scene's conclusion shows Michael and Apollonia dancing to Carmine Coppola's *Mazurka alla Siciliana* [01:50:29-A-I-44] until it dissolves to the bridal suite in Don Tommasino's villa where bride and groom spend their wedding night. I discuss Rota's music to this episode in Chapter 5.

I turn now to a choral scene that occurs in Part II. It shows the arrival at Ellis Island of hordes of immigrants in the year 1901. This crowded episode evokes vividly Henry James' impression of Ellis Island that I quoted in Chapter 3.

NEW YORK 1901 (PART II)

The scene begins with a shot of the ship *Moshulu*[29] sailing in past the Statue of Liberty. Hundreds of immigrant families are huddled together with all their earthly possessions on deck; the stowaway boy Vito Andolini (Oreste Baldini) is among them. A previous scene taking place in Sicily showed Vito being loaded on a mule hiding in a large chest together with his belongings as he prepared for a secret escape to

America. For this pivotal scene in the film's narrative Rota composed *The Immigrant Theme*, a piece whose moods combine feelings of ethnic longing and hope [00:07:01-A-II-3].

Ex. 4.3. *The Immigrant Theme.* Composer: Nino Rota. Copyright © 1974 (renewed 2002) by Famous Music LLC. International Copyright Secured. All Rights Reserved.

The Immigrant Theme, Rota's new important musical contribution to Part II, is a work filled with romantic ardor, echoing the nostalgic yet hopeful mood of certain Slavic music like Tchaikovsky's *Marche Slave* for instance. That is not an uncommon trait in Rota's music since he, a great admirer of Russian composers from Mussorgsky to Shostakovich, often quoted them without reservation.

Rota's spotting notes reveal that he planned to score this important scene as follows:

The music must begin softly—starting even a little earlier if neces-
sary—Music should start building up from when we see the donkey
carrying Vito along a tiny street. It should underscore the fact that he
has escaped to America, thus it should show the joy. Ship's steerage
crowded with emigrants (various ambiance noises), music builds up.
Statue of Liberty (music quieter, more sustained) underscoring the
fact that he [Vito Andolini] has escaped. End. Music takes us to
America.

[Rota's notebooks are notated in an interesting mixture of Italian and English, reflecting the composer's involvement with the characters, moods, and dialogues in the film and his own private thoughts. When originally written in Italian, all quotes have been translated into English by the author. Rota's notes are always indicated in italics.]

This piece, which Rota originally entitled *Gli emigranti*, is in effect a miniature tone poem that evokes feelings of ethnic longing and hope experienced by emigrants on their voyage to faraway lands. Divided into five short sections, it concludes with a reprise of the second section and a coda. Here is an analysis of this piece in the piano reduction published on pages 30 (Mus. Ex. 4.3) and 31 of *The Godfather Trilogy: Music Highlights from I, II & III* (see appendix). The genesis of section one (measures 1–4) can be traced back to Rota's *Preludio No. 4* (Andante sostenuto ed espressivo) from *Quindici preludi per pianoforte*, composed in 1964.[30] This opening section possesses a Verdian doleful choral quality that leads to the principal theme of ethnic longing in E minor (anacrusis to measure 5 to measure 9), then another anacrusis to measure 10 leads to the theme of hope in A minor. The theme of hope, though, is followed by harmonic modulations punctuated by minor seventh chords culminating in a G sharp diminished seventh that stretches the sequence through further modulations until the reprise of section two and the restoration of the theme of ethnic longing in the familiar opening key of E minor. It is clear that Rota's musical narrative aims at underscoring the reality that for the emigrants hope is indeed a variable state of mind while longing for the abandoned country; that is, loss of one's national identity may remain a constant for the rest of their lives. The coda concludes this remarkable piece with a "sigh" of accepted resignation. The orchestral version of *The Immigrant Theme* heard in the film cue contains a brief joyous tarantella-like fragment symbolizing the immigrants' jubilation as they catch sight of the Statue of Liberty upon the ship approaching the Hudson Bay. At this point Rota celebrated the meaning of the whole piece by stating in his notebook: *Music takes us to America.*

Indeed, *The Immigrant Theme* that takes the viewer to America does so through the eyes of young Vito Andolini. The camera frames him while he gazes at the Statue of Liberty from the window of his Ellis Island quarantine cell. Vito hears diegetically implied harbor noises that traumatically remind him of the drumbeats he heard at his father's Sicilian funeral procession that opened Part II [00:01:13-A-II-2], then he sings to himself *Lu me sceccu* (My Little Donkey), a nostalgic Sicilian folk song [00:10:39-A-II-5].[31] The concluding measures of this song are accompanied by the non-diegetic sound of a church organ, which accompanies the dissolve to a grand family/choral scene: Anthony's First Communion Celebration and the ensuing festivities taking place in Nevada at Lake Tahoe's Corleone Estate. The screen shows the following caption: His Grandson Anthony Vito Corleone, Lake Tahoe, Nevada, 1958.

LAKE TAHOE, NEVADA, 1958 (PART II)

This scene begins with young Anthony Corleone (James Gounaris) moving down the aisle of a church decorated for his First Communion. The now diegetic sound of the organ carried over from the previous scene and the voice of Father Carmelo (Father Joseph Medeglia) reciting the Communion Sacraments in Latin begin this long Lake Tahoe sequence whose music consists of pieces composed/arranged by Carmine Coppola.

The lawns of the great estate on the shore of Lake Tahoe, Nevada, are covered with guests gathered for a wonderful party to honor Anthony Corleone's First Communion. A full dance orchestra plays tunes of the period on a pavilion bandstand built especially for the occasion. A couple performing Carmine Coppola's exhibition tango called *Italian Eyes* [00:12:18-A-II-7] is seen as guests continue to arrive and attendants park their cars.

A long shot of the party leads the viewer to a close-up of Mama [Carmela] Corleone (Morgana King) who says: "Look who's here" addressing her daughter, Connie, escorted by her latest fiancé Merle Johnson (Troy Donahue). Father Carmelo soon joins them while the music background is enlivened by the strains of *Heart and Soul* [00:12:52-A-II-9], a very popular tune by Frank Loesser and Hoagy Carmichael.[32] Then, the bandleader, preceded by the blaring of a fanfare and a drum roll, announces the presence of U.S. Nevada Senator Geary (G. D. Spradlin) who thanks the Corleone family for their generosity in endowing the University of Nevada as the Sierra Boys Choir diegetically intone *Mr. Wonderful* [00:15:12-A-II-12], a Tin Pan Alley song by Jerry Bock.[33] This song is directed at Michael Corleone, the signified Mr. Wonderful, who, as the boys sing, poses for the photographers holding a commemorative plaque he has just received from the Senator. The lyrics of this song allude ironically to Michael's officially acquired "whiteness" through the means of opportunistic philanthropy as Senator Geary's explicit remarks spoken behind close doors strongly suggested. However, the reader may recall Michael's very sharp reply which reminded the Senator that although politics and Mafia business were part of the same hypocrisy, it never applied to his family.

This terse dialogue between Michael and Senator Geary in the presence of Al Neri (Richard Bright), Tom Hagen (Robert Duvall), and Rocco Lampone (Tom Rosqui) is underscored by the faintly heard strains of *I Love to Hear That Old Time Music* [00:17:11-A-II-13] by Carmine Coppola. What "that old time music" is meant to signify remains open to one's imagination as it is also the subsequently heard tune by Carmine Coppola *Stumbleloo* [00:19:55-A-II-14][34] that underscores the "stumbling" appearance on the scene of the inebriated old Mafia boss Frank Pentangeli (Michael V. Gazzo). He makes his presence obnoxiously evident by mounting the bandstand and forcing the musicians to play an Italian tarantella, which turns instead, as the musicians' joke on the *mafioso*, to the American *Pop Goes the Weasel* [0024:11-A-II-16].[35] The whole scene is a demonstration of how *La Via Vecchia*, the old spirit of Italianicity embedded in Pentangeli—the Mafia boss who had succeeded Don Corleone and Peter Clemenza in the control of the New York City territory—is completely lost to the cultural Americanization; that is, gentrification of the Italian-Americans present at the gathering.

A host of tunes by Carmine Coppola continues to be heard during the remainder of the scene underscoring minor episodes. For instance, *Sophia* [00:24:48-A-II-17] is heard when Merle is introduced to Michael as Connie's new beau; *In a Paris Café* [00:27:18-A-II-18] is played by the orchestra in and out of diegesis as guests and family drink a toast at the dinner table; *Ho bisogno di te* (*Gelosia, When I'm with You*) [00:28:30-A-II-19], a song written by Francesco Pennino but arranged by Coppola, underscores a drunken and rebellious Deanne Corleone, Fredo's American wife, who dances and makes some racially charged remarks belittling her husband before guests and family[36]; *Pink Champagne* [00:30:13-A-II-20] underscores the argument taking place between Michael and Pentangeli in the presence of Neri, Rocco, Tom, and Willi Cicci (Joe Spinell), Pentangeli's bodyguard. They argue about the elimination of the Rosati Brothers in New York City[37]; and finally, at the conclusion of the evening, Michael and pregnant Kay dance to the tune *Ev'ry Time I Look in Your Eyes* [00:32:38-A-II -21]. A comparison between Connie's wedding and Anthony's First Communion choral scenes clearly shows how the Corleones' cherished Italian traditions have deteriorated in the span of 14 years.

NEW YORK CITY 1917 (PART II)

Sound, color, and ambiance change dramatically in the next familial choral scene shot in sepia tints and golden soft light. Francis Coppola takes the viewer back to 1917 New York City for a visit with his maternal grandfather, songwriter Francesco Pennino who emigrated from Naples to America in 1905. Pennino was active in the New York Italian American Community as a theater operator, composer of songs, and piano player in cafes. Some of his tunes achieved notoriety and entered the repertoire of well-known recording artists, including—it seems—Enrico Caruso. Pennino's songs belong to a Neapolitan genre called *sceneggiata*, literally meaning "staged and acted song," exactly as it is performed in this film sequence. The *sceneggiata* song can be considered an heir to the eighteenth century's *azione tragica* or *azione drammatica* or even the *melologue*. *Sceneggiate* were composed and performed on Neapolitan stages until the late 1970s. Authentic tear jerker, the most famous *sceneggiate* deal with the loss of maternal love—by death or forced separation—a sentiment very strongly felt among emigrant males. For the Neapolitan (Italian) emigrant, nostalgia for the abandoned country also assumed the oxymoron connotation of mother-country rather than father-country, thus placing a great deal of emotional weight upon learning about the physical loss of one's mother. In this film episode, the performance of Pennino's song *Senza Mamma* (*Without a Mother*) is particularly effective as the audience in the theatre assumes a participatory role like that of the chorus in an ancient Greek tragedy.[38] Pennino's *sceneggiate* songs are heard in the following order: *Napule ve salute* (*Lassanno Napule*) [*Goodbye to Naples*] [00:44:00-A-II-26], arranged by Carmine Coppola. The scene unfolds as follows: a man and a woman are finishing dancing on stage. The audience, poor Italian-Americans, sings, applauds, and whistles. Vito walks down the aisle with his friend Genco (Frank Sivero). They find seats and watch/listen to *Senza Mamma* already in progress. As part of this *sceneggiata*, Carla (Kathy Beller) delivers to Peppino (Livio Giorgi), the tenor, a letter from Naples, which conveys bad news: Peppino's mother is dead. Reprise of *Senza Mamma* after the tenor says: "*Morta! Mamma mia*" Dead! Oh, my mother! Then he weeps and sings the rest of the song which most of the audience knows by heart.[39] While Peppino and his audience pour their hearts out in Pennino's song, the action switches backstage where a real drama unfolds. Don Fanucci (Gastone Moschin), the neighborhood's Black Hand, is threatening Carla at knifepoint if her father, the theatre impresario (Ezio Flagello), does not pay up his "protection" fee. In the end, Don Fanucci lets the girl go but helps himself from the cash box. Vito and Genco witness the scene while hiding behind a corner.

Now, before moving to the next choral episode, the colorful Festa di San Rocco, Francis Coppola pays homage to his paternal grandfather Augusto and to his father Carmine with a scene which was ultimately deleted.[40] In this scene, grandfather Augusto is a mechanic who repairs guns while his young son Carmine displays his talent as a flautist in his father's workshop for the clients' delight—Vito, Clemenza, and Tessio (Abe Vigoda) in this case.[41]

The Festa di San Rocco opens with strains of the *Marcia Reale Italiana* (Italian Royal March) [01:55:07-A-II-50][42] played by an Italian-American marching band in front of the church to commemorate the first night of this annual traditional community event. Clemenza and Tessio give money to Vito as the sound of the *Marcia Reale* is followed by that of *The Star-Spangled Banner* [01:55:29-A-II-51].[43] To emphasize the musical Italianicity of this scene, Carmine Coppola introduces his *Marcia Stilo* [*sic*] *Italiano* [01:55:49-A-II-52], a march in the Italian style whose misspelled title, although probably a slip of the pen in Carmine's case, was typical of the immigrant who was no longer familiar with the correct spelling of his own language. After Vito makes Don Fanucci an offer he cannot refuse, the music track switches to Carmine Coppola's *Marcia religioso* [*sic*] [01:58:33-A-II-53], a substantial piece for large marching band followed by *Festa March* [02:02:56-A-II-55] by Coppola as well. These two pieces underscore the entire street festival episode, the murder of Don Fanucci, and the transformation of Vito Corleone from honest breadwinning family man to assassin. I return to this episode in Chapter 5.

The band's sound that one hears throughout this scene takes on a second, non-diegetic function which, according to Marcia Citron, accompanies Vito as he hops across rooftops on the way to kill Fanucci. Furthermore, she writes:

As with Verdi's structural use of the *banda* dances in *Rigoletto*, here the *banda* reinforces the fear and suspense that we experience in anticipation of what is to come. In other words, its function as a continuous stream in which dramatic strands are embedded and counterpointed is thoroughly Verdian. The grand nature of the occasion, which includes Catholic icons and ritual as well as crowds and general spectacle, recalls the *concertato* scenes of Verdi.[44]

NEW YORK CITY 1979 (PART III)

In this choral scene it is important to notice how Carmine Coppola's *Marcia religioso* is heard again in a choral arrangement, this time accompanying Michael's "Order of St. Sebastian" induction ceremony at the beginning of Part III immediately following the opening Main Title [00:05:11-A-III-4]. I do not know how intentional this was on the part of both Francis and Carmine Coppola, but it seems a curious coincidence that this very music, which underscored Vito's transition to a life of crime, is now dressed in the new clothes of the religious choral setting and serves to accompany Michael's transition to legitimacy with the blessing of no less than an archbishop.

The religious initiation ceremony is followed by a sumptuous reception that takes place in Michael's opulent New York City penthouse. Connie, now the Corleone family matron, holding a microphone in hand as if it were a commanding scepter, leads the guests in a sing along rendition of *Eh, Cumpari!* [00:05:55-A-III-5] by Julius La Rosa and Archie Bleyer while Carmine Coppola conducts a sizable diegetic orchestra. The party song *Eh, Cumpari!*, launched to great acclaim in 1953 by La Rosa,[45] enabled Francis Coppola to create another memorable operatic familial choral scene and refresh those elements of Italianicity that had been lost during the family's Americanization (gentrification) process that was already very evident in the First Communion Party episode seen in Part II. Following *Eh, Cumpari!*, one hears *El Cha Cha Cha di Santo Domingo*, consisting of *Tu* by Fernan Sanchez Fuentes, arranged by Carmine Coppola [00:07:54-A-III-6]. The Cuban song is followed by *Notturno* from String Quartet #2 in D by Alexander Borodin, arranged by Carmine Coppola [00:08:38-A-III-7].[46]

The sound of trumpets diegetically playing in unison the Sicilian folk song *Vitti 'na crozza* [00:11:11-A-III-9] by Francesco Li Causi creates a moment of down-to-earth authenticity—be it Italianness or Italianicity—to an overall rather gaudy scene. The song introduces, fanfare-like, Mary Corleone (Sofia Coppola), who speaks about the foundation that Michael has created in her name to help poor Sicilian children. As a link to earlier familial choral scenes, Johnny Fontane arrives on the premises. There is no "bobby socks" hysteria this time as the aging Johnny nostalgically sings *To Each His Own* [00:12:35-A-III-10] by Jay Livingston and Ray Evans[47] while Kay looks at family pictures on the walls and fireplace mantel until Michael joins her in his study to discuss the future of their son, Anthony, who is planning to abandon law school to become an opera singer. The discussion between Kay, Michael, and later Anthony (Franc D'Ambrosio) is underscored by Carmine Coppola's *Sophia* [00:16:05-A-III-11], a song previously heard in Part II at Anthony's Lake Tahoe First Communion Party, perhaps reminding the viewer about Anthony's determining moments in his life, such as the First Communion and seeking his father's approval for a singing career. After some convincing, Michael decides to let Anthony pursue the career he wishes for.

The diegetic party music continues with more songs by Carmine Coppola: *Dimmi, dimmi, dimmi* [00:18:44-A-III-12], which introduces the old *mafioso* Don Altobello (Eli Wallach), and *On Such a Night* [00:21:28-A-III-13], which ushers to the scene Vincent Mancini (Andy Garcia). Then, the presence of young New York Mafia boss Joey Zasa (Joe Mantegna) is underscored by the same cue Rota used to underscore Luca Brasi in Part I [00:22:55-A-III-14]. The re-use of Luca's cue establishes some affinity between Luca and Zasa and their similar "departure" from the film's narrative. As Zasa presents Michael with an award from the Meucci Foundation, followed by a settlement between Zasa and Vincent, the strains of Carmine Coppola's *In a Paris Café* [00:23:50-A-III-15], a melody previously used in Part II's Lake Tahoe First Communion Party, concludes the episode.

After business is taken care of in Michael's study, the camera pans to the party scene proper where commemorative family photographs are being taken while the orchestra ironically plays *Beyond the Blue Horizon* [00:29:40-A-III-16] by W. Franke Harling, Leo Robin, and Richard A. Whiting.[48] Finally, the scene concludes with a touch of nostalgia: Michael and Mary dance to the diegetic performance of Rota's *The Godfather Waltz* [00:30:26-A-III-17] just as Don Corleone and Connie did at the end of the familial choral scene in Part I. But the sense of nostalgia does not end in Michael's penthouse apartment; another choral scene takes the viewer to the streets of New York City's Little Italy where a colorful religious festival replicating the Festa di San Rocco observed in Part II is in progress. On this occasion, Vincent, impersonating a horse-mounted policeman, shoots Joey Zasa to death. The music underscoring the scene is *Siciliana* [01:19:24-A-III-35], a piece for large marching band written by Carmine Coppola that brings to mind the scene in Part II when Vito kills Don Fanucci.

Again, Marcia J. Citron reflects on this episode's *mise-en-scène* with appropriate words:

> In *Godfather III*, a Titian-like palette of rich maroon replaces darkness in many scenes, such as when Michael conducts business in his study during the opening party scene. The change reflects Michael's turn toward redemption and is meant to suggest his nobility and his-torical connectedness. Beyond these local inflections, the studied to-nal arrangement in the trilogy gives a feeling of artfulness. This in it-self is operatic.[49]

HAVANA, CUBA, 1959 (PART II)[50]

This episode takes place in Havana on the eve of the Cuban Revo-lution. It culminates in a chaotic choral finale, which, aside from being essential to the film's narrative, symbolizes the end of an era in Cuban history and the installation of the Fidel Castro regime.

Local color, movement of people, ambiguities, and political over-tones filling the scene are underscored by a variety of diegetic and non-diegetic music cues provided by Rota and Carmine Coppola.

The first episode begins with a spectacular shot of the Caribbean surf that dissolves to Michael, his bodyguard Busetta, and a chauffeur riding in a car through the bustling streets of Havana. The episode con-cludes with the arrival of Fredo (John Cazale) in Michael's hotel room carrying a briefcase containing some two million dollars. The music track throughout this episode consists of Rota's colorful orchestral cue entitled *Havana* [01:25:56-A-II-38].

Rota's first impressions upon viewing this cue were: *Havana (we see a mixed guitar ensemble playing). [They play] "Santa Fe" with guitars and orchestra in Habanera tempo with one saxophone or more.*

It is possible that the "Santa Fe" Rota referred to was *A Santa-Fè*, a successful song he had composed for the film *Gli uomini sono nemici* (Ettore Giannini, 1947). Next, as Fredo and Michael are seated at an outdoor café table discussing the motives behind the Cuban trip, Mi-chael explains to Fredo his plan of action that includes the killing of Hyman Roth. In the meantime, one hears a Cuban traditional tune called *Guantanamera* [01:27:49-A-II-39] arranged by Carmine Coppola and performed diegetically by roving street musicians. It is interesting to note that although Carmine Coppola copyrighted the use of *Guantanamera*, the song had been suggested by Rota in the first place. In fact, he wrote the following in a memo-to-self: *Guantanamera*

[is] *a beautiful Cuban song. I could use it for the scenes of the Revolution, especially toward the end when everybody is running scared. It is a one hundred year old song in the Public Domain and very meaningful to Cubans.*

The scene continues with an episode occurring at Aqua Luz, a plush Havana nightclub. The music heard is *Music for Aqua Luz* [01:34:56-A-II-40] by Carmine Coppola, followed by *El Cha Cha Cha di Santo Domingo*, consisting of *Tu* by Fernan Sanchez Fuentes, arranged by Carmine Coppola with new lyrics by Italia Coppola [01:35:17-A-II-40]. Fictitious Cuban star Yolanda, impersonated by singer/actress Yvonne Coll, performs the song. From the plush nightclub the scene moves to Havana's red-light district for a sex show. There, Michael, Senator Geary, and other notable guests from the United States join Fredo and his party.

This is an episode of pivotal importance because it confirms to Michael that Fredo is indeed the traitor in the family. In fact, it was Fredo who allowed Roth and his thugs to attempt the assassination of Michael, Kay, and their children in their home in Lake Tahoe following Anthony's First Communion celebration. I discuss the details of this scene in Chapter 5.

During the nightclub episode the viewer hears *Danza esotica (Rumba di Amor)* [01:36:39-A-II-41] by Carmine Coppola while a large room with platforms is arranged around a circular area. Men—tourists and businessmen—stand on different levels forming the audience. Fredo leads his party into the dive. Superimposed on the diegetic sultry sound of an alto saxophone playing Coppola's *Danza esotica* is the non-diegetic glacial tone of a bass clarinet articulating the opening notes of *The Immigrant Theme* (Mus. Ex. 4.3) as the camera closes up on Michael's face [01:38:08-A-II-42]. It shows Michael's disdain for the whole scene and for Fredo's foolish behavior. I consider Rota's use of the deep sound of the bass clarinet as an excellent psychological brush stroke to express Michael's glacial inner feelings of contempt toward his brother.

Next scene takes place in the presidential palace where Cuban President Fulgenzio Batista (Tito Alba) and his guests are celebrating New Year's Eve. They dance to *My Tropical Love* consisting of *La Paloma* by Sebastian Yradier[51] arranged by Carmine Coppola [01:40:07-A-II-45]. While Michael and his group are seated at a table, this episode intercuts to the killing of Busetta at the hands of the Cuban police as he attempts to murder Roth at the hospital.

A brief yet highly dramatic and fundamental episode takes place in the presidential palace's ballroom at the sound of Carmine Coppola's *El Padrino* [01:41:34-A-II-46]. As the guests kiss each other celebrating the New Year, Michael kisses Fredo in Sicilian fashion on the mouth while telling him that he knew he had betrayed the family. Then, the strains of *Guantanamera* [01:43:10-A-II-47] take the viewer from the ballroom to the streets of Havana where Fidel Castro's Revolution has indeed erupted. Michael gets into a car that will take him to a plane bound for the United States.

This frantic choral episode was annotated by Nino Rota as follows:

> *"Rite of Spring" at [0:58] a whole phrase built on Michael's Theme high and tragic. Sequence of the exit. Starting to build. Encounter Michael and Fredo. As Michael's automobile leaves, music builds. Man thanks Michael Corleone. Guantanamera (perhaps this song is now too happy). Man asks to board Roth's plane. Close up of Michael whose facial expression is similar to that in the end of Part 1 of Godfather I. Michael's Theme played softly, then even less, ending heartbroken, empty. This is a piece formed by themes that come and go among noises and people running all over the place. The music has to emerge through all this.*

For the Revolution pandemonium, Rota employs rhythmic and thematic material borrowed from the opening measures of Stravinsky's ballet *The Rite of Spring*, whose premiere in 1914 generated a riot among the Parisian audience as the work ushered a new beginning in modern music. This is not the first time that Rota resorted to quoting Stravinsky's masterpiece; in fact, his score for the ballet *La strada* (1966) quotes liberally a long stretch of *The Rite of Spring*. Rota was perhaps correct in thinking about *Guantanamera* as too happy a song for the occasion. However, irony could have played an important role under the circumstances as the Castro Revolution did promise "New Happiness" to the Cuban people.

NEW YORK CITY 1920s (PART II)

I have inserted this ensemble scene here because of a remark I found in Rota's notebook regarding the challenge he was experiencing while underscoring this episode. He wrote:

> *. . . the music must bring [the viewer] from Havana to the present point. Leopoldo's sequence is sad yet a little humorous in order to provide a bit of relief. [Music from when] Vito leaves Leopoldo with the words "I will remember" and Leopoldo answers "What a character!" (light transition with a little bit of humor), Leopoldo looks at*

the legs of a female passerby—interior of shop—dialog; we see Leopoldo outside the shop's glass door, then he walks in. Leopoldo speaks.

It seems that in August 1974 when Rota saw the rough cut of Part II, the transition from the Cuban Revolution to a flashback in early 1920s New York City had been put together rather abruptly. Instead, the final montage shows a charming ensemble episode whose music, written in operetta style, brings to my mind lighthearted moments from Rota's opera *Il cappello di paglia di Firenze*.

This scene takes place on the crowded streets of New York City's Italian neighborhood where Signor Roberto (Leopoldo Trieste) and Vito Corleone (Robert De Niro) stand on the sidewalk discussing Signora Colombo's situation. The problem at hand is that Signor Roberto, the landlord, dislikes the fact that his tenant Signora Colombo (Saveria Mazzola), a friend of the Corleones, wishes to keep a dog in her apartment. She has appealed to Vito for intervention.

In underscoring this scene Rota re-adapts a short tap dance piece evocative of the *Fox-Trot* in William Walton's *Façade* [00:10:44-A-II (disc 2)-61],[52] a variant of which Rota had used in 1965 for Federico Fellini's *Giulietta degli spiriti* (see Mus. Ex. 4.4). Furthermore, Leopoldo Trieste, the Italian actor playing Signor Roberto the landlord, co-starred in *Lo sceicco bianco* (1952), the film that launched the Rota–Fellini collaboration, and later in *I vitelloni* (1953). Thus, this short episode, aside from providing Part II with a rare moment of humor, becomes Rota's homage to Fellini as well. Parenthetically, it should be pointed out that in the notebook quoted above, Rota's subconscious objectivity made him refer to Signor Roberto as Leopoldo [Trieste].

Ex. 4.4. Theme from *Giulietta degli spiriti*.

Another ensemble scene entitled "The New Carpet" is characterized like "The Landlord" by a veiled sense of humor as Peter Clemenza (Bruno Kirby Jr.) and Vito Corleone steal a carpet from a wealthy neighbor's house. Amid the colorfully crowded streets of the Italian neighborhood so masterfully re-created by the trilogy's set designer Dean Tavoularis, Clemenza and Vito are shown standing at the front door of a house. Clemenza rings the bell. Nobody is home, so he looks for the key under the mat. Ultimately, Clemenza opens the door with a knife to gain access to the house. The twosome then roll up and carry out a valuable Persian rug destined to ornament Vito's apartment. This is, in fact, Clemenza's way of thanking Vito for having hidden his guns in an earlier episode.

The score used for this cue is identical to the *Allegretto Natalizio* Rota originally composed for the Christmas scene in Part I, which I describe in Chapter 5. In the present cue [00:13:38-A-II (Disc 2)-62] the music underscores the mischievous character of Peter Clemenza (Richard Castellano in Part I) portraying him as a kind of Sancho Panza figure at the side of the emerging Don (Quixote) Vito Corleone. The episode continues as Vito and Clemenza carry the rolled-up rug on their shoulders; they go up the steps, enter Vito's apartment, and install the new carpet. An early music suggestion sheet noted that after having spread the rug on the floor, Clemenza would have sung without accompaniment to baby Santino in a direct recording. Although deleted in the 2001 DVD Collection, this little scene can be viewed in the 1981 Epic. Here are Rota's notes pertaining to this scene:

> *They are carrying the rug through the streets—they have stolen a rug. Interior of Vito's house where he plays with the baby ends when he sees the baby. The family of Vito on the way up. The family of Michael on the way down. One should always keep in mind that this is a memory of simple taste "on the way up." The dialogue between Vito and Clemenza sitting at the kitchen table should have a sustained music background very mysterious like a child who says something: and it is the truth. Vito's pondering expression (because inside he has not accepted the situation) should be characterized by silence—then when he sits at the table (a low third) but not too dark—sufficiently to show that he is thinking. Dialogue around the table and dissolve.*

It is a pity that the voice of Clemenza singing to Santino was not included in the 2001 DVD Collection. It would have added a touch of humanity to the behavior of these young people who were about to turn their lives from that of petty thieves to cold-blooded murderers. Rota's observation about creating for this episode a musical background very mysterious "like a child who says something and it is the truth" is another manifestation of the composer's determination to find candor in any human being and situation. It seems that Rota wanted to emphasize such rare moments in both Parts I and II. This scene, ending with a very romantic rendition of *The Immigrant Theme* [00:58:49-A-II-33], is suddenly interrupted by the sight on screen of a high-speed train honking in the night. The carefree atmosphere created by "The New Carpet" music brings the viewer, through a very brief account of *The Immigrant Theme*, immediately into the sinister world of Michael Corleone. As Michael is shown sitting in his compartment in the train, the diegetic sound of water being poured into a glass is heard. That sound brings back memories of the baptism scene in Part I and its symbolic washing of one's sins.

THE FORTIES (PART II)

This last familial choral scene takes place at the end of Part II. It begins with a flashback of the Corleones' dining room in the year 1941. The family gathers at the dining room table to celebrate Don Vito Corleone's birthday: Sonny (James Caan), Carlo Rizzi—being introduced by Sonny to Connie—Tom, Michael, Fredo, and Tessio, who comes in carrying a large box containing the birthday cake. Sonny argues with Michael about his decision to enlist in the Army. There is a great deal of scurrying in the adjoining room as Sonny rises. Tom and Michael remain seated, then Tom and Sonny exit arguing while Michael sits alone at the table drinking wine. A whispering warns the group that Don Vito has entered the vestibule; they all exclaim "Surprise!" and sing "for he's a jolly good fellow." Don Vito Corleone is not shown, however the viewer can certainly feel his presence through the excitement transpiring from the family group.

The music heard throughout this scene [01:05:00-A-II (Disc 2)-70] emanates from a radio situated somewhere in the dining room or in the adjoining parlor. An early music suggestion sheet informed the music editors that the temporary track used for this scene was Glenn Miller's *Sunrise Serenade*, alerting them that Francis Coppola would have selected another tune arranged by Carmine Coppola in 1941 style. Rota, on the other hand, jotted down in his notebook the following: *I must do this piece about the family in 1940—radio—piece in the style of Glenn Miller as in "source music."*

Rota did compose a cue entitled *The Forties*, which was recorded on October 30, 1974, but it was not used. Carmine Coppola's Glenn Miller style arrangement, also recorded on October 30, 1974, was used instead.

N. 29 –

Siena d'amore (vedi tempi altro quaderno)

musica suonata da fuori
da mandolini e chitarre

motivo come di romanza siciliana
o d'opera

Chapter 5

The Sound of *The Godfather Trilogy*: Tales of Love and Death

I am not close to the world of The Godfather *because I don't understand violence. The assumptions of those films—stealing and murders—are for me psychological abjections.*

—Nino Rota[1]

If the Mafia is the collective metaphor overshadowing the familial choral scenes discussed in Chapter 4, can love play a role in them? Intuitively, my answer would tilt toward the negative; however, given the operatic approach chosen to analyze the trilogy's music track, manifestations of love and their sonic representations may account for supportive, essential components of the film's narrative. In this chapter, I plan to investigate the function of the music Rota used to underscore the relationships between Michael and his wives Apollonia and Kay.

MICHAEL, KAY, AND APOLLONIA: LOVE BETWEEN REALITY AND MYTH

At the beginning of the trilogy, Kay appears to be totally and tenderly in love with Michael, then her feelings turn tragically into contempt for the man, who although professing to reciprocate her total and tender love, tragically and repeatedly shuts her out of his life. I believe that these were the reasons why Rota did not compose a love theme that reflected the couple's feelings for each other. Instead he underscored their relationship with the following icy descending chromatic sequence of intervals of parallel fifths:

Ex. 5.1. Parallel Fifths.

With this simple harmonic devise and its diaphanous instrumentation (flutes and celesta), Rota wanted to emphasize how the Michael/Kay relationship was indeed devoid of a "tonal" body, stability, and passion like a quasi motto for sterility. Furthermore, Rota's use of parallel fifths conveys an operatic allusion to Puccini's opening of Act III of *La bohème*, a moment in the opera when the impulsively passionate Mimí/ Rodolfo relationship had become ambiguously cold.[2] Thus, without a love theme, Rota abandons Michael and Kay's musical characterization to be represented by their own individual themes, as I demonstrate in the course of this chapter. But first, I follow Michael Corleone and Kay Adams' appearances in the film's chronological context.

They met as fellow students at Dartmouth College in New Hampshire and became engaged. They are "officially" seen together for the first time in August 1945 at Connie and Carlo Rizzi's wedding and again at Christmastime in a New York City hotel room. Michael and Kay are in bed basking in the afterglow of lovemaking. They cajole about what excuse to give to the Corleone family regarding their absence at the family compound in Long Island as overnight guests; the reason for not going to Long Island is as an unmarried couple Don Corleone's strict moral standards would have required them to sleep in separate rooms. No music is heard during this "pink comedy" scene[3] until they come out of Best & Co., a fashionable New York City department store. They look very much like any young American bourgeois couple buying Christmas presents. The non-diegetic music accompanying this episode is a seasonally appropriate song by Hugh Martin and Ralph Blane entitled *Have Yourself a Merry Little Christmas*, performed by Al Martino impersonating the fictional celebrity Johnny Fontane encountered at Connie's wedding [00:39:45-A-I-19]. The couple's bliss is caught by a medium shot of traffic and pedestrians showing them kissing as they walk.

After Christmas shopping Michael and Kay adjourn for a late afternoon at the movies. Next they exit Radio City Music Hall where they watched *The Bells of St. Mary's*, a film by Leo McCarey starring Ingrid Bergman and Bing Crosby.[4] While walking, Michael and Kay engage in a dialogue underscored by the non-diegetic strains of *The Bells of St. Mary's*, the film's title song written by A. E. Adams and Douglas Furber [00:45:46-A-I-24], which offers to the viewer the impression that the tune was still ringing in their ears.[5] In the course of their dialogue Kay asks Michael if he would have liked her better if she were Ingrid Bergman or a nun, thus advancing the idea that she, a Protestant, would contemplate converting to Catholicism if "Michael would have liked her better"! Michael and Kay's attention, though, is suddenly caught by a newspaper stand where they read the headlines of the *Daily Mirror* announcing that Vito Corleone is feared dead.

Following Don Corleone's assassination attempt and the Don's hospitalization, Michael and Kay are shown having dinner in their hotel room. This episode is underscored by a diegetically implied rendition of Irving Berlin's 1944 hit song *All of My Life* [00:59:45-A-I-29].[6] The song's lyrics, *"I just want the right to love you/All of my life/Just the right to take care of you/All of my life,"* sung by a female vocalist, reflect more Kay's love for Michael than vice versa. In fact, this scene signals the first time that Michael separates Kay from the rest of his family when he insists on wanting to visit his father at the hospital without her. The Michael/Kay relationship is interrupted without explanation by Michael's secret escape to Sicily after he murders Sollozzo and McCluskey. At least two years pass before the couple meets again, this time at the play yard near a New Hampshire elementary school where Kay now teaches. Michael is a changed man; he is the new Godfather of the Corleone family, a crucial moment in the film for Rota to introduce *Michael's Theme*, a melody of poignant beauty.

Ex. 5.2. *Michael's Theme.* Composer: Nino Rota. Copyright © 1972 (renewed 2000) by Famous Music LLC. International Copyright Secured. All Rights Reserved.

This very important theme, which will be heard through the very end of the trilogy, was previously used by Rota as Fischietto's *Funeral March* in the 1970 film *I clowns* by Federico Fellini. Thus, I venture to say that the composer wanted the viewer to see Michael, the "new" Godfather, as a tragic *persona* wearing a mask, a costume like a Fellinian clown or even an operatic one like Verdi's Rigoletto's.[7] Very often in the trilogy, *Michael's Theme* is presented underlined by a funereal dotted thumping rhythm (Mus. Ex. 5.3) or by a steady beat emanating from the low register of a piano or played by timpani (Mus. Ex. 5.4).

Ex. 5.3. Pounding Beat A.

Ex. 5.4. Pounding Beat B.

I will point out the symbolic applications of these two rhythmic patterns as they occur. Now, I return to Michael and Kay and their reunion in New Hampshire. A medium long shot shows Kay leading a group of children into the schoolyard path. She sees Michael standing beside a parked black Cadillac, then they engage in a dialogue underscored by *Michael's Theme* [02:12:41-02:14:40-A-I-47-48-49]. At this point, Michael asks Kay to become his wife, the mother of his children.

The beautifully wrought *Michael's Theme* and the concluding *Godfather Waltz*, symbolically representing the son "becoming" his own father, are followed by the descending sequence of fifths as Michael and Kay exit the scene. The latter musical code symbolizes Kay's perplexity at Michael's marriage proposal. In fact, she gives him no immediate answer. Rota labeled this pivotal cue "Autumn," referring to the "changing" visual reflections of the characteristic autumnal New England landscape in which the scene takes place. Furthermore, Autumn is intended in this instance as a psychological season of self-reflection in one's life: Michael replacing his father, thus getting older prematurely, then seeking a wife to build a nuclear family of his own. The reader should remember that in the course of their dialogue Michael says "*I love you Kay*" only at the conclusion of his plea; otherwise he emphasizes that *he needs her, he cares for her*! As Michael becomes the new Godfather, his theme foreshadows murders just as *The Godfather Waltz* underscored Don Vito Corleone's deeds. A year after this episode takes place, the couple marries in New England: "A quiet wedding, with only her family and a few of her friends present," wrote Mario Puzo.[8] Michael and Kay have two children, Anthony and Mary.

As Rota's sequence of parallel fifths predicted, their marriage turns into a tragic affair especially after Michael learned from Kay that she had had an abortion, not a miscarriage as he had previously been led to believe. In the course of a *verismo*-drenched operatic duet, although one without a music track (00:31:05-A-II (Disc 2)], Kay yells at Michael about her refusal to bring into the world another child of his, a son no less. By uttering such a dramatic revelation Kay knew all too well that for a woman to abort her child was, in Italian-American cultural terms, the ultimate act of contempt against the child's father and a mortal sin in the eyes of the Roman Catholic faith she had embraced.

The theme that Rota composed to portray Kay is heard for the first time during the "Bedroom Shooting" episode in Part II [00:34:44-A-II (Disc 1)-22]:

Ex. 5.5. *Kay's Theme.* Composer: Nino Rota. Copyright © 1974 (renewed 2002) by Famous Music LLC. International Copyright Secured. All Rights Reserved.

Kay's Theme is characterized by melodic and harmonic structures that "sound" American, sophisticated, and bluesy as this theme serves to distinguish Kay's WASP (White, Anglo-Saxon, Protestant) upbringing from that of the Italian-Americans in the film. Interestingly though, Rota used the same thematic incipit when he characterized the figure of Maria (The Virgin Mary) in his 1968 *Sacra rappresentazione "La Vita di Maria."*[9] I view such a coincidence as a sign that Rota considered Kay like a secular Madonna; see, for instance, Deleted [Additional] Scene 26 in the DVD Collection in which Kay, having converted to Catholicism, lights candles in church praying for Michael's redemption with the fervor of a newly found zeal which often obfuscates the boundary between the sacred and the secular. At that moment in the film the Kay/Maria's theme is heard played by the full orchestra with great fervor as the end credits begin to crawl. This revelatory scene would have concluded Part II as it concluded Puzo's original novel. Deleted from the released commercial prints of the film, the scene was restored in 1977 to end the nine-hour NBC television mini-series entitled *Mario Puzo's* The Godfather: *The Complete Novel for Television.*

Another powerful scene involving Michael and Kay occurs in Part II at the Lake Tahoe family estate upon Michael's return from his trip to Havana. Rota's music carries on this episode's narrative since it has no dialogue [00:00:03-00:01:37-A-II (Disc 2)-57-58]. The scene unfolds as follows: It is a cold winter day and the ambiguous descending sequence of fifths is heard again, suggesting that Michael and Kay's relationship has remained as incorporeal as ever. Then Rota offers a version of *Michael's Theme* in a manner strongly resembling certain anxiety-laden moments one finds in the music of Schumann or Brahms. In this instance the violas' syncopated accompaniment support the violins passionately playing *Michael's Theme*, thus evoking feelings of intense longing or regret, especially when Michael looks at Kay busy at the sewing machine. She does not notice his presence. Michael walks away, crosses the snowy ground of the estate, and reaches his mother's quarters to confide in her by conversing in Sicilian, their ancestral language. Coppola states in his voice-over commentary in the DVD set that this episode is reminiscent of Penelope in the *Odyssey*, a point of view I elaborate upon later in my analysis. For now, I want to emphasize that the power of Rota's score in this melodramatic episode is breathtaking as Michael renounces Kay in order to seek comfort in his mother's arms.

Just as powerful as the episode described above is the closing scene of Part I [02:48:01-A-I-56] when Kay asks Michael whether he had ordered the killing of Carlo Rizzi. After Michael's staunch denial, Al Neri closes Michael's office door, thus blocking Kay from interfering with the business side of the family.

A similar scene occurs in Part II [00:58:27-A-II (Disc 2)] when Kay, now divorced from Michael and forbidden to see her children, manages, with Connie's consent, to visit with Anthony and Mary at the Lake Tahoe compound. However, as she procrastinates saying goodbye to Anthony, Michael enters the room. He looks contemptuously at Kay and shuts the door on her face in a very operatic fashion as it concludes Part II.

Many years pass by before Michael and Kay see each other again—this time at the ceremony and party in honor of Michael's induction in the Order of St. Sebastian at the beginning of Part III. On that occasion, Mary and Anthony accompany Kay and her husband Douglas, a New York lawyer. Kay greets Michael with respect, although when alone she does not mince words about her feelings of the hypocrisy pervading the entire induction ceremony. She pleads with Michael for their son Anthony's case of wanting to pursue a career as an opera singer. Ultimately Michael grants Anthony his consent to do as he wishes.

On another occasion Kay is shown visiting Michael at the hospital after he suffers a diabetic attack. Their conversation is affectionate, and the fact that *Kay's Theme* underscores Kay's appearance on the scene [01:10:41-A-III-31] conveys the notion that she still has ambiguous yet affectionate feelings for him.

Michael and Kay reunite again in Palermo, Sicily, to attend Anthony's debut as Turiddu in Pietro Mascagni's opera *Cavalleria rusticana.* Although the May 10, 1989, first draft of Part III script indicates that at this time the couple physically rekindles their love or whatever was left of it, the film shows the couple just enjoying a cordial middle-aged if gallant relationship in the course of a daytime excursion through the Sicilian countryside and into the town of Corleone, a scene strangely underscored by the *Love Theme from Part I* [01:53:53-A-III-54]. I interpret Coppola's dramaturgical choice of the non-diegetic use of Rota's *Love Theme* in terms of Joseph Kerman's imaginative reminiscence, in this case as a reminder of things past revolving around Michael's exclusion of Kay from his intimate thoughts. More appropriately, though, one hears during the same episode some Sicilian folk music accompanying rustic wedding festivities and a puppet show playing the old Sicilian legend called *La baronessa di Carini*, the dreadful 16th-century story about a young bride killed by her father because she had fallen in love with her cousin [01:55:16-01:56-A-III-55]. The puppet show does make an ironic allusion to the love affair actually blossoming between Mary and Vincent in the film's plot. Michael and Kay dance at the rustic wedding party to the sound of diegetic music performed by a trio of trumpet, guitar, and accordion [01:54:53-A-III-54].

During their lunch break at Don Tommasino's villa, Michael learns that the old Don has been assassinated. The tragic news brings back many years of bad memories, crimes, blood, and endless vendetta. Kay's calvary-like relationship with Michael does not end here though but at the very conclusion of the trilogy, as I describe at the end of the chapter.

THE MYTH OF APOLLONIA'S THEME

> *I remained a little perplexed, thinking that it would have been super-*
> *fluous to invent something new. So, I selected four or five themes I*
> *had composed for other films of Southern Italian flavor and em-*
> *barked—as usual—upon inflicting my friends with a choice of their*
> *own about the most suitable of those themes. Finally, we concluded*
> *that a theme composed some fifteen years earlier had the right poten-*
> *tial. It was a theme originally conceived as a sprightly, teasing little*
> *march.*[10]

With this quote, Rota dispelled the notion about any inspirational epiphany one would have searched for regarding the genesis of *Apollonia's Theme*. If a bit disingenuous, Rota's comments correspond to reality. In an Italian newspaper article dated December 24, 2005, 100-year-old Prudenzina Giannelli reminisced about her old friend Nino Rota. Ms. Giannelli, for whom I had played the violin when I was a little boy, recalled that Rota never released publicly a piece of his music without her affectionate approval. Thus, I would assume that Prudenzina and other friends could have had a say in Rota's adaptation of the little march from the film *Fortunella* to what became the mythical *Apollonia's Theme*, one of the most famous love themes in the history of film music. Music examples 5.6 and 5.7 give a comparison of the two themes:

Fortunella's:

Ex. 5.6. Theme from *Fortunella*.

Apollonia's:

Ex. 5.7. Love Theme from *The Godfather.* Composer: Nino Rota. Copyright © 1972 (renewed 2000) by Famous Music LLC. International Copyright Secured. All Rights Reserved.

The uproar generated in 1972 by the inclusion of this tune in the soundtrack of Part I disappointed Rota very much, especially since, due to such adverse publicity, the American Academy of Motion Pictures withdrew the composer's 1973 Oscar nomination for Best Original Score.[11]

Apollonia's Theme is heard for the first time halfway through Part I (96 minutes and 31 seconds into the picture). At first, the theme serves to underscore the geographical transformation of the visual landscape from the preceding scene that took place in Don Corleone's hospital room in New York City to the Sicilian countryside [01:36:31-A-I-37]. Appropriately, Rota's melody, lushly orchestrated, possesses a serene, sunny, pastoral character punctuated by the sporadic sound of cowbells. However, Rota's original cue, entitled *Sicilian Pastorale,* started in Don Corleone's hospital room with an *arioso* English horn solo (see Mus. Ex. 5.8) whose melodic progressions reflect indeed a Mediterranean/Arabic *melopea* with which Rota intended to set the mood for the whole Sicilian episode as a mythical outlook sprawling out of the ailing Don's imagination: a vision about Michael—his favorite hero son—walking through their ancestral land. This cue can be heard in its entirety in CD 1, Track 6.

Ex. 5.8. English Horn Solo.

The above melody, introduced during the lap dissolve that takes the viewer to Sicily, is a reminder of the English horn solo (Shepherd's Call) heard at the start of act 3 of *Tristan und Isolde*—"die alte Weise"—which expresses Tristan's memories of his ancient homeland and the death of his father when he was a boy. In the film's final cut though, after a brief olio-like graphic pastoral landscape, Michael and his bodyguards Calo (Franco Citti) and Fabrizio (Angelo Infanti) are now walking through the fields as the landscape unfolds, while *Apollonia's Theme*, played by a solo oboe, evokes the sound of an Arcadian land as it had metamorphosed from the atavistic trumpet solo motif heard at the beginning of the film. My interpretation of Rota's application of *Apollonia's Theme* is that it signifies more a mythological love for *Triskelion*, the ancient Greek symbol for Trinacria/Sicilia (Sicily) rather than that for a mortal human being. After all, Apollonia, whose name is the feminine of Apollo, may have never existed, just like other mythical creatures resembling Penelope or Nausicaa or even a sort of Botticellian Venus born out, as I said before, of Don Vito Corleone's near-death experience as he rested on his hospital bed. The reader should remember Calo's expression when he attempted to describe Apollonia to her own father: "Her beauty was more Greek than Italian!" A validation of this interpretation can be found in Part III when Francis Coppola makes Anthony Corleone sing for his father a special song, "an authentic Sicilian song" entitled *Brucia la terra* (This Burning Soil). The "authentic Sicilian song" is, of course, Rota's *Apollonia's Theme* sung to Sicilian verses by Giuseppe Rinaldi [01:30:02-A-III-41]. The enormous popularity this theme had achieved in "real" life certainly contributed to its "acquired" mythical status, especially if one considers the 17-year lapse (25 years in the fictional narrative) between the trilogy's Part I and Part III. In that scene Michael is brought to tears by the evocative power of the song whose diegetic and non-diegetic rendition underscores his flashback reverie about the mythical Apollonia.[12]

In Part I, beautiful, young Apollonia and a group of her village maidens are shown accompanied by two stocky matrons garbed in black. They walk along the field gathering pink and purple flowers, which they mix with orange and lemon blossoms. The group intones a Sicilian folk song entitled *Sciuri, Sciuri* or *Fiuri, Fiuri* (Flowers, Flowers) [01:39:10-A-I-39].[13] The women are unaware that Michael, Calo, and Fabrizio are watching them in admiration. Then Fabrizio says in Sicilian, "Mamma mia what a beauty," and, looking at Michael who cannot take his eyes off Apollonia, "I think you got hit by the thunderbolt." Calo, also speaking Sicilian, intervenes by saying: "Michael, in Sicily women are more dangerous than shotguns." At this point Apollonia looks back toward Michael.

Apollonia's Theme is heard next when Michael meets her father to propose marriage and again in an extended version played by the full orchestra during the couple's engagement party. Finally it is heard at their wedding night played very poetically *sottovoce* like a nocturnal serenade by mandolin, guitar, and accordion [01:50:51-A-I-45].[14]

This Sicilian love episode, containing the most poetic scenes of the trilogy, does not end as tragically as it appears on screen. The mythical Apollonia perhaps did not die blown up in an automobile; she just vanished in the same way she had appeared on the scene. In fact, there are no Sicilian funerals or traditional Mediterranean theatrics associated to such episodes of mourning. Apollonia remained hidden in Michael's soul until Part III when, broken down upon hearing Anthony singing *Brucia la terra* (*Apollonia's Theme*), Michael finally said: "I loved her!"

VENDETTA, OMERTÀ, AND DEATH

Vendetta and *Omertà* are two main precepts ruling the Mafia underworld. *Omertà* is the vow of silence as well as the code of honor a *mafioso* swears to at the time of induction; vendetta is the inevitable consequence one faces when breaking the codes of *omertà*. There is no timetable establishing when vendetta follows the violation of *omertà*; it happens unexpectedly and so the transgressor lives in constant fear. *The Godfather Trilogy's* metanarrative is based on such fear, even when it is ameliorated by the mantra "it's business, not personal"—all *mafiosi* in the film euphemistically refer to themselves as businessmen. This means that the family and love scenes described in the first portion of this chapter are to be kept separate from the premeditated vindictive death scenes I analyze in the pages ahead. Francis Coppola has accomplished an unprecedented task in directing dozens of murder episodes, while Nino Rota, despite his proclaimed contrariness toward such "psychological abjections," composed music that often underscores sinister actions but, more often, counterpoints them. There is a great deal of cause and effect governing the chain of murders that occur in the trilogy; therefore, in the interest of clarity I have opted to analyze them by placing each occurrence in the chronological order established by Coppola in *The Godfather 1902–1959: The Complete Epic* version of the film's Parts I and II.

Thus, the saga begins in the year 1901 when, in the Sicilian town of Corleone,[15] Antonio Andolini, a family man of principles, insulted or crossed the local Mafia chieftain Don Ciccio. As a consequence, Don Ciccio ordered Antonio's death and placed a premium on the head of his older son Paolo who, having sworn to avenge his father, disappeared into the hills. As the film begins, drums and undistinguished, brassy, sinister sounds are heard coming from very far away announcing a funeral procession slowly passing over the rocky Sicilian soil. As the procession gets closer, musicians become visible and clearly the viewer hears their harsh and blaring instruments becoming progressively louder. A priest, two altar boys, and six peasant men carrying a wooden coffin on their shoulders follow the musicians. Behind them are the widow Andolini (Maria Carta), a strong woman dressed in black, and her nine-year-old son Vito accompanied by relatives, children, and town folks. Suddenly, shots are fired and the musicians stop playing. The small crowd disbands, seeking shelter. A woman announces with dramatic flare that Paolo, Vito's older brother, has been killed.[16] Carmine Coppola provides the sound underscoring this funeral and murder scene [00:01:13-A-II-2]. When Rota viewed this scene, he jotted down in his notebook the following regarding the music he was to compose[17]:

> *1. Faraway drums then small band approaching with funeral [cortege] until gun shots [are heard]. 2. Man playing an old Sicilian song on the ocarina.[18] (The same song should be played on the ocarina some 2 hours later [in the film], thus reconnecting [the viewer's] memory to this initial scene.) 3. One of this film's themes is America with the interwoven presence of the Mafia.*

In order to appreciate Rota's comments, it is necessary to view the deleted [additional] scene, "Searching for Vito," which includes an old Sicilian folk song played on the ocarina by one of the two men searching door-to-door for young Vito. Furthermore, Rota's important mnemonic suggestion that the tune should have been heard again "two hours later in the film" finds a point of reference in Deleted [Additional] Scene #9, "Vito's Revenge," discussed later. Thus, if the film's narrative is considered in chronological order, this old Sicilian folk tune becomes an authentic leitmotiv that also anticipates Cue #42 in Part I when the same tune would have been heard played by a communal marching band at Michael and Apollonia's wedding [01:49:02-A-I-42].

In the present description, the action moves to 1917 in New York City where the murder scene that turns Vito Corleone into an assassin takes place.[19] An Italian marching band plays in front of the church to commemorate the opening night of the Festa di San Rocco.[20] Clemenza and Tessio give Vito some money and then Vito meets with Don Fanucci, a member of the Black Hand organization, in a nearby café to discuss protection terms. Back in the neighborhood, people jam the street lined up with vendors' booths. Don Fanucci appropriates an orange[21] from a cart; a passerby kisses Fanucci's hand; Vito jumps from one roof to another. Finally, Vito arrives at Don Fanucci's building and enters the building from the roof.

Vito stands looking down near a window at the top of the stairs. He starts down the steps. Once outside Don Fanucci's apartment Vito turns off the light and places a cloth over his gun. Meanwhile, as the camera switches to the street festivities, a priest is seen offering a benediction. Suddenly the camera returns to Fanucci standing by the door of his apartment tapping the lightbulb which Vito has loosened. The light flickers. Don Fanucci tightens the bulb and the light comes on as Vito steps behind Fanucci, who turns around to face him just as Vito fires the gun. Again, the camera turns to the priest amid the crowd and the smoke of celebratory fireworks. Vito comes down a ladder onto another roof; he holds the gun and the cloth. He throws away the cloth, takes money out of Don Fanucci's wallet, and smashes the gun and drops pieces of it down various vent pipes. Marcia J. Citron considers this scene to be eminently operatic, as I have already pointed out. Furthermore, she writes:

> . . . Cinematographer Gordon Willis' creation of stunning chiaroscuro, with dark background and half-lit faces—a prime element in Kael's observation about "operatic contrast" between dark and light in the films. Darkness is also used thematically. It characterizes the interior scenes, where business is conducted, while the outdoor scenes, especially celebrations, are in light-filled places where women and children operate. Many scenes display the dark palette.[22]

Ten years elapse since the murder of Don Fanucci. Vito is now a "man of respect" in New York City's Italian-American neighborhood, where he is known as Don Vito Corleone. He and his friend Genco Abbandando have established a successful olive oil import business, and Vito's wife Carmela (Francesca De Sapio) has given him four children: Santino (Sonny) born in 1916, Fredo in 1919, Michael in 1920, and Costanza (Connie) in 1927. Following Connie's birth the young family takes a holiday to the town of Corleone to visit with relatives and business associates. They arrive by train at the Corleone railroad station greeted by relatives and friends to the music of a brass band [00:37:16-A-II (Disc 2)-64]. Vito's trip to Corleone, though, includes a dark agenda: vendetta! He seeks to avenge the murder of his father Antonio, brother Paolo, and his mother, who had also been killed in front of young Vito by Don Ciccio's henchmen. This extended episode comprises Deleted [Additional] Scene #9 in which Vito kills Don Ciccio's accomplices Strollo and Mosca. Mosca is the man who played the ancient Sicilian tune on the ocarina in Deleted [Additional] Scene #1. Two hours into the film's original montage of Part II, Rota's psychological assessment that the ocarina sound emanating metaphorically from the Sicilian soil from which the instrument was made places ethnological importance on this tune's significance. In the meantime, Vito moves ahead with his vendetta plans by arranging for his host and partner Genco to introduce him to Don Ciccio (Giuseppe Sillato). When Vito meets the *mafioso* face-to-face he plunges a knife into the old man's stomach.[23] For this vendetta scene Rota uses fragments from the *Love Theme* from *The Godfather*, *Michael's Theme*, and *The Immigrant Theme* followed by a nine-second combination of *The Immigrant Theme* and *Michael's Theme* + *The Godfather Waltz* [00:37:56-00:43:04-A-II (Disc 2)-65-66]. Rota conceived the music track for this vendetta episode in rather *verismo* operatic terms as clearly expressed in his spotting notes:

> *[when] Vito's boat approaches Strollo's and hits the fisherman on his head, hold a chord to which should be superimposed the sound of faraway church bells (like in Cavalleria rusticana). [Then as the camera focuses on the] Church's piazza we hear the bells closer. [When Vito reaches the] home of the second fisherman [underscore the moment with a] low register chord, [additionally] one must hear the noise of Vito's little saw cutting the net surrounding the sleeping fisherman.*

After the killing of Don Ciccio, Rota concluded: *"La commedia è finita"* Vito has accomplished the vendetta he desired.

The composer's reference to Mascagni's *Cavalleria rusticana* (evoked by the *ethnos* of the sound of Sicilian church bells) and to Leoncavallo's *I pagliacci* (quoting the disheartened dramatic utterance with which the clown Canio concludes that opera after killing his wife Nedda) shows how prophetic Rota's comment was as Coppola returned to *Cavalleria rusticana* to conclude the trilogy 17 years later.[24]

THE HORSE'S HEAD

By the year 1945 (beginning of Part I), Don Vito Corleone's "Genco Olive Oil Company" is nothing more than a front for illicit operations, including gambling and prostitution but excluding the smuggling of narcotics. The Don, now officially addressed as "Godfather," built a financial empire during the Prohibition era by nationally distributing liquors imported from Canada. The *famiglia* Corleone is now the most powerful and feared branch of New York City's five-headed *mafioso* hydra. Puzo and Coppola provide a clear idea about the Godfather's sphere of influence during Connie's wedding,[25] when Don Corleone engaged in an animated discussion with godson Johnny Fontane about an important role the singer/actor wished to have in an up-coming film production. The problem was that Hollywood producer Jack Woltz (John Marley) had no intention of entrusting the role to Fontane; therefore, the Don's intervention was hastily requested. Don Corleone dispatched Tom Hagen to Hollywood at once with the charge to make Woltz an offer he could not refuse. This episode, known in the film as "The Horse's Head," was commented upon by Rota as follows:

> *Coppola wished me to underscore the continuous string of murders occurring in the film with the notes of some kind of waltz, a leitmotiv signifying a recurring cycle devoid of closure. In fact, every time there is a shootout or a death or a wounded person or many dead or many wounded, what one hears is a waltz theme.*[26]

With these words, the composer summarizes the charge given to him by Francis Coppola to give the film, Part I in this case, a definite sound imprimatur identified with *The Godfather Waltz.*[27] After this theme is heard played by a solo trumpet in the film's Main Title and danced to by Don Corleone and daughter Connie, it is hard to imagine how it could have been used to underscore murder if not playing against the action. This contrapuntal procedure is particularly effective in the episode under discussion in which, although no one is killed but a horse, the extremely cruel and bloody scene conveys to the viewer the idea that the Mafia and *mafiosi* stop at nothing to get what they want.

The scene begins with a long shot of a TWA Constellation aircraft landing as the image dissolves to a long, down shot of Hollywood panning right over Grauman's Chinese Theatre[28] while the noted song *Manhattan Serenade* underscores the plane's landing shots.[29] Strains from the same tune are briefly heard again when Tom Hagen's limousine arrives at Jack Woltz's mansion. Once at the exterior of the luxurious villa, the camera focuses on a medium shot of the fountain in the atrium, then it continues moving in toward an outside staircase, up toward a window, and finally dissolves to the interior of Woltz's bedroom. It is now daytime. A medium shot of the bed shows Woltz still asleep under the covers. The camera continues to move in slowly toward the bed, then it pans slightly to the left as it continues moving forward to show Woltz lying with his back to the camera. He stirs. He feels under the covers; he reacts as he feels something. He sits up, then withdraws his hand which is covered with blood. Sitting up straighter, he pushes the covers back, camera panning down to his blood-soaked pajamas, and sees the horse's head lying at the foot of the bed. Woltz screams. The camera moves to the exterior of the mansion through a long shot of the home and pool while Woltz's screams continue to be heard.

This episode, which pays homage to a famous scene in *Dr. No* (Terence Young, 1962) when James Bond (Sean Connery) was awaked in his bed by a tarantula crawling from under the sheets, remains one of the most memorable moments in American cinema since the shower scene in *Psycho* (Alfred Hitchcock, 1960). The music cues underscoring this scene [00:29:03-A-I-15-00:32:18-A-I-16a-00:32:42-A-I-16b], though, are not heard as Rota conceived them but are a creation of sound editor Walter Murch who explained:

> The music, as it was originally written, was a waltz and it played against the horror of the event. It was sweet carousel music. You were seeing those horrible images, but the music was counterpointing the horror of the visuals. Perhaps it needed to be crazier a little earlier. So I tried something I had done on *THX 1138*[30]—layering the music, playing records backwards, turning them upside down, and slowing them down—a version of what I'd done when I was eleven years old. Nino's music for the horse's-head scene had an A, B, A musical structure. That is to say, it had an opening, then a variation, and then a return to the opening statement. This structure allowed me to make a duplicate of the music, slip the sync of the second copy one whole musical statement, and then superimpose them together. The

music started off A, as it was written, but then became A+B, simultaneously, and then B+A. You now heard, superimposed on each other, things that were supposed to be separate in time. So it starts off as the same piece of music, but then begins—just as Woltz realizes that *something* is wrong—to grate against itself. There is now a disorienting madness to the music that builds and builds to the moment when Woltz finally pulls the sheet back.[31]

My thesis is that Rota viewed this episode as if it were a classical fairy tale, something in the mold of Apuleius' *The Golden Ass*. I envision him assuming the role of the *Lector in fabula*, the reader/narrator waiting for the metaphorical wolf in the fable, which he now recognizes in Jack Woltz. Woltz is a "Hollywood rough-spoken, rapaciously amorous, raging wolf ravaging helpless flocks of young starlets," wrote Mario Puzo (54). A 12-year old starlet named Janie (see Deleted [Additional] Scene #11) becomes the lamb who is fed to the wolf by her own witch-mother. Janie, as the reader can see in the deleted [additional] scene, received from Woltz a beautiful pony as a birthday present with the implication that the pony would continue to "discharge the fabled gold" as long as Janie remained in Woltz's grasp. Tom Hagen quickly discovers Woltz's true colors, and when he reports the episode back to Don Corleone, a disgusted Godfather utters only one word: INFAMIA! Then, he gives the order leading to the beheading of the horse.[32] The episode brings to mind the opening line of Kafka's *Metamorphosis* which reads: "As Gregor Samsa awoke one morning from uneasy dreams he found himself transformed in his bed into a gigantic insect."[33] Surely enough, the anthropomorphic transformation of the horse, whose name was Khartoum,[34] into Woltz's alter ego becomes a portent of more atrocious things to come for the famous film producer, including the specter of castration as a lifelong alternative to beheading. That very morning Woltz called Hagen in New York, and Johnny Fontane reported to work on the film's set the following Monday.[35]

Elements of my fairy-tale account of Rota's interpretation are indeed present in the composer's original cue.[36] Rota's spotting notes about this scene reveal that he intended to weave a magic sonic tapestry full of distortions as psychic motions. Therefore, the jazzy motif that forms the original cue was first played as notated (see Mus. Ex. 5.9) and then in "augmentation" by a wailing saxophone (see Mus. Ex. 5.10).

Ex. 5.9. Jazzy Motif.

Ex. 5.10. Alto Sax Motif.

Later, the same material, this time notated in "expanded augmentation," is heard played *tremolando sul ponticello* by the strings:

Ex. 5.11. String Tremolando.

This transforms the jazzy motif into the metaphorical, mysterious "woods" in which the fairy tale's narrative begins to unfold.[37] The composer wrote:

> *The Hollywood theme* [see Mus. Ex. 5.11] *is played with wide tremolando, then we hear just two phrases from the second part of the Corleone waltz (measures 12-21). Then, from the bedroom's interior begins a distortion of the first incipit (measure 22). It continues by*

repeating the same this time in contrary motion one octave above and below. Finally, raise the whole thing up a step.

All things considered, Rota's original cue would have been just as effective as Murch's manipulation; however, one must take into account the cut of two dramaturgically important scenes and the urgency to make this episode appear as horrific as possible.

THE DON IS DEAD

I detect another fairy-tale soundscape in the next scene as well, the attempt on Don Corleone's life. This long and complex episode occurs during Christmas Eve 1945. It begins in Don Corleone's office at the Genco Olive Oil Company where a meeting is in progress between the Don, Tom, Fredo, Sonny, Tessio, and Virgil Sollozzo, head of a rival clan who proposes to the Corleones a partnership in the manufacturing and distributing of narcotics. At the meeting's conclusion, Don Corleone thanks Sollozzo for the offer but rejects the deal. The appearance on the scene of Sollozzo, a sinister figure destined to cause a lot of trouble for the Corleone clan, is underscored by Rota with an ominous series of low-register chords periodically suspended by holds and culminating with permutations of *The Godfather Waltz* played by stinging muted brass [00:34:40-A-I-17].

During the course of this meeting, Coppola cuts away twice to show first Michael and Kay Christmas shopping and having dinner in their hotel room, then Luca Brasi (Lenny Montana) in his apartment getting ready for a meeting later in the day with Sollozzo and the Tattaglia brothers (Tony Giorgio and Victor Rendina). These brief cutaways are underscored by the tune *Have Yourself a Merry Little Christmas* [00:39:45-A-I-19][38] that emanates diegetically from a radio receiver or phonograph heard simultaneously in Michael and Kay's room and Luca's apartment. It juxtaposes Michael and Kay's bourgeois, American way of life with the upcoming, atrociously graphic murder of Luca Brasi, whose appearance, although accented by Rota with a thematic variation of *The Godfather Waltz*, is also highlighted by the same strains of the radio song enjoyed by Michael and Kay. Thus, in a twist of irony, Coppola manipulates the viewer into believing that a thug like Luca Brasi is also allowed to feel the Christmas spirit. Furthermore, while still horrified by having watched Brasi's death by garroting at the hands of Sollozzo and the Tattaglia brothers, the viewer hears another Christmas favorite, *Santa Claus Is Coming to Town*,[39] blaring forth from the department store where Michael and Kay have done their Christmas shopping [00:43:32-A-I-21]. The film's action then returns to Don Corleone's office where, upon the conclusion of the meeting with Sollozzo and the departure of the other attendees, an office clerk helps Don Corleone put on his overcoat. The Don exits onto the street.

The sound of this remarkable scene, which signals the beginning of Don Corleone's downfall, is ushered in by random warm-up notes played by a trumpet in one of the many apartments overlooking the crowded streets of New York City's Little Italy [00:44:08-A-I-22]. It is nighttime when Don Corleone leaves the Genco Olive Oil office building; he walks across the street to a fruit stand and buys oranges from a deferential vendor. Suddenly, two gunmen appear and shoot the Don, who sprawls against the hood of a car. Fredo, who was waiting for his father by the sidewalk, gets out his gun, which is shot out of his hand. The two gunmen run off.

I could argue that this scene is as much about Don Corleone's toughness as it is about Fredo's weak character. The incident provided Fredo with a great opportunity to save his father's life and preserve the family's honor. However, as a foreshadowing of things to come, the trumpet's warm-up scales did not evolve into a triumphal tune for Fredo. Instead, after the Don was hit, the sound of *The Godfather Waltz* is heard played by an oboe. Rota's instrumental code, changing from trumpet to oboe clearly denotes the gap between Don Corleone, who needed a "warmed-up" trumpet heralding his appearance, and the plaintive sound of an oboe underscoring the pathetic showing of Fredo sitting on the sidewalk, head in his hands crying "Papa, Papa!"[40]

Following Sollozzo's attempt on Don Corleone's life, Coppola presents a series of short scenes focusing on the anxiety-ridden family members. Rota underscores each of the short clips with iconic motifs. For instance, he uses a triplet on the notes *G-A flat-G-A flat*, a quirky ominous variant of *The Godfather Waltz*, which he refers to in his notebook as "Hospital Theme."

Ex. 5.12. Hospital Theme.

This musical "twitch" expresses fear, anxiety, and uncertainty in film noir style when Michael and Kay pick up a copy of the *Daily Mirror* bearing the headline: VITO CORLEONE FEARED MURDERED [00:46:40-A-I-25]. Michael's hands open the paper to reveal a picture of Don Corleone and a story headed "Assassins Gun Down Underworld Chief." Michael then rushes to a phone booth to contact his brother Sonny. While Sonny absorbs the news, Rota fills the atmosphere with a tender version of *The Godfather Waltz* played by an unaccompanied cello, underscoring Sonny's sad feelings about his father with whom he had quarreled during the Sollozzo meeting. However, Sonny's notoriously hot temper is quickly emphasized by Rota's menacing chord sequence [01:23:20-A-I-30]:

Ex. 5.13. *The Halls of Fear.*

This cue conveys the desire for vendetta, and mounting rage levels are evoked by the sequence's chromatic progressions. *Michael's Theme*, heard here for the first time, follows this chord sequence. It is a clear sign that because of Fredo's failure to save Don Corleone's life, Michael will be the one, not Sonny, to execute the family's vindictive scheme and eventually become the new Godfather.

It is interesting to note here that, upon viewing this scene for the first time, Rota conceived a much gentler, almost innocent Christmas atmosphere, despite the attempted murder and consequent mounting rage for vindication. He composed a 77-measure piece called *Natale* (Christmas) scored for 8 boy sopranos, 2 flutes, 2 oboes, 2 clarinets, 1 bassoon, 2 French horns, 1 harp, 1 piano, 1 celesta, 1 cordovox, and strings (12-4-3-2), thus continuing the fairy-tale soundscape initiated with *The Horse's Head* episode.

MICHAEL KILLS

A pivotal scene in the film is Michael's transformation from decorated war hero to cold-blooded murderer, a situation parallel to his father's killing of Don Fanucci in Part II. In this scene, Michael, having been coached by Clemenza, is ready to meet with Virgil Sollozzo and Captain McCluskey to kill them both. A drone-like sinister chord underscores the scene.

A medium long shot shows Michael at night standing on the sidewalk in front of Jack Dempsey's Restaurant waiting for Sollozzo and McCluskey's car. When the car arrives Michael gets in. McCluskey frisks him as the car heads towards the Triborough Bridge to New Jersey. Midway across the bridge the driver turns the car around towards New York. Inside Louis's Restaurant in the Bronx, Michael, after retrieving a gun hidden behind the restaurant's toilet, kills Sollozzo and McCluskey, drops the gun on the floor, and leaves the premises. Rota's music begins exactly when Michael drops the gun. It consists of a grave peroration of *Michael's Theme* that concludes the film's first half and marks Michael's successful transformation into the new Godfather [01:29:07-A-I-35]. Sound editor Walter Murch provided the scene with one of the most effective sound montages in the cinematography of the period. Here is Murch's account of his intervention:

> It is always a balance for me, between something being authentic, and celebrating that authenticity, and yet at the same time trying to push the sound into the metaphorical areas. Think of the screech of the elevated subway train in *The Godfather* when Michael Corleone murders Sollozzo and the policeman, Captain McCluskey, in the Italian restaurant. It's an authentic sound because it's a real subway train and because it seems authentic to that neighborhood of the Bronx, where the restaurant is located. We don't wonder what the sound is, because we've seen so many films set in the Bronx where that sound is pervasive. But it's metaphorical, in that we've never established the train tracks and the sound is played so abnormally loud that it doesn't match what we're looking at, objectively. For a sound that loud, the camera should be lying on the train tracks.[41]

However, for this very important dramaturgical episode, Rota had conceived a cue dense with references (it can be heard on CD 1, Track 3 as *The Pickup*). In the original cue Rota underscored Michael's Faustian metamorphosis by quoting the foreboding opening measures from his 1962 oratorio *Mysterium* followed by an extended version of the jagged jazzy theme originally conceived as the beginning of the original (not used) *Horse's Head* episode (see Mus. Ex. 5.9). After Michael committed murder, the peroration of *Michael's Theme* played by brass instruments is "as melodramatic as the over-the-top moments of *Tosca* or *Cavalleria rusticana*—a real catharsis," commented Marcia Citron.[42] As in the best of operas, musical climaxes close off the dramatic strands developed thus far and usher in changes in tension level which in this case reveal Michael's complete transformation from war hero to assassin. Or, one may interpret the whole episode as Michael's act of self-immolation and damnation in replacing his father to oversee his family's destiny, a most important trope in all Mafia stories.

THE BAPTISM

Each part of the trilogy reaches a climax in which Puzo and Coppola deal with the seven Catholic sacraments—Baptism, Eucharist (Communion), Reconciliation (Confession), Confirmation, Marriage, Holy Orders, and the Anointing of the Sick (Last Rites)—as tropes for explicit metaphors by juxtaposing them to scenes showing vendetta by assassination. Coppola brilliantly realizes these juxtapositions by means of cutaways that jump back and forth from one occurrence to another. *The Baptism Scene* in Part I [02:36:17-A-I-54] constitutes one such climactic moment. A very long shot shows the interior of a large church where the officiating priest, assisted by a monsignor and a cleric, surround the Corleone family. Then, a medium shot of the priest and family shows Kay carrying Carlo and Connie's baby toward the altar, followed by Michael. The atmosphere is solemn, drenched in Catholic mysticism. The church is too vast for the small group of celebrants and the sound of the organ is overbearing for a scene during which, while baby Michael receives the sacrament that symbolizes his embrace with God, nine people are assassinated without the comfort of the Last Rites. When Rota viewed this scene for the first time, its temp track consisted of a potpourri of organ music incorporating fragments from Poulenc's *Organ Concerto* and Bach's *Passacaglia in C Minor.* Therefore, the challenge for the composer was to provide an original organ score that could coherently synthesize both the diegetic and non-diegetic elements making up the episode. The task must have been a complex one since Rota composed two different organ pieces to fit the episode. The first, entitled *Il battesimo* (The Baptism) is a 159-measure piece based on the grave, sinister thematic transformation of *The Godfather Waltz*:

Ex. 5.14. Theme from *Il battesimo*.

The second is an organ fantasy constructed on rhythmic and thematic elements derived from *The Godfather Waltz*, a *Passacaglia* in the
style of J. S. Bach:

Ex. 5.15. Rota's *Passacaglia.*

Ex. 5.16. Bach's *Passacaglia in C minor.*

and by a fragment imitating Bach's *Prelude in D Major* BWV 532:

Ex. 5.17. Rota's *Prelude.*

Ex. 5.18. Bach's *Prelude in D major.*

Finally, a full-stopped peroration on the *The Godfather Waltz* and *Michael's Theme* interwoven concludes the cue:

Ex. 5.19. Rota-Organ Finale.

With this piece, Rota solved the music track problem presented by the scene in an exemplary fashion. However, what the viewer actually hears on the film's soundtrack is a manipulation of the second Rota score in which material taken from *The Godfather Waltz* and *Michael's Theme* have been substituted by random improvisations. The final "montage" of the piece created by music editor Peter Zinner was probably suggested by a wish on Coppola's part to keep the already dense double narrative of baptism and simultaneous murders flowing unencumbered through abstract music, thus exonerating the viewer from decoding any extra musical narrative.[43] I point out that this sequence, aside from the two concurrent narratives mentioned above, contains further layers of cultural meanings oscillating between physical and metaphysical realms, such as the use of a real Italian-American Church (old St. Patrick's Church on Mulberry Street in New York's Little Italy); a real priest (Father Medeglia); a "real" baby, Sofia Coppola, who receives here her own "baptism" of sorts as future actress and successful filmmaker. Then there is the symbolic speaking of Latin (a "dead" language spoken by the priest to baby Michael) and English spoken to adult Michael, who pronounces his renunciation vows for the baptized baby Michael as a Christian and for himself vicariously "baptized" as Godfather in both meanings of the word. At the end of the sequence, as blood is shed, the sound of pure (holy) water is heard being poured on the baby's head from the basin. Perhaps, in Michael Corleone's mind, this act represents the full cleansing of his sins and the realization of his father's dream: a march toward legitimacy through a compellingly antithetical juxtaposition of murder and Catholic creed.[44]

MURDER ATTEMPT ON MICHAEL AND HIS FAMILY

The 1959 segment of *The Godfather Part II* begins with Anthony's First Communion, the elaborate choral scene I described in Chapter 4. The scene ends showing Michael and Kay tenderly dancing before retiring to their quarters. They put Anthony and Mary to bed and adjourn to their bedroom. This scene of familial bliss is underscored by Rota's poetic version of *The Godfather Waltz* played in *concertante* style by two clarinets and viola accompanied by a mandolin and pizzicato strings [00:34:05-A-II-22]. When the camera focuses on Kay's face resting on the pillow, *Kay's Theme* is heard played by the full orchestra for the first time on the soundtrack [00:34:44-A-II-22]. Then, the camera turns toward Michael who is about to close the window's drapes, when machine-gun bullets rip into the room. Michael crawls on the floor and rolls Kay off the bed, holding her in his arms. The atmosphere created by Rota's music through the romantic portrayal of Michael and Kay is shattered by the bullets meant to wipe out Michael and his most precious possessions: Kay and the children. Rota's notes reflect the composer's sense of urgency provoked by the anxiety pervading this scene. He scribbled the following:

*After the shooting in Michael's and Kay's room—alarming music—
great commotion in the night [on the part] of Michael's security people—music begins as from a distance to culminate on Michael's wife
and children. The family is terrorized while Michael is sad and perplexed as he makes decisions; here is the principal motive of the film.
Michael walks into the night followed by other men, tragedy, Michael's dilemma until he stops in front of the door—[music] thought-
ful—[music] builds up—cue stopped—Kay's chord held—men
searching for the body in the dark—just steps—music—slow building
—simple (similar to the end of Godfather I)—tragedy—held chord,
when the body is found, music returns as before. Hagen walking in
the dark toward Michael's residence—transition to Michael—end of
scene.*

FREDO'S EXECUTION

The second part of this scene, consisting of the search for the per-
petrators, is underscored by what Rota characterizes as "alarming music," an arsenal of string tremolos, *sul ponticello,* accented chords
played by muted brass, and a recurring nervous rhythmical twist placed
on the first measure of *Michael's Theme.* Although Michael, Kay, and
the children remain unscathed by the attempted murder, and the assassins are found dead in a ditch on the estate, Michael begins to consider
the idea that Fredo had betrayed him. Ultimately, the axe of Michael's
vendetta fell on Fredo's head with tragic consequences when Michael
uttered the words "You're nothing to me now. You're not a brother;
you're not a friend. I don't want to know you or what you do" upon
learning that it was Fredo who informed Johnny Ola (Dominic
Chianese)—Hyman Roth's henchman—about him and his family quarters' location on the estate. Thus, although Fredo claimed that he did
not know that Ola and Roth were planning an execution, he became
responsible for the attempted murder. In one of the most climactic moments of the entire trilogy, Michael orders the murder of his brother.
Here is how Rota's score penetrates Michael's psyche during the un-
folding of this astonishing vendetta scene: *The Godfather Waltz,* gla-
cially played by a bass clarinet, is heard with an added *ostinato* beat
pounding every quarter note [00:26:09-A-II (Disc 2) 63]. It provides a
strong pulsating effect resembling the opening measures of Johannes
Brahms' *First Symphony.* The composer commented:

*After Fredo has forcefully argued with Michael about being the older
brother deserving respect, Michael feels pain for his brother [while
at] the same moment he excommunicates him—Michael reacts quietly*

*—silence—[Michael] walks away toward Connie—[Michael] says at
the end: "I will not do anything to him while mother is alive"—End.
Music similar to Tessio's farewell in The Godfather [Part I] but more
passionate because [Fredo] is his brother. Music strained (strings à
la Bartok—something pulled but still based on family problem).*

This heart-stopping scene shows Fredo sitting in the fishing boat
reciting the Hail Mary as Al Neri points the gun at the back of his head.
The sight of Michael looking at the boat and listening to the gunshot
from the deck of his desolate Lake Tahoe estate concludes Part II, accompanied by the sound of a solitary French horn intoning the *The Immigrant Theme* in a tragic and longing fashion [01:02:40-A-II (Disc 2)
69]. There is a strong perception in this scene that Michael has so inter-
nalized the role of the Godfather, has adopted the mantra "it's business,
not personal" so completely, that he thereafter denies having ordered
Fredo's murder until he confesses to Cardinal Lamberto (Part III) that
he had indeed ordered the murder of his brother, his father's son, as he
repentantly and repeatedly put it.

FINALE ON THE STEPS

Nino Rota died in 1979. Consequently, some of the music he wrote
for Parts I and II was readapted to underscore selected scenes in Part III
(see appendix). In general, Rota's music was reused judiciously
throughout Part III. Take, for instance, *Michael's Theme* which, played
with a pounding beat, alternates and overlaps with Mascagni's diegetic
strains of *Cavalleria rusticana* during the murder of Michael's enemies
while the opera is in progress. This situation may remind many a reader
of the 1934 Hitchcock film *The Man Who Knew Too Much* for which
Australian composer Arthur Benjamin composed the *Storm Cloud Cantata* for chorus and orchestra. In the Hitchcock film, murder occurred
during the diegetic performance of the cantata as a pistol shot was fired
backstage synchronically with a diegetic cymbal crash in the orchestra
on stage. I believe that Coppola wanted to add a Hitchcock touch to his
trilogy, cymbal crash included, as well as to pay homage to two members of his own family—father Carmine and uncle Anton.[45] The choice
of *Cavalleria rusticana* to conclude the trilogy, another virtuoso tour de
force of cinematographic editing (see cues 65 to 80 in the appendix),
raises many questions. I agree that *The Godfather* epic needed to end in
Sicily where it began. After all, "Sicily is opera," Michael told Kay
during their excursion in the Sicilian countryside (Part III). Therefore,
it would have been appropriate to conclude the saga with a Pirandellian

theatrical twist insomuch as Anthony, Michael's son, was to debut in Palermo as an opera singer. Had Rota been alive and willing to score a *Godfather* music track one more time, he would have solved the problem differently, probably excluding the cinematic montage of a large portion of a very popular opera such as *Cavalleria rusticana.* A solution à la Hitchcock/Benjamin would have been a much more auspicious one, and it would have saved Coppola—by 1990 one of the most sought-after Hollywood directors—the embarrassment of being compared to directors who made "Opera on Film" their specialty, like Jean-Pierre Ponnelle (*Madame Butterfly,* 1974; *Tristan und Isolde,* 1983), Gianfranco de Bosio (*Tosca,* 1976), Francesco Rosi (*Carmen,* 1984), and, above all, Franco Zeffirelli (*Cavalleria rusticana,* 1982; *La traviata,* 1983). Italy's most authoritative film musicologist, Sergio Miceli, judged Coppola's final episode excessively long and confusing, describing it as closer to a television serial than a cinematic sequel. Furthermore, Miceli criticized tenor/actor Franc D'Ambrosio (Anthony Corleone in the film) as a less-than-credible Turiddu and attacked what he called the "laughable inadequacy of American cinema when it steps out of its cultural traditions,"[46] thus making Coppola a scapegoat for certain failures of American cinema.

On the other hand, cultural critics and musicologists like Deborah Anders Silverman, Naomi Greene, Marcia J. Citron, and Lars Franke have written enthusiastically about *Cavalleria rusticana* as the best way to conclude the saga. Silverman observed:

> The theme of star-crossed lovers appears throughout the *Godfather* films, perhaps a carryover from Sicilian folk songs as described by folklorist Carla Bianca. In *Godfather I,* Michael's first wife, Apollonia, is murdered by Michael's enemies in Sicily; in *Godfather II,* Michael and his second wife, Kay, split up; and in *Godfather III,* Mary's death comes shortly after Vincent heeds Michael's advice to end the "kissing cousins" relationship. The opera *Cavalleria rusticana* also addresses the topic of forbidden love in a slightly different form, the violent end of an adulterous relationship.[47]

It must be added here that allusions to Mascagni's opera were signaled at the very beginning of the first flashback in *The Godfather Part II* when a peasant woman uttered the words "Hanno ammazzato Paolo" echoing the "Hanno ammazzato compare Turiddu" in the opera and portending the "Hanno ammazzato la signorina Maria" heard when Mary is shot on the steps of the Teatro Massimo.

Naomi Greene, in an essay entitled "Family Ceremonies: or Opera in The Godfather Trilogy,"[48] aside from discussing Mascagni's *Cavalleria rusticana* as the all-encompassing metaphor for concluding the trilogy, brings forth another strong operatic parallel, Giuseppe Verdi's *Rigoletto*. She writes:

> [*Rigoletto*] portrays the tragic death of a beautiful and cherished daughter who perishes because of the sins of her father. Although *Rigoletto* is never mentioned explicitly, one of the many performances that punctuate the trilogy—in this case, a Punch-and-Judy show witnessed in Sicily—hints at the father/daughter drama informing both *Rigoletto* and *Godfather III*.

In her essay, Greene refers to *La baronessa di Carini* as she describes the plot of the show and the Michael/Vincent/Mary triangulation. Rigoletto, of course, does not perform such a heinous deed himself. But there is never any doubt that he—like Michael in Part III—is responsible for his daughter's death. In Verdi's opera, which is based upon a play by Victor Hugo, *Le roi s'amuse* (1832), Rigoletto is a mean-spirited, hunchbacked jester at the court of a corrupt Renaissance prince, the Duke of Mantua, who is just a puppet in Rigoletto's hands.

On the other hand, Francis Coppola could be viewed as the ultimate puppet master who becomes both Michael/Rigoletto and the Duke (King) as he sacrifices his own daughter Sofia/Mary in order to end his play. Greene would have been delighted to know that a "live" performance of *Rigoletto*'s vocal quartet *Bella figlia dell'amore* was planned to be inserted in the divertissement taking place during Anthony's First Communion celebration party at Lake Tahoe in *The Godfather Part II*. Aside from somewhat bringing *Rigoletto* into the film's diegesis, it could have been the only touch of Italianness/Italianicity added to the entire episode.[49]

Marcia Citron's exhaustive essay, *Operatic Style and Structure in Coppola's Godfather Trilogy*,[50] leaves only a few stones unturned in her analysis of the subject. She writes the following about the use of *Cavalleria rusticana*:

> [*Cavalleria rusticana*] restores both period culture and the nostalgia and idealism that are associated with opera. By this point in the trilogy we are ready to be immersed in an aesthetic world and let feeling take over. By choosing this particular opera, set in Sicily, and staging it in this place, the main opera house in Palermo, Sicily, Coppola reinforces the ethnic-origins theme of the saga and brings it home to the literal place of origin.

Ironically, the opera portion of the film was not shot in Palermo's Teatro Massimo but in Rome at a Cinecittà soundstage,[51] thus reinforcing the feeling that the opera sets seen in the film, in addition to the director's altering of *Cavalleria rusticana*'s original order of scenes to suit a number of intercuts, constitute just another mega puppet show exclusively controlled by Francis Coppola while the reuse of Nino Rota's music (*Michael's Theme* with ostinato pounding quarter-beats) invades ominously Mascagni's score. Now, moving from inside the Cinecittà reconstructed operatic stage to the real steps of Giovanni Battista Basile's great neo-classical structure of Teatro Massimo, much has been said about Michael's spine-chilling *Urschrei* "silent scream." Well, the scream was not silent until sound editor Walter Murch partially shut it off to create a gasping effect. On the other hand, Al Pacino's scream could have been dubbed over by a striking sung version of *Michael's Theme* or "Fate Motive," as Citron labeled it. It would have been anticlimactic for sure, but enticing from a sophisticated puppeteer's standpoint, reminding the viewer that Rota had used a sung version of that very theme in the closing scene of Federico Fellini's *Il Casanova*, the ultimate cinematic puppet show.

Finally, Franke's study entitled *"The Godfather Part III:* Film, Opera, and the Generation of Meaning"[52] analyzes the last 30 minutes of the film on three levels: literal, cultural, and dramatic, with the addition of an intriguing discussion of Mascagni's *Intermezzo* viewed as the underscoring device for the film's narrative closure. He writes:

> The events that unfold on the steps [of the Teatro Massimo] are deeply symbolic. At its simplest, the destruction of the protagonist by robbing him of that which is most dear to him is a basic dramatic device, a theatrical as much as an operatic technique. More subtly, however, Mary is both the concrete sacrifice that this effect dictates, and a symbolic commentary on the internal destruction of Michael. If only through her name, she becomes the direct representation of uncorrupted faith, and consequently her death marks the ultimate moral fall of her father.

At this point Franke adds a footnote taken from Coppola's verbal commentary in the bonus video in which he remarks that he felt it would be "too easy and too kind" to Michael to conclude with his getting shot, and Coppola wanted "something more ironic and more devastating." However, later on Franke brings forth the issue of opera, Italian Catholicism, and the film's "real life" becoming fused. He writes, "By a common ritualism which cuts across genres and time, thus situating

the film's 'reality' both historically and culturally," one may argue that
the film does not really end with the fatal shooting on the steps of the
Teatro Massimo.

Franke is absolutely right; in fact, at the end of the film Michael is
shown dying alone of old age in the garden of his Sicilian villa. While
he had certainly paid the supreme price by losing his beloved daughter,
he had also received absolution for his sins by Cardinal Lamberto (Raf
Vallone), a future pope no less, and had seen his own son Anthony becoming an opera star completely liberated from the family business,
thus realizing the kind of American Dream that Don Vito Corleone had
wished for him.

It would have been a great *coup de théâtre* if Coppola had regaled
his audience with a scene or two from his uncle Anton's *Sacco and
Vanzetti*, the post-*verismo* opera premiered by Opera Tampa in 2001.
Francis Ford Coppola encouraged his uncle to complete the opera after
listening to pieces that Anton had prepared in 1995 for a television
documentary Francis intended to shoot about the two Italian anarchists.
The documentary was never made. The opera, however, did express
deep sentiments about a most compelling story turned into a *cause cé-
lèbre* that dealt with issues of immigration, stereotyping of Italian-
Americans, and, ultimately, the inadequacies of the American social
and justice system that led to the execution of Ferdinando Nicola Sacco
and Bartolomeo Vanzetti on August 23, 1927. I remind the reader that
the words uttered by Amerigo Bonasera at the very beginning of the
trilogy—"I believe in America"—reflected the above-mentioned sentiments. Thus, why not conclude the epic by reiterating the same trope
underscored by Anton Coppola's music that would have been much
more organic than Mascagni's?

My task, though, is to bring to a close a book about Rota's music
for *The Godfather* films, not Mascagni's or Anton Coppola's. My observations on the film's final episode are confined to the very effective
re-use of Rota's *Michael's Theme* that underscored with the macabre
persistence of a death knell the scenes showing Keinzig's body hanging
from a bridge; a bodyguard stabbed by Mosca backstage; Pope John
Paul I dying under mysterious circumstances; Spara stabbing the twin
bodyguards; Connie poisoning Don Altobello; Calo killing Lucchesi;
Lucchesi's bodyguard shooting Calo; Spara shooting Mary; Vincent
killing Spara and Neri killing Archbishop Gilday—while the screen
ultimately shows Michael, Rota's signified, dying of old age like real-
life Mafia patriarch Joseph Bonanno, who passed away in 2002 in Tuc-
son at the age of 97.

Nonetheless, fictitious character Michael Corleone died in Sicily, the land he loved so much. The inherited *Italianicity* he had lost through the slow and long process of Americanization had finally turned into the original *Italianness* embedded in the Andolini family.

Appendix

Abbreviations

MM (Musical Material)
A = Piano reductions and/or short scores (PMA [Paramount Music Archive, Hollywood])
B = Photocopies of the scores used by Carlo Savina for the recording sessions that took place in Hollywood on January 17–20, 1972 (PMA)
C = Autograph scores (ANR [Archivio Nino Rota–Fondazione Cini, Venice])
The sign -------- means that no musical material has been found regarding a particular cue.
CD = Compact Disc of original soundtrack
PSM = (Published Sheet Music by Famous Music Corporation)

Primary Sources

1. Rota's autograph scores for *The Godfather* and *The Godfather Part II*.
Archivio Nino Rota (ANR). Fondazione Giorgio Cini. Venice, Italy.
2. Rota's notebooks (ANR) for *The Godfather* and *The Godfather Part II*.
3. Scores and other pertinent material in photocopies marked for recording and synchronization.
Paramount Music Archives (PMA). Hollywood, California.
4. Musical Suggestions Cue Sheet compiled by Hammell, Reynolds, and Murch dated December 17, 1971 (PMA & ANR).
5. Cue Sheet dated March 7, 1972 (PMA).
6. Cue Sheet to Part II.
7. Cue Sheet to Part III.

Published Material

1. Published Film Scripts:
Sam Thomas. *Three Best American Screenplays* (New York: Crown Publishers, 1992).

2. Video Recordings:
a) *The Godfather 1902–1959: The Complete Epic.* 3 VHS Cassettes. Paramount Home Video, 1981.
b) *The Godfather—The Godfather Part II—The Godfather Part III.* 6 VHS Cassettes. Paramount Home Video, 1997.
c) *The Godfather DVD Collection.* Paramount Pictures, 2001.
d) *The Godfather–The Coppola Restoration.* Paramount Pictures, 2007.

3. CD Recordings marked as CD 1–CD 2–CD 3:
These CDs comprise selections from the original soundtrack recordings. All other versions have been excluded.

The Godfather (MCAD–10231. Paramount Records 1972): CD 1
Content:
Track: 1. Main Title (*The Godfather Waltz*) (3:04)
                 2. *I Have But One Heart* (Farrow & Symes). Sung by Al Martino (2:57)
                 3. The Pickup (2:56)
                 4. Connie's Wedding (Carmine Coppola) (1:33)
                 5. The Halls of Fear (2:12)
                 6. Sicilian Pastorale (3:01)
                 7. Love Theme from *The Godfather* (2:41)
                 8. *The Godfather Waltz* (3:38)
                 9. Apollonia (1:21)
                 10. The New Godfather (1:58)
                 11. The Baptism (1:49)
                 12. *The Godfather* Finale (3:50)

The Godfather Part II (MCAD–10232. Paramount Records 1974): CD 2

Content:

Track: 1. Main Title/The Immigrant (3:25)
2. A New Carpet (1:58)
3. Kay (2:58)
4. *Ev'ry Time I Look in Your Eyes* (Carmine Coppola)/After the Party (2:33)
5. Vito and Abbandando (2:36)
6. *Senza Mamma* (Francesco Pennino). Sung by Livio Giorgi/Ciuri-Ciuri (Traditional)/Napule Ve Salute (Francesco Pennino) (2:34)
7. The Godfathers at Home (2:33)
8. Remember Vito Andolini (2:59)
9. Michael Comes Home (2:18)
10. Marcia Stilo Italiano (Carmine Coppola) (2:00)
11. Ninna Nanna a Michele. Sung by Nino Palermo (2:18)
12. The Brothers Mourn (3:18)
13. Murder of Don Fanucci (Marcia Religiosa and Festa March) (2:48)
14. End Title (3:51)

The Godfather Part III (CK 47078. CBS Records 1990): CD 3

Content:

Track: 1. Main Title (0:42)
2. *The Godfather Waltz* (1:10)
3. Marcia Religioso (Carmine Coppola) (2:51)
4. Michael's Letter (1:08)
5. The Immigrant and Love Theme from *The Godfather Part III* (Rota & Coppola) (2:36)
6. *The Godfather Waltz* (1:24)
7. *To Each His Own* (Livingston & Evans). Sung by Al Martino (3:21)
8. Vincent's Theme (Rota & Coppola) (1:49)
9. Altobello (Rota & Coppola) (2:09)
10. *The Godfather* Intermezzo (Rota & Coppola) (3:22)
11. Sicilian Medley: *Va Pensiero/Danza Tarantella//Mazurka alla Siciliana* (Verdi & Coppola, Coppola) (2:10)

12. *Promise Me You'll Remember* (Love Theme from *The Godfather Part III*) (Carmine Coppola & John Bettis). Sung by Harry Connick Jr. (5:11)

13. *Preludio and Siciliana* [Turiddu]/*A casa amiche* [Turiddu and Chorus]/*Preghiera* (8:15 + 1:59 + 5:30)

14. Finale [Alfio, Turiddu, Lola, Lucia, Santuzza, Chorus] (8:12)

15. Coda: *The Godfather* Finale (2:28)

4. Published Sheet Music marked as PSM:

The Godfather Trilogy: Music Highlights from I, II & III (Miami, FL: CPP/Belwin, 1991).

Content:

1. *Promise Me You'll Remember* (Love Theme from *The Godfather Part III*), F Major, composed by Carmine Coppola

2. *Godfather II* (*The Immigrant Theme*), E Minor, composed by Nino Rota

3. *Antico Canto Siciliano* (Wedding Procession–Sicilian Love Song), E-flat Minor, composed by Carmine Coppola

4. *Come Live Your Life with Me* (*The Godfather Waltz*), C Minor, composed by Nino Rota, lyrics by Larry Kusik

5. *The Godfather Mazurka*, G Minor, composed by Carmine Coppola

6. *The Godfather Tarantella*, A Minor, composed by Carmine Coppola

7. *Kay's Theme*, C Major, composed by Nino Rota

8. *Michael's Theme*, A Minor, composed by Nino Rota

9. *Speak Softly, Love* (Love Theme from *The Godfather*), C Minor, composed by Nino Rota, lyrics by Larry Kusik

PART I

1. I Believe in America

1. MAIN TITLE (1M1X) [00:00:06-00:00:45]
   It consists of *The Godfather Waltz* #1 (N. Rota)–Trumpet Solo.
   Music starts on black screen. It ends before fade to office.
   MM:
   A) *Main Title* consisting of a piano reduction of the first 11
   measures dated Jan. 10, 1972. The music is notated in 6/8 time.
   B) *Titolo* [Main Title] consisting of the first 11 measures from
   The Godfather Waltz notated in 6/8 time. It is scored for 2 Fl, 1
   Ob, 1 E. Hn, 2 Cl, 2 Bsn, 3 Hn, 2 Tpt, 2 Trbn, 1 Tb, 2 Perc, 1
   Hp, 1 Pn, 1 Org, Strings (6-6-4-3-2). Recorded on 1/18/72.
   C) Original orchestral score and piano reduction of the above.
   CD 1–Track 1 *Main Title*
   PSM: *The Godfather Waltz* complete piano reduction consisting
   of 43 measures notated in 3/4 time. The same piece is also
   known as *Come Live Your Life with Me* with lyrics by Larry
   Kusik and Billy Meshel: 20–21.

2. ORCHESTRA TUNING [00:06:39-00:07:00]
   From after Don Corleone says: "... my daughter's wedding day"
   until he says: "I want reliable people."

2. The Wedding

3. THE GODFATHER TARANTELLA (C. Coppola) [00:07:00-
   00:09:12]
   From cut to exterior mall until music ends and guests applaud.
   CD 1–Track 4 *Connie's Wedding*
   PSM: *The Godfather Tarantella* piano reduction: 16–19.

4. THE GODFATHER MAZURKA (C. Coppola) [00:09:19-
   00:10:38]
   From cut to close-up of feet dancing until Luca Brasi says
   "... invited me to your home ..."
   CD 1–Track 4 *Connie's Wedding*
   PSM: *The Godfather Mazurka* piano reduction: 37–39.

5. THE GODFATHER FOX TROT (C. Coppola) [00:10:58-00:11:45]
   From after Sonny says: "Goddam FBI don't respect nothing" until after Don Corleone says: "... your daughter to be married."

3. Johnny Fontane

6. EV'RY TIME I LOOK IN YOUR EYES (C. Coppola) [00:12:03-00:14:28]
   It starts when Bonasera leaves Don Corleone's office. It ends when Michael says: "Very important to the family."

7. THE GODFATHER FOX TROT (C. Coppola) [00:15:14-00:15:53]
   It starts when Luca Brasi says: "I'm gonna leave you now ..." It ends when girls at table laugh.

8. LUNA MEZZ'O MARE (P. Citarella) [00:15:58-00:17:22].
   It begins shortly after the end of the preceding cue until cut to Don Corleone's office.

9. I HAVE BUT ONE HEART (Symes & Farrow) [00:18:40-00:20:54]
   This song begins when Kay says: "He did?" Then, Fontane sings until after Michael says: "That's my family, Kay, it's not me."
   CD 1–Track 2 *I Have But One Heart* sung by Al Martino

10. THE GODFATHER MAZURKA (C. Coppola) [00:21:17-00:22:19]
    From when Fontane talks with Don Corleone until Fontane says: "But this uh–this man ..."
    CD 1–(see Cue #4)

11. NON SO PIÙ COSA SON (Mozart/C. Coppola) [00:23:04-00:23:14]
    From when woman sings until the office door is closed.

12. THE GODFATHER TARANTELLA (C. Coppola) [00:24:43-00:25:01]
    It starts on cut to mall as cake is carried in. It ends when Don Corleone says: "... leave with bridegroom?"
    CD 1–(see Cue #3)

13. THE GODFATHER WALTZ #4 (3M2]) (N. Rota) [00:25:51-
00:26:32]
It begins after the photographer's flash goes off and ends when
scene fades out on dance.
MM:
A) 1. *The Godfather Waltz* (Main Title, same as Cue #1) consist-
ing of a piano reduction of 26 measures from *The Godfather
Waltz* notated in 6/8 time. This manuscript is dated Jan. 25,
1972. 2. *The Godfather Waltz* (version #4) consisting of a piano
reduction of *The Godfather Waltz* dated Jan. 20, 1972, and bear-
ing the annotation "Revised as recorded on January 19, 1972 as
Corleone Waltz #1."
B) Same version scored for 2 Cl, 1 Trp in C, 1 Accordion, 1
Mandolin, 1 Gt, 1 Perc.
Recorded on 1/19/72.

4. Tom Hagen Goes to Hollywood

14. MANHATTAN SERENADE (4M1) (Louis Alter) [00:26:33-
00:27:31]
From when camera fades in airfield until stage bell rings.

15. MANHATTAN SERENADE (4M1) (Louis Alter) [00:29:03-
00:29:33]
It starts on dissolve to limousine on street until Tom Hagen says:
"Very nice." Cues 14 and 15 were arranged by Peter King on
Jan. 2, 1972, and recorded in New York City on Jan. 10, 1972.

16. MAIN TITLE (1M1X) [00:32:18-00:32:42]
It consists of *The Godfather Waltz* #1 (N. Rota). It begins when
camera dissolves to fountain until it pans to horse's head on the
bed.
+
THE HORSE'S HEAD (4M3) [00:32:42-00:33:30]
It consists of *The Godfather Waltz* (N. Rota).
MM:
A) *The Horse's Head* consisting of 38 measures in piano reduc-
tion.
B) Same scored for 2 Fl, 1 Ob, 2 Cl, 2 Bsn, 2 Hn, 2 Tpt, 1 Pn, 1
Org, 1 Accordion, Strings (6-6-4-3-2). Recorded on 1/18/72.

C) 1. Main Title (*The Godfather Waltz*) and *The Horse's Head* consisting of 38 measures penciled in short score. 2. *Il cavallo* (The Horse) consisting of 24 measures with a note saying: "to be re-done!"

Note: What is heard on the soundtrack is not the entire Rota score but a sound montage prepared by Walter Murch.

5. Meeting with Sollozzo

17. SOLLOZZO THE TURK (4M4) (N. Rota) [00:34:40-00:35:36]
It begins when Don Corleone says: "How about his prison record?" It ends when the camera cuts to Genco offices.
MM:
A) *Sollozzo the Turk* consisting of 18 measures in piano reduction dated Jan. 14, 1972. It comprises a series of low-register sustained chords.
B) Same scored for 2 Cl, 2 Bsn, 2 Hn, 1 Hp, 1 Pn, 4 Vla, 3 Vlc, 2 Cb. Recorded on 1/18/72.
C) Same consisting of 19 measures scored as above.

18. LUCA BRASI (5M1) (N. Rota) [00:39:19-00:38:44]
From a close shot of Luca Brasi until camera fades to a street.
MM:
A) *Luca Brasi* consisting of an 8-measure thematic variation of *The Godfather Waltz*'s incipit in piano reduction.
B) Same scored for 12 Vl, 4 Vla, 3 Vlc, 2 Cb. Recorded on 1/18/72.
C) *Luca Brasi* consisting of an 8-measure thematic variation of *The Godfather Waltz*'s in piano reduction.

6. Shooting of Don Corleone

19. HAVE YOURSELF A MERRY LITTLE CHRISTMAS (Martin & Blane) [00:39:45-00:40:41]
From the beginning of scene until cut to the interior of Genco office. Sung by Al Martino in 1945 style.

20. WHISTLED FRAGMENTED MELODY [00:41:03-00:41:23]
It is heard echoing through the lobby of the building until Brasi puts coat over his arm.

21. SANTA CLAUS IS COMING TO TOWN (Gillespie & Coots)

[00:43:32-00:44:04]
From when the camera cuts to the exterior of a toy store until it cuts to the exterior of Genco Co.
It was arranged and recorded by Peter King in New York City on Jan. 10, 1972.

22. TRUMPET WARM-UP SCALES [00:44:08-00:44:46]
It is heard from when Don Corleone says: "I'm goin' to buy some fruit" until the camera cuts to running gunmen.

23. THE AFTERMATH (5M5) [00:45:16-00:45:44]
It consists of *The Godfather Waltz* (N. Rota).
It begins when Fredo looks down and ends when he yells: "Papa."
MM:
A) *The Godfather Waltz* consisting of 16 measures in piano reduction dated Jan. 21, 1972, bearing the annotation: "Recorded as Revised."
B) *The Aftermath* scored for 1 Ob, 1 Gt, 1 Accordion, 2 Vlc, 1 Cb. Recorded on 1/19/72.
C) Same consisting of 20 measures scored for 1 Ob, 1 Mandolin, 1 Gt.

24. THE BELLS OF ST. MARY'S (Adams & Furber) [00:45:46-00:46:38]
This song is heard when the camera cuts to the exterior of the theatre until a car honks at Michael.
It was arranged and recorded by Peter King in New York City on Jan. 10, 1972.

   Deleted [Additional] Scene #15 *The Don's Been Shot* is underscored by 0:30 of music featuring a dramatic triplet motif part of *The Halls of Fear* identified by Rota as "Hospital Theme." It will be heard later in cues #26 and 30.
   Deleted [Additional] Scene #16 *Sonny Absorbs the News* features a 0:26 version of *The Godfather Waltz* played by solo cello which will be heard again in cue #28 and *The Halls of Fear* which will be heard in cue #26.

25. BAD NEWS (6M2) [00:46:40-00:46:56]
It consists of *Michael's Theme* (N. Rota).

From after auto horn is heard until Sonny says: "Michael, where you been?"
MM:
A) *Michael's Theme* consisting of 21 measures in piano reduction dated Jan. 12, 1972.
B) Same scored for 2 Fl, 2 Ob, 2 Cl, 2 Bsn, 3 Hn, 1 Pn, Strings (6-6-4-3-2). Recorded on 1/18/72.
C) Same consisting of 19 measures.

7. Luca Brasi Sleeps with the Fishes

26. BAD LUCK (6M3) [00:52:05-00:52:58]
    It consists of *The Halls of Fear Part I* and *Michael's Theme* (N. Rota).
    From after Virgil Sollozzo says: "… if you don't make that deal" until the camera dissolves to office.
    MM:
    A) *Bad Luck* consisting of a piano reduction of 12 measures from *Michael's Theme* dated Jan. 14, 1972.
    B) Same scored for 2 Fl, 2 Ob, 2 Cl, 2 Bsn, 3 Hn, 1 Pn, Strings (6-6-4-3-2). Recorded on 1/19/72.
    C) *Bad Luck* consisting of 12 measures from *Michael's Theme*.

27. SICILIAN MESSAGE (7M1) (N. Rota) [00:55:15-00:55:23]
    From after Peter Clemenza says: "… sleeps with the fishes" until after the camera cuts to his home.
    MM:
    A) *Sicilian Message* consisting of 3 measures in piano reduction dated Jan. 13, 1972.
    B) Same scored for 1 Tpt, 2 Hn, 1 Pn, 1 Gt, Strings (4-4-3-3-2). Recorded on 1/19/72.
    C) --------

8. Michael at the Hospital

28. TOO LITTLE TIME (17M1) [00:57:16-00:58:07] consisting of *The Godfather Waltz* (N. Rota).
    From when Clemenza reacts to shots until Michael says: "Hello, Kay?"
    MM:
    A) --------
    B) --------

C) *Too Little Time* consisting of 64 measures from *The God-father Waltz #2* scored for 2 Ob, 1 Cl, 1 Pn, 1 Gt, 1 Accordion, Strings (4-4-3-3-2). Recorded on 1/17/72.

29. ALL OF MY LIFE (I. Berlin) [00:59:45-01:01:00]
    From dissolve to interior of hotel room until camera cuts to lobby.
    It was arranged and recorded by Peter King in New York City on Jan. 10, 1972.

30. THE HALLS OF FEAR (7M4) [01:01:04-01:04:08]
    It consists of *Michael's Theme* (N. Rota) + *Meditation* (N. Rota).
    From when the camera cuts to the hospital exterior until after Michael says: "No help me, please."
    MM:
    A) *The Halls of Fear Part 1* followed by *Michael's Theme* consisting of 24 measures in piano reduction.
    B) Same scored for 2 Fl, 2 Ob, 2 Cl, 2 Bsn, 3 Hn, 1 Tpt, 1 Perc, 1 Pn, 1 Hp, Strings (6-6-4-3-2). Recorded on 1/18/72.
    C) Same consisting of 50 measures.
    Recorded on 1/18/72
    CD 1–Track 5 *The Halls of Fear*
    Recorded on 1/19/72.
    Meditation consisting of 3 measures comprising a triplet motif scored for 1 E. Hn, 2 Cl, 1 Bsn, 4 Vl, 3 Vla, 2 Vlc. It was recorded on 1/19/72.

31. MICHAEL'S DECISION (8M2) [01:06:12-01:06:36]
    It consists of *The Godfather Waltz* (N. Rota)
    +
    BAD LUCK (6M3) (N. Rota)   [01:06:36-01:07:40]
    consisting of *The Halls of Fear*
    +
    THE WAITING GAME (8M3) (N. Rota) [01:07:40-01:08:13]
    consisting of *Michael's Theme*.
    From after Michael says: "I'm with you" until after police cars stop.
    MM:
    A) *Michael's Decision* consisting of 17 measures from *The God-father Waltz* in piano reduction dated Jan. 14, 1972 + *The Wait-*

ing Game consisting of *The Godfather Waltz* and *Michael's Theme* totaling 27 measures in piano reduction.
B) Same scored for 1 Ob, 2 Fl, 2 Bsn, 1 Hp, 1 Pn, Strings (4-4-3-3). Recorded on 1/19/72.
C) Same as above.

9. It's Strictly Business

32. ARMED AND READY (8M4) (N. Rota) [01:09:49-01:10:20]
+
SET THE MEETING (8M5)
It consists of *The Godfather Waltz* (N. Rota).
From after McCluskey says: "Go on" until Clemenza says: "What's with all the new faces?"
MM:
A) *Armed and Ready* consisting of 14 measures of non-thematic material + *Set the Meeting* consisting of 21 measures from *The Godfather Waltz* in piano reduction.
B) *Armed and Ready* scored for 2 Fl, 1 Ob, 2 Cl, 2 Bsn, 2 Hn, 2 Tpt, 1 Trbn, 1 Tb, 1 Pn, 1 Gt, Strings (6-6-4-3). Recorded on 1/18/72 + *Set the Meeting* scored for 1 Bsn, 2 Tpt, 2 Hn, 1 Gt, Strings (4-4-3-3-2). Recorded on 1/19/72.
C) Same consisting of 14 measures.

10. How's the Italian Food in This Restaurant?

33. MARRY ME KAY (15M2) [01:20:36-01:20:55]
It consists of the first 6 measures from *Michael's Theme* (N. Rota).
It begins after Sonny says: "... when I think the time is right" until car drives off.
The New Godfather consisting of 24 measures from *Michael's Theme* followed by *Autumn* and pounding quarter-note beats. Recorded on 1/19/72.
CD 1–Track 10 *The New Godfather*
+
BAD LUCK (6M3) (N. Rota)   [01:20:55-01:21:18]
It consists of 12 measures from *The Halls of Fear*, 2 Fl, 2 Ob, 2 Cl, 2 Bsn, 3 Hn, 1 Pn, Strings (6-6-4-3-2). Recorded on 1/19/72.

34. BAD LUCK (6M3) (N. Rota) [01:23:20-01:23:43]
From after Sollozzo says: "Nice work, Lou" until after car stops.

MM:
Continuation of Cue #33.

35. THE GETAWAY (10M3) (N. Rota) [01:29:07-01:29:21]
From after Michael drops a gun until first dissolve.
MM:
A) *The Getaway* consisting of 5 measures from *Michael's Theme* in piano reduction dated Jan. 13, 1972.
B) Same, scored for 1 Ob, 1 E. Hn, 2 Cl, 2 Bsn, 3 Hn, 2 Tpt, 2 Trbn. Recorded on 1/18/72.
C) Same, 6 measures scored as above.

11. The Don Returns Home

36. THIS LONELINESS (C. Coppola) [01:29:21-01:30:49]
From above dissolve until dissolve to the hospital exterior.

12. The Thunderbolt

37. LOVE THEME FROM THE GODFATHER (12M2) (N. Rota) [01:36:31-01:37:44]
It begins on dissolve to Sicily. It ends when Michael says: "Corleone."
MM:
A) --------
B) *Apollonia* consisting of 81 measures scored for 2 Fl, 2 Ob, 2 Cl, 2 Bsn, 3 Hn, 2 Tpt, 2 Trbn, 1 Tb, 1 Hp, 1 Pn, 1 Gt, 1 Accordion, 2 Mandolins, Strings (10-8-6-6-4). Recorded on 1/17/72.
C) --------
CD 1–Track 9 *Apollonia*
PSM: *Love Theme from The Godfather* also known as *Speak Softly Love* (lyrics by Larry Kusik): 6–7.

Deleted scenes #20 and 21 extend Cue #37 as Michael and his bodyguards explore the Sicilian countryside underscored the *Love Theme* from *The Godfather*. They come across a political rally singing *Bandiera Rossa*, the Italian Communist Party song, followed by a tender version of the *Love Theme* played by an oboe accompanied by wind instruments, accordion, and cowbells. The scene continues as Michael and his companion look for Vito Andolini's ancestral home. The episode is underscored by the *Love Theme* played by the accordion with mandolin and guitar. It is fol-

lowed by the "sequence of fifths" which would have been heard
here for the second time had the original cue intended for Cue #37
been used. See *Sicilian Pastorale* (Track #6 in CD 1).

38. SICILIAN PASTORALE PART 3 (11M4–12M1) [01:37:54-
    01:39:25]
    It consists of *Love Theme* from *The Godfather* (N. Rota).
    From when camera dissolves to countryside until after girls are
    seen.
    MM:
    A) --------
    B) *Sicilian Pastorale Part 3* consisting of 41 measures scored
    for 1 Ob, 1 Bsn, 1 Accordion. Recorded on 1/19/72.
    C) *Love Theme* from *The Godfather* consisting of 39 measures
    of which 24 are scored for 1 Ob, 1 Bsn, 1 Accordion, and last 15
    measures are scored for 1 Fl, 1 Ob, 1 Bsn, 1 Accordion, 1 Gt,
    1 Celesta, Strings (4-4-3-3-2).

39. SCIURI SCIURI (Sicilian Folk Song) [01:39:10-01:39:39]
    Starting on above action until close-up of Apollonia looking at
    Michael.
    Recorded on location by Carmine Coppola.

40. APOLLONIA (13M3) [01:39:50-01:40:22]
    It consists of *Love Theme* from *The Godfather* (N. Rota).
    From when camera dissolves to town until fade-out under Sicil-
    ian dialogue.
    MM:
    A) --------
    B) --------
    C) *Apollonia* consisting of 42 measures scored for 2 Mandolins,
    2 Gt + 1 Accordion in the last 17 measures.
    Recorded on 1/17/72 (see Cue #37).

13. Sonny Gives Carlo a Warning [no music]
14. Michael Marries Apollonia

41. LOVE THEME FROM *THE GODFATHER* (12M2) (N. Rota)
    [01:43:18-1:45:43]
    From when the camera dissolves to the villa's courtyard until it
    cuts to the exterior of a building in New York City.
    MM:
    Same as Cue #37.

42. ANTICO CANTO SICILIANO (C. Coppola) [01:49:02-01:50:05]
From after the priest finishes his benediction until the camera cuts to town square.
PSM: *Antico Canto Siciliano* (*Wedding Procession Sicilian Love Song*), arranged and adapted by Carmine Coppola: 12–13.

43. LIBIAMO from *LA TRAVIATA* (Verdi/C. Coppola) [01:50:05-01:50:28]
It starts on above cut until music ends.
Recorded on location by Carmine Coppola.

44. MAZURKA ALLA SICILIANA (C. Coppola) [01:50:29-01:50:50]
From when Michael and Apollonia dance until the camera dissolves to bedroom.
PSM: see Cue #4.

45. APOLLONIA (13M3) [01:50:51-01:52:08]
It consists of *Love Theme* from *The Godfather* (N. Rota).
From after above dissolve until the camera cuts to the Corleone's compound in Long Island.
MM:
Same as Cue #40.

15. I Don't Want His Mother To See Him This Way

46. SONNY'S DEAD (14M2) [01:58:12-01:59:02]
It consists of *The Godfather Waltz* (N. Rota).
From when the camera dissolves to the office until Don Corleone drinks.
MM:
A) *The Godfather Waltz* consisting of 35 measures in piano reduction.
B) Same scored for 1 Ob, 2 Cl, 1 Bsn, 1 Hn, Strings (6-4-3-3-2). Recorded on 1/19/72.
C) *Sonny's Dead* consisting of *The Godfather Waltz*. Same as above.

16. Apollonia's Murder [no music]

17. We Are All Reasonable Men Here [no music]
18. The Don Puts Michael in Charge

47. REUNION (15M1) (N. Rota) [02:12:41-02:13:30]
   From after Don Corleone says: "... Barzini all along" until
   Michael says: "It's good to see you, Kay."
   MM:
   A) *Michael's Theme + Autumn* (descending chromatic sequence
   of parallel fifths) consisting of 22 measures in piano reduction.
   B) Same scored for 2 Fl, 1 Ob, 2 Cl, 2 Bsn, 1 Hn, 1 Hp, 1 Pn,
   1 Celesta, Strings (8-6-4-3-2).
   C) *Reunion* consisting of 22 measures bearing the annotation
   "Autunno" (Autumn). Recorded on 1/17/72.
   Note: *Michael's Theme* heard here is taken from a portion of
   Cue #49 entitled *The New Godfather*.

48. MAIN TITLE (17M1) [02:13:30-02:14:19]
   It consists of *The Godfather Waltz #2* (N. Rota).
   On above line until Michael says: "Who's being naïve, Kay?"
   MM:
   A) --------
   B) *The Godfather Waltz #5* consisting of 16 measures scored for
   1 Ob, 2 Cl, 1 Pn, 4 Vla, 3 Vlc, 2 Cb.
   C) --------

49. THE NEW GODFATHER #1 (15M2) [02:14:40-02:15:53]
   It consists of *Michael's Theme* (N. Rota).
   From when Michael says: "Kay ..." until he gets in his car and
   the camera fades out.
   MM:
   A) *The New Godfather #1* or *Marry Me Kay* consisting of 25
   measures from *Michael's Theme* in piano reduction.
   B) Same scored for 2 Fl, 1 Ob, 2 Bsn, 1 Hp, 1 Pn, Strings (8-6-4-
   3-2). Recorded on 1/17/72.
   C) Same. *The New Godfather* consisting of 25 measures from
   Michael's Theme.
   CD 1–Track 10 *The New Godfather*
   PSM: *Michael's Theme*. Piano reduction: 40–41.

19. I'm Moe Green

50. LUCKY (16M1B) (C. Coppola) [02:19:00-02:19:35]
From when the camera dissolves to Las Vegas until after it dissolves to corridor.
Arranged and recorded by Peter King in New York City on Jan. 10, 1972.

51. FOR HE'S A JOLLY GOOD FELLOW (Traditional/C. Coppola) [02:19:51-2:20:02]
From when Fredo opens the door until he says: "It's all his idea ..."
Arranged and recorded by Peter King in New York City on Jan. 10, 1972.

52. MONA LISA (16M3) (Livingstone & Evans) [02:20:05-02:20:44]
From when Fredo says: "Girls?" until he yells: "Scram!"
Arranged and recorded by Peter King in New York City on Jan. 10, 1972.

20. I Never Wanted This for You

53. MAIN TITLE (17M1) [02:28:01-02:29:51]
It consists of *The Godfather Waltz* #2 (N. Rota).
From after Michael says: "... I'll handle it" until the camera dissolves to the garden.
MM:
A) *Main Title* (*The Godfather Waltz*) #2 consisting of 64 measures scored for unaccompanied cello (originally with English Horn) followed by accompaniment scored for 2 Ob, 1 Cl, 1 Bsn, 1 Tpt, 1 Gt, 1 Accordion, 1 Pn, Strings (4-4-3-3-2). Recorded on 1/17/72.
B) --------
C) *Main Title* (*The Godfather Waltz*) consisting of 64 measures same as A.

Deleted [Additional] Scene #24 *Talking in the Garden* if inserted at the beginning of Cue #53 would extend this scene underscored by the music heard in Cue #47, this connecting somewhat the Kay/Michael reunion with Michael having a heart-to-heart talk with his father.

21. Baptism and Murder

54. THE BAPTISM (18M1ZZ) [02:36:17-02:41:22]
consisting of *Improvisation* (N. Rota) [measures 1–12]
+
Passacaglia in C Minor (J. S. Bach) [measures 13–16]
+
Improvisation (N. Rota) [measures 17–22]
+
Passacaglia in C Minor (J. S. Bach) [measures 23–29]
+
Improvisation (N. Rota) [measures 30–46]
+
The Baptism (N. Rota) [measures 47–49]
+
Prelude in D Major (J. S. Bach) [measures 50–59]
+
Improvisation (N. Rota) [measures 60–61]

This scene begins when the camera cuts to the interior of the
church until it cuts to the exterior.
MM:
A) 1. *The Baptism* and *Godfather Waltz* dated Jan. 14, 1972. Recorded on 1/20/72. 2. 2nd version revised on Feb. 7, 1972, incorporating: Poulenc's *Organ Concerto* (measures 1–12 + 17–23
+ 34–47); Bach's *Passacaglia in C Minor* (measures 13–16 +
24–33); Rota's *The Baptism* (measures 48–50); Bach's *Prelude
in D Major* (51–61). 3. 3rd version revised by Rota and Coppola
dated Feb. 10, 1972.
B) --------
C) 1. 3rd version as listed above. 2. *Il battesimo* consisting of a
159-measure piece different from all of the above.
CD 1–Track 11 *The Baptism* (abbreviated version of A1)

22. Don't Ask Me about My Business, Kay

55. NO TEARS FOR TESSIO (18M2) [02:43:37-02:44:04]
It consists of *Michael's Theme* (N. Rota).
From after Tom Hagen says: "Can't do it, Sally" until the end of
the scene.

MM:

A) *No Tears for Tessio* consisting of 8 measures from *Michael's Theme* in piano reduction.

B) Same scored for 2 Cl, 1 Bsn, 2 Hn, 4 Vla, 3 Vlc. Recorded on 1/18/72.

C) Same as above.

56. MAIN TITLE (1M1X) [02:48:01-02:48:38]

It consists of *The Godfather Waltz* #1 (N. Rota).

From after the car leaves until after another car arrives with women.

MM:

A) --------

B) --------

C) --------

23. End Credits

57. FINALE (19M2) [02:51:25-02:52:25]

It consists of *The Godfather Waltz* (N. Rota).

From when Michael and Kay embrace until the screen goes black.

MM:

A) *Finale* consisting of 64 measures from *The Godfather Waltz* in piano reduction.

B) Same scored for 1 Ob, 2 Cl, 3 Hn, 1 Tpt, 1 Gt, 1 Pn, 1 Accordion, Strings (8-6-4-3-2). Recorded on 1/18/72.

C) --------

58. THE GODFATHER FINALE (19M3) [02:52:26-02:54:56]

It consists of *Michael's Theme* (N. Rota)

+

Love Theme from *The Godfather* (N. Rota)

+

The Godfather Waltz (N. Rota).

From after preceding cue until the camera fades out before Paramount logo appears on the screen.

MM:

A) *The Godfather Finale* (*End Credits*) consisting of 116 measures in piano reduction.

B) Same, scored for 2 Fl, 1 Ob, 1 E. Hn, 2 Cl, 2 Bsn, 3 Hn, 2 Tpt, 2 Trbn, 1 Tb, 1 Hp, 1 Pn, 1 Gt, 1 Accordion, 2 Mandolins, Strings (10-8-6-6-4). Recorded on 1/17/72.
C) *The Godfather Finale* consisting of 102 measures in short score comprising *Michael's Theme*, *The Love Theme* from *The Godfather*, and *The Godfather Waltz*.
CD 1–Track 12 *The Godfather Finale* [extended version with dubbed chorus]

Music Cues Recorded but Not Used

January 17, 1972

THE PICKUP PART 2 consisting of 27 measures scored for 2 Fl, 2 Cl, 1 Bsn, 2 Tpt, 2 Hn, 1 Perc, 1 Pn, 1 Gt, 1 Xyl, 1 Cel, 1 Org, Strings (10-8-6-6-4).
CD 1–Track 3

THE PICKUP PART 1 consisting of 31 measures scored for 2 Fl, 4 Cl (Sax), 1 Perc, 1 Pn, 1 Gt, 1 Accordion, Strings (10-8-6-6-4).
CD 1–Track 3

THE BELLS OF ST. MARY'S

January 18, 1972

XMAS AND LUCA scored for 8 Boy Sopranos, 2 Fl, 2 Ob, 2 Cl, 1 Bsn, 2 Hn, 1 Hp, 1 Pn, 1 Cel, 1 Cordovox, Strings (6-6-4-3-2).

PRELUDE TO MURDER consisting of 19 measures marked *Allegretto Natalizio* scored for 2 Fl, 2 Ob, 1 Hp, 1 Xyl, 1 Cel, 1 Accordion, Strings (6-6-4-3-2).

THE HORSE'S HEAD consisting of *The Godfather Waltz* scored for 2 Fl, 1 Ob, 2 Cl, 2 Bsn, 2 Hn, 2 Trp, 1 Acccordion, 1 Hp, 1 Pn, Strings (6-6-4-3-2).

SICILIAN PASTORAL PART 1 consisting of the *Love Theme* from *The Godfather* scored for (--------).
CD 1–Track 6

FIRST CONTACT consisting of 4 measures scored for 1 Cl, 1 Pn, Strings (6-6-4-3-2).

THE HALLS OF FEAR PART 2 consisting of 18 measures scored for 2 Fl, 2 Ob, 2 Cl, 2 Bsn, 1 Tpt, 3 Hn, 1 Perc, 1 Hp, 1 Pn, 3 Vlc, 1 Cb).
CD 1–Track 5

CORLEONE WALTZ #2 {5} consisting of 16 measures from *The Godfather Waltz* scored for (--------).
CD 1–Track 8

SICILIAN PASTORAL PART 2 consisting of *Love Theme* from *The Godfather* scored for (--------).
CD 1–Track 6

HOLLYWOOD consisting of 44 measures scored for 2 Fl, 3 Cl (Sax), 1 B. Cl, 3 Tpt, 2 Trbn, 1 Perc, 1 Pn, 1 Gt, 1 Accordion.

THE MANSION consisting of 16 measures scored for 2 Fl, 3 Cl (Sax), 1 B. Cl, 3 Tpt, 2 Trbn, 1 Perc, 1 Pn, 1 Gt, 1 Accordion.

LAS VEGAS STRIP consisting of 25 measures scored for 2 Fl, 3 Cl (Sax), 3 Tpt, 2 Trbn, 1 Perc, 1 Pn, 1 Gt, 1 Org, 1 Cb.

Peter King arranged, orchestrated, and recorded in New York City on January 10, 1972, the following source music for possible use in the film. The titles marked in bold were not used.

1. *Manhattan Serenade* (Adamson & Alt)
2. **Dinner Decision,** consisting of *Etude,* op. 30 #3 by Chopin
3. *Santa Claus Is Coming to Town* (Gillespie & Coots)
4. *The Bells of St. Mary's* (Adams & Furber)
5. **To Each His Own** (Livingston & Evans)
6. **Be My Love** (Cahn & Brodszky)
7. **Sam's Song** (Elliott & Quasling)
8. **That Old Black Magic** (Mercer & Arlen)
9. **That's Amore** (Brooks & Warren)
10. *For He's a Jolly Good Fellow* (Traditional)
11. *Mona Lisa* (Livingston & Evans)
12. **Stella by Starlight** (Washington & Young)

13. *All of My Life* (Berlin)
14. *Tangerine* (Mercer & Schertzinger)
15. *Lucky* (Coppola)

PART II

DISC 1
1. Funeral in Sicily

1. MAIN TITLE (1M1) [00:00:15-00:01:11]
   It consists of *The Godfather Waltz* (N. Rota)
   +
   Michael's Theme (N. Rota) [00:00:52].
   The music starts on black screen until the camera fades to the Sicilian countryside.
   MM:
   C) *Titles* (same as Cue #1 in Part I) consisting of 20 measures from *The Godfather Waltz* and *Michael's Theme* scored for 1 E. Hn, 2 Cl, 1 Bsn, 2 Hn, 1 Tpr, 3 Trbn, [1 Hp], Strings (6-4-3-3-2). Recorded on 10/30/74.
   CD 2–Track 1 *Main Title/The Immigrant*

2. MARCIA FUNEBRE (C. Coppola) [00:01:13-00:02:25]
   From when the above cue fades in until shots are fired killing Paolo Andolini. Recorded by Carmine Coppola on location in Sicily.

   Deleted [Additional] Scene #1 "Searching for Vito" shows two men searching for young Vito Andolini. As one man knocks at Andolini's door asking about the boy's whereabouts, the other crouches leaning against a wall and plays on the ocarina[1] the *Antico Canto Siciliano.*
   Recorded by Carmine Coppola on location in Sicily.

   PSM: *Antico Canto Siciliano* (Wedding Procession–Sicilian Love Song, arranged and adapted by Carmine Coppola): 12–15.

---

[1] The ocarina is a simple, small wind instrument made out of terra-cotta or wood.

2. It's Not His Words I'm Afraid Of [no music]
3. "Ellis Island, 1901"

3. THE IMMIGRANT (1M2) [00:07:01-00:08:02]
   It consists of *The Immigrant Theme Part I* (N. Rota)
   +
   The Immigrant Theme Part II (N. Rota) [00:07:16]
   +
   The Immigrant Theme Part I (N. Rota) [00:07:31]
   From before the camera dissolves to New York Harbor until view of Ellis Island.
   MM:
   C) *Gli emigranti* [*The Emigrants*] consisting of 32 measures scored for 2 Fl, 2 Ob, 2 Cl, 2 Bsn, 2 Hn, [1 Tpt], 3 [2] Trbn,1 Tb, 1 Perc, 1 Hp, 1 Pn, Strings (8-8-6-6-4). Recorded on 10/29/74.
   CD 2–Track 1 *Main Title/The Immigrant*
   PSM: *Theme from Godfather II* by Nino Rota: 30–31.

4. THE FIDDLER (1M4) (C. Coppola) [00:08:48-00:08:53]
   From when the camera moves past waiting immigrants.

5. LU ME SCECCU (Sicilian Folk Song) [00:10:39-00:11:12]
   From after young Vito sits and sings until after the camera dissolves to interior of a church.

6. ANTHONY'S FIRST COMMUNION (2M2) (N. Rota)
   [00:10:56-00:11:46]
   +
   The Godfather Waltz (N. Rota) [00:11:23] (organ solo)
   From above dissolve until the camera cuts to the Lake Tahoe estate.
   MM:
   C) 26 measures scored for voice and organ.

4. Party at Lake Tahoe[2]

---

[2] All cues marked by an * were recorded by Carmine Coppola on location at Kings Castle in Incline, Nevada. Those marked ** were recorded at Paramount Studios in Hollywood.

7. ITALIAN EYES (C. Coppola) [00:12:18-00:12:11]*
   From above cut until the dance exhibition ends.

8. ITALIAN EYES (2M7X) (C. Coppola) [00:12:18-00:12:30]**
   From a long shot of the party until before Carmela Corleone
   says: "Look who's here."

9. HEART AND SOUL (Loesser & Carmichael) [00:12:52-
   00:13:12]
   From when Connie Corleone says: "Here I am" until Carmela
   says: "Like everybody else."

10. FANFARE (C. Coppola) [00:13:15-00:13:19]
    After the above line is spoken.

11. DRUM ROLL [00:14:44-00:14:49]
    From when Senator Geary says: "... a real Nevada thank-you
    ..."

12. MR. WONDERFUL (Bock, Holofcener &Weiss) [00:15:12-
    00:16:00]*
    A choir begins until the camera cuts to the interior of the boat-
    house.

5. You Can Have My Answer Now

13. I LOVE TO HEAR THAT OLD TIME MUSIC (C. Coppola)
    [00:17:11-00:18:26]*
    From after above cut until after Geary says: "... your whole
    fucking family."

14. STUMBLELOO (C. Coppola) [00:19:55-00:21:00]*
    From a long shot of the party until Frank Pentangeli says: "...
    gives me a Ritz cracker ..."

15. INDISTINGUISHABLE MELODY [00:21:14-00:21:33]
    From after Pentangeli says: "Bring out the peppers and sausage"
    until he says: "No, no, that was no heart attack."

16. PAUL JONES TARANTELLA (POPS GOES THE WEASEL)
    (Traditional/C. Coppola) [00:24:11-00:24:48]
    From when Pentangeli tries to get the orchestra to play until the
    camera cuts to the boathouse interior.

17. SOPHIA (C. Coppola) [00:24:48-00:26:17]*
From the above cut until Michael says: "I want to be reasonable with you."

6. Frankie Pentangeli's Complaint

18. IN A PARIS CAFÉ (C. Coppola) [00:27:18-00:28:20]
From cut to the party at night until Pentangeli says: "With all respect ..."

19. HO BISOGNO DI TE (GELOSIA) (WHEN I'M WITH YOU) (Pennino/C. Coppola) [00:28:30-00:29:43]
From cut to Deanna Corleone dancing until the camera cuts to the boathouse interior.

20. PINK CHAMPAGNE (C. Coppola) [00:30:13-00:31:31:22]
From above cut until Pentangeli says: "Junk. Dope."

21. EV'RY TIME I LOOK IN YOUR EYES (C. Coppola) [00:32:38-00:34:05]
From after Al Neri says: "You want him to leave now?" until a long shot of the party.

Deleted scenes #27–31.

7. Bedroom Shooting

22. AFTER THE PARTY (4M4) [00:34:05-00:35:15]
It consists of *The Godfather Waltz* (N. Rota)
+
Kay's Theme (N. Rota) [00:34:44]
From above cut until machine gun starts firing.
MM:
C) *After the Party* consisting of 31 measures from *The Godfather Waltz* and *Kay's Theme* scored for 2 Fl, 2 Cl, 1 Perc, 1 Hp, 1 Pn, 1 Mandolin, 1 Gt, Strings (6-4-3-3-2).
Recorded on 10/30/74.

23. FINDING THE MAN (4M5) (N. Rota) [00:35:46-00:36:44]
From cut to the exterior of estate until after cut to the interior.

MM:

A) *Finding the Man* consisting of 26 measures based on a thematic variation of the incipit of *Michael's Theme* scored for 2 Fl, 2 Ob, 2 Cl, 1 B. Cl, 2 Bsn, 3 Hn, 2 Tpt, 2 Trbn, 1 Timp, 1 Xilophone, 1 Hp, 1 Pn, Strings (8-8-6-6-4). Recorded on 10/29/74.

C) *Ricerca dell'uomo* [Finding the Man] consisting of 43 measures from *Michael's Theme* scored for 2 Fl, 2 Cl, 2 Bsn, 2 Hn, 1 Perc, Strings (6-4-3-3-2). Recorded on 10/30/74.

24. THE SEARCH CONTINUES (5M1)–FINDING THE MAN
[00:37:07-00:37:26]
It consists of *Michael's Theme* (N. Rota).
From cut to the exterior of estate until long shot of motorboat.
MM:
C) 1. *The Search Continues–Finding the Man* consisting of 8 measures from same as above scored for 2 Fl, 2 Cl, 2 Bsn, 2 Hn, 1 Perc, Strings (6-4-3-3-2).

25. MICHAEL AND ANTHONY (5M3) [00:42:11-00:44:00]
It consists of *The Godfather Waltz* (N. Rota).
From after Michael kisses his son until camera dissolves to the interior of vaudeville theatre.
MM:
C) Michael and Anthony consisting of 69 measures from *The Godfather Waltz* and *Michael's Theme* scored for 2 [1] Fl, 2 [1] Ob, 2 [1] Cl, 1 B. Cl, 1 Bsn, [1 Hn], 1 Tpt, 2 Perc, 1 Pn, 1 Celesta, {1 Gt}, {1 Accordion}, Strings (6-4-3-3-2).
Recorded on 10/30/74.
Note: *The Godfather Waltz* is played on Glockenspiel (or amplified Celesta) while *Michael's Theme* is played by Viola and Bassoon beginning at 00:43:26.

8. New York City, 1917[3]

26. NEW YORK, 1917
NAPULE VE SALUTE (LASSANNO NAPULE) (GOODBYE TO NAPLES) (F. Pennino) [00:44:00-00:44:43]
From dissolve of preceding cue until performers finish.

---

[3] Cues #26–28 were recorded by Carmine Coppola on location in New York City at A&R Recording Studio.

27. SENZA MAMMA (F. Pennino) [00:44:48-00:45:01]
From when the curtain rises until after the actor begins.

28. SENZA MAMMA (F. Pennino) [00:46:00-00:48:24]
From after the actor says: "Morta. Mamma mia" until the theatre's owner says: "Not my daughter."

Deleted [Additional] Scene #2 "Fanucci Attacked" takes place after the backstage episode described in Cue #28 in which Fanucci holds at knifepoint the daughter of the theatre owner. Later, Vito witnesses Fanucci being attacked and having his throat slashed by two youngsters. We hear 0:44 of music taken from *The Immigrant Theme*.

CD2–Track 6 *Senza Mamma* sung by Livio Giorgi

29. VITO AND ABBANDANDO PART III (6M2) [00:49:12-00:50:04]
It consists of *The Immigrant Theme* (N. Rota).
From after cut to Abbandando's store until after the camera dissolves to the interior of Vito's flat.
MM:
C) 27 measures from *The Immigrant Theme* scored for 2 Fl [Piccolo], 2 Cl, 1 B. Cl, 3 Perc, 1 Pn, 1 Tack Pn, 1 Hpsc, 1 Org, 1 Mandolin, 1 Gt, 1 Cb. Recorded on 10/30/74.
CD 2–Track 5 *Vito and Abbandando*

9. Vito Meets Clemenza

30. CELESTE AIDA from *AIDA* (Verdi/C. Coppola) [00:50:06-00:51:03]
From when Vito says: "Forget it" until after he opens a package containing guns.
Scored for 2 Fl, 2 Ob, 1 E. Hn, {2 Cl}, 2 Bsn, 2 Hn, 1 Tb, Strings (6-4-3-3-2). Recorded on 10/30/74.
2nd version with tenor solo recorded at Paramount Studios, Hollywood.

31. VITO AND ABBANDANDO PART I (6M4) [00:53:19-00:54:43]

It consists of *The Immigrant Theme* (N. Rota).
From after Vito says: "And I won't forget it" until camera cuts to the street.
MM:
C) 22 measures from *The Immigrant Theme* scored for 1 Fl, 1 Ob, 1 E. Hn, 2 Cl, 1 B. Cl, 2 Bsn, 2 Hn, [1 Hp], {1Fender Bass}, {2 Gt}, Strings (6-4-3-3-2). Recorded on 10/30/74.
CD 2–Track 5 *Vito and Abbandando*

Deleted [Additional] Scene #3 "I'm My Own Boss" portrays young Clemenza asserting himself in the eyes of Vito. The scene takes place in a cafè where a piano player performs diegetically a tune by Francesco Pennino.
Deleted Scene #4 "Playing the Flute" shows Clemenza, Vito, and Abbandando in Augusto Coppola's gunsmith shop. As the foursome discuss the accuracy of the pistols under scrutiny, Augusto asks his young son Carmine to play a favorite tune on the flute. The boy plays an unaccompanied serenade composed (and played) by Carmine Coppola.
Recorded by Carmine Coppola at Paramount Studios, Hollywood.

32. A NEW CARPET PART II (7M1) (N. Rota) [00:55:46-00:56:09]
From the beginning of the scene until Clemenza bends to look for the key.
MM:
C) *A New Carpet Part II* consisting of 30 measures from *Allegretto mosso* in 6/8 "like a kind of tarantella" and *The Immigrant Theme* scored for 1 Fl, {2 Ob}, 2 Cl, 1 B. Cl, {2 Bsn}, {2 Hn}, 2 Tpt, 2 {1} Trbn, 1 Celesta, [1 Vibraphone], 1 Tack Pn, 1 Hpsc, 1 Org, {2} Gt, 1 Fender Bass. Recorded on 10/30/74.
CD 2–Track 2 *A New Carpet*

33. A NEW CARPET (7M2) [00:58:34-00:59:30]
It consists of *A New Carpet Part I* (N. Rota)
+
The Immigrant Theme (N. Rota) [00:58:49]
From cut to the street until cut to the countryside and train.
MM:
C) *A New Carpet Part I* consisting of 10 measures from *A New Carpet* (see Cue #32) and 28 measures from *The Immigrant Theme* scored for 1 Piccolo, 1 Fl, 2 Cl, 1 B. Cl, [2 Hn], 2 Tpt, 1 Trbn, 1 Tack Pn, 1 Fender Gt, 1 Gt, 1 Fender Bass, 1 Celesta

[1 Vibraphone], [1 Org], Strings (6-4-3-3-2).
Recorded on 10/30/74.
CD 2–Track 2 *A New Carpet*

10. Keep Your Friends Close, but Your Enemies Closer

34. A VISIT TO ROTH (7M3) (N. Rota) [01:00:10-01:01:53]
From cut to a Miami hotel exterior until Michael opens a screen
door.
MM:
C) *A Visit to Roth* consisting of 26 measures of non-thematic
material including *Autumn* (see Cue #47 in Part I) scored for
1 Piccolo, 1 Fl, 1 Ob, 1 E. Hn, {2 Cl}, [2 Bsn], 1 Hp, 1 Celesta,
1 Pn, Strings (6-4-3-3-2). Recorded on 10/30/74.

35. DEATH OF THREE (N. Rota) [01:09:08-01:10:33]
From after Michael says: "... who the traitor in my family was"
until cut to the exterior of a bar.
MM:
A) --------
B) --------
C) *Death of Three* consisting of 36 measures of non-thematic
material, 2 Fl, 1 Ob, 2 Cl, 1 Bsn, 1 Hn, 1 Perc, [1 Hp], [1 Ce-
lesta], [1 Pn], Strings (6-4-3-3-2). Recorded on 10/30/74.

11. I Remember She Was Laughing

36. AUTUMN (8M1) (N. Rota) [01:15:44-01:16:51]
    +
KAY'S THEME (N. Rota) [01:15:44] (Violin solo)
From after Tom Hagen says: "All that's left is our friendship"
until cut to Havana.
MM:
C) *Autumn* and *Kay's Theme* consisting of 39 measures scored
for 2 Fl, [2 Ob], 2 Cl, [1 Bsn], [1 Hn], {1 Perc}, [1 Celesta],
1 Hp, {1 Pn}, {1 Gt}, {1 Mandolin}, Strings (6-4-3-3-2).
Recorded on 10/30/74.

12. Welcome to Havana

37. EL CHA CHA CHA DI SANTO DOMINGO [01:16:51-01:18:16]
Consisting of *Tu* (Sanchez Fuentes/C. Coppola).
From preceding cue until cut to the interior of the presidential palace.
Recorded by Carmine Coppola on location in Santo Domingo.

13. I Know It Was You, Fredo

38. HAVANA (8M6) (N. Rota) [01:25:56-01:27:23]
From cut to a hotel exterior until after Michael says: "Johnny Ola."
MM:
C) *Havana* consisting of 57 measures scored for 2 Fl, {1 Cl}, 1 Tpt, [1 Alto Sax], 1 Fender Gt, 1 Gt, 1 Fender Bass, 5 Perc. Recorded on 10/30/74.

39. GUANTANAMERA (Traditional/C. Coppola & new lyrics by Italia Pennino) [01:27:49-01:30:49]
From cut to garden café until cut to hotel suite.
Recorded by Carmine Coppola on location in Santo Domingo.

40. MUSIC FOR AQUA LUZ (C. Coppola) [01:34:56-01:36:29]
+
EL CHA CHA CHA DI SANTO DOMINGO [01:35:17]
Consisting of *Tu* (Sanchez Fuentes/C. Coppola). Vocal version sung by Yvonne Coll.
From cut to interior of nightclub until cut to interior of another club. Recorded by Carmine Coppola at Criteria Recording Studios in Miami, Florida.

41. DANZA ESOTICA (C. Coppola) [01:36:39-01:38:28] (Alto Sax and Percussion)
From after above cut until cut to interior of hotel suite.
Recorded by Carmine Coppola on location in Santo Domingo.

42. VITO AND ABBANDANDO PART II (6M3) [01:38:08-01:38:18] (Bass Clarinet solo)
It consists of *The Immigrant Theme* (N. Rota).

MM:

C) 27 measures scored for 1 Piccolo, 1 Fl, 2 Cl, 1 B. Cl, 1 Tack Pn, 3 Perc, 1 Mandolin, 1 Gt, 1 Org, 1 Hpsc, 1 Cb.
Recorded on 10/30/74.

43. OLA'S DEATH (11M5) (N. Rota) [01:38:29-01:39:31]
From preceding cue until a doctor says: "... to the hospital."
MM:
C) *Ola's Death* consisting of 19 measures scored for 2 Cl, 1 B. Cl, 2 Bsn, 2 Hn, 1 Perc, 1 Celesta, 2 Pn, Strings (6-4-3-3-2).
Recorded 10/30/74.

44. ROTH IS NEXT PART III (12M4) [01:40:03-01:40:05]
From when the bodyguard reenters until cut to the interior of the presidential palace.
MM:
C) *Roth Is Next Part III* consisting of fragments from 7 measures of non-thematic material scored for {3 Saxophones}, [2 Cl, 1 B. Cl], [2 Bsn], 2 Hn, 2 Tpt, 3 Perc, 2 Pn.
Recorded on 10/30/74.

45. MY TROPICAL LOVE (12M3) [01:40:07-01:40:56]
It consists of *La Paloma* (Yradier/C. Coppola).
From above cut until cut to hospital.
La Paloma scored for 5 Saxophones, 3 Tpt, 3 Trbn, 1 Perc, 1 Pn, 1 Cel, 1 Accordion, 6 Vl, 2 Vlc, 1 Cb.
Recorded on 10/30/74.

46. EL PADRINO–BUSETTA'S DEATH
(C. Coppola) [01:41:34-01:42:06]
From cut to the interior of the presidential palace until cut to the hospital.
Recorded by Carmine Coppola on location in Santo Domingo.

47. GUANTANAMERA (Traditional/C. Coppola) [01:43:10-01:44:05]
From cut to the interior of the presidential palace until cut to the street.
Fireworks + Cuban Revolutionary Song [01:44:12-01:44:26]
Recorded by Carmine Coppola on location in Santo Domingo.

48. FREDO'S PANIC (12M9) (N. Rota) [01:45:46-01:46:58]
    +
    The Godfather Waltz (N. Rota) [01:46:21]
    +
    Fredo's Panic (N. Rota) [01:46:24]
    +
    Michael's Theme (N. Rota) [01:46:46]
    MM:
    C) *Fredo's Panic* consisting of 60 measures including "Rite of
    Spring"-like material scored for 2 Fl, 1 Ob, 1 E. Hn, {2 Cl},
    {2 Bsn}, [2 Hn], [2 Tpt], [1 Fender Gt], 1 Hp, [1 Pn], [1 Ce-
    lesta], Strings (6-4-3-3-2) + a montage of various pre-recorded
    versions of *The Godfather Waltz* and *Michael's Theme*.
    Recorded on 10/30/74.

14. Was It a Boy? [no music]
15. Fanucci Wants to Wet His Beak

49. MICHAEL AND ANTHONY (5M3) [01:49:45-01:50:30]
    It consists of *The Godfather Waltz* (N. Rota).
    From after Tom Hagen says: "I really don't know" until cut to
    street.
    MM: Same as Cue #25.

16. Murder of Fanucci

50. MARCIA REALE ITALIANA (Gabetti/C. Coppola) [01:55:07-
    01:55:28]
    From cut to the street festival until Clemenza moves to a booth.
    Recorded by Carmine Coppola at A&R Recording Studio in
    New York City.

51. STAR-SPANGLED BANNER (Smith & Key/C. Coppola)
    [01:55:29-01:55:46]
    After above until Clemenza says: "His family's out of the
    house."
    C) *Stars and Stripes* scored for 1 Fl, 3 Cl, 2 Hn, 3 Tpt, 5 Perc,
    1 Pn, 1 Org, 2 Gt.
    Recorded on 10/30/74.

52. MARCIA STILO ITALIANO (13M4/14M1) (C. Coppola)
    [01:55:49-01:57:49]
    From when Abbandando says: "Here's my fifty dollars" until
    Don Fanucci says: "You've got a lot of guts."
    Recorded on 10/30/74.
    C) *Marcia Stilo Italiano* scored for 1 Fl, 2 Cl, 2 Hn, 3 Tpt,
    5 Perc, 1 Pn, 1 Org, 2 Gt. Recorded on 10/30/74.
    CD–Track 10 *Marcia Stilo Italiano*

53. MARCIA RELIGIOSO (C. Coppola) [01:58:33-02:01:51]
    From cut to the street festival until cut to Vito covering his gun
    and turning the lightbulb off.
    Recorded by Carmine Coppola at A&R Recording Studio in
    New York City.
    CD 2–Track 13 *Murder of Don Fanucci*

54. MURDER OF DON FANUCCI (C. Coppola) [02:02:06-
    02:02:56]
    It consists of drum roll and footsteps alternating with the priest
    reciting rituals.
    From when Vito steps behind Don Fanucci until he kills him.

55. FESTA MARCH (C. Coppola) [02:02:56-02:05:08]
    From preceding cue until Vito nears his flat.
    Recorded by Carmine Coppola at A&R Recording Studio in
    New York City.
    CD 2–Track 13 *Murder of Don Fanucci*

56. NINNA-NANNA A MICHELE (14M4A1) [02:05:08-02:06:10]
    It consists of *The Godfather Waltz* (N. Rota & lyrics by Italia
    Pennino)
    +
    Michael's Theme (N. Rota) [02:06:04]
    From preceding cue until the end of the scene.
    MM:
    C) *Ninna-Nanna* consisting of *The Godfather Waltz* and *Mi-
    chael's Theme* scored for voice, 2 Fl, 2 Ob, 2 Cl, {1 B. Cl},
    2 Bsn, 3 Hn, {2 Tpt}, {3 Trbn}, {1 Tb}, 1 Gt, 2 Perc, 1 Hp,
    Strings (8-8-6-6-4). Sung by Nino Palermo with guitar accom-
    paniment, then by full orchestra. Recorded on 10/29/74.
    CD 2–Track 11 *Ninna-Nanna a Michele* sung by Nino Palermo

DISC 2
1. You Can Never Lose Your Family

57. THE CORLEONE ESTATE (15M1X) (N. Rota) [00:00:03-
    00:00:24]
    From the beginning of the scene until a car drives through the
    gates.
    MM:
    C) *Autumn* consisting of portions of Cue #47 in Part I.

58. MICHAEL COMES HOME–THE GODFATHER AT HOME
    PART I (15M2) [00:00:46-00:01:53]
    It consists of *Michael's Theme* (N. Rota)
    +
    Kay's Theme (N. Rota) [00:01:37]
    From when Michael stops by Anthony's red toy car until he
    looks through the open door.
    MM:
    C) *Michael Comes Home* consisting of 32 measures from *Mi-
    chael's Theme* and *Kay's Theme* scored for 2 Fl, 1 Ob, 1 E. Hn,
    2 Cl, 2 Bsn, 2 Hn, 1 Hp, Strings (6-4-3-3-2).
    Recorded on 10/30/74.
    CD 2–Track 7 *The Godfather at Home*

59. FREDO'S STAY OF EXECUTION–THE GODFATHER AT
    HOME PART II (16M1) [00:04:22-00:04:49]
    It consists of *Michael's Theme* (N. Rota).
    From cut to the exterior of the estate until after Michael sits by
    Carmela.
    MM:
    C) *Michael's Theme* consisting of 17 measures marked *Lento,
    funereo* scored for 2 Fl, 1 Ob, 1 E. Hn, 2 Cl, 1 B. Cl, [2 Bsn],
    3 Hn, 1 Perc, 1 Tack Pn, 3 Vlc, 2 Cb. Recorded on 10/30/74.

60. MICHAEL AND HIS MOTHER (16M2) [00:05:40-00:07:06]
    It consists of *The Immigrant Theme* (N. Rota).
    From after Carmela says: "… about the baby you lost" until Vito
    says: "… why did you come to see me?"
    MM:
    C) *The Immigrant Theme* consisting of 23 measures scored for
    2 Fl, 1 [2] Ob, 2 Cl, 2 Bsn, 3 Hn, 1 Perc, 1 Hp, 1 [Tack] pn,
    2 Mandolins, 1 Gt, Strings (6-4-3-3-2).

2. The Dog Stays

61. THE LANDLORD (16M3) (N. Rota) [00:10:44-00:11:17]
    From after a man says: "What a character" until he enters shop.
    MM:
    C) *The Landlord* consisting of 18 measures from a *Fox-Trot*
    marked *Allegro comodo* scored for {1 Fl}, [1 Alto Sax], 1 B. Cl,
    {1 Bsn}, 1 Org, 1 Tack Pn, 1 Gt, 1 Cb. Recorded on 10/30/74.

    Deleted [Additional] Scene #7 "Don Vito Corleone" shows
    Signor Robert (the landlord) searching for Vito, whom he ad-
    dresses as Don for the first time in Part II's flashback episodes.
    Deleted [Additional] Scene #8 "Introducing Hyman Roth," al-
    though deprived of music soundtrack, continues "The Landlord"
    episode after Signor Roberto's clumsy exit from Vito's shop.

62. A NEW CARPET PART III [(7M1) (N. Rota) [00:13:28-
    00:14:00]
    +
    The Immigrant Theme (N. Rota)
    +
    A New Carpet Part III (N. Rota)
    +
    The Immigrant Theme (N. Rota)
    From cut to exterior of Genco's store until cut to the interior of
    the Senate Hearing Room.
    MM:
    C) *A New Carpet* consisting of 28 measures scored for 1 Piccolo,
    [1 Fl], 2 Cl, 1 B. Cl, [2 Tpt], 4 Trbn, 1 Celesta, [1 Vibraphone],
    [1 Tack Pn], 1 Hpsc, [1 Hp], 1 Fender Gt, 1 Gt, 1 Fender Bass,
    Strings (6-4-3-3-2). Recorded on 10/30/74.
    Note: *The Immigrant Theme*'s fragments heard in this cue are
    taken from pre-recorded versions of same.
    CD 2–Track 2 *A New Carpet*

3. Senate Hearing [no music]
4. You're Nothing to Me Now

63. FREDO'S STAY OF EXECUTION (16M1) [00:25:18-
    00:26:26]

It consists of *Michael's Theme* (N. Rota) same as Cue #59

+

The Godfather Waltz (N. Rota) (Bass Clarinet solo) [00:26:09]
on steady beat.

From after Michael says: "Fredo, you're nothing to me now" until the camera pans to another entrance of an Army base.

MM:

C) *Michael's Theme* (*Lento funereo*) same as Cue #59.

5. Pentangeli Sees His Brother [no music]
6. Michael, You Are Blind [no music]
7. My Father's Name Was . . . Antonio Andolini

64. SICILY, 1927–CIURI-CIURI (Sicilian Folk Song/C. Coppola)
    [00:37:16-00:37:57]
    From cut to train station until dissolve to road.

> Deleted [Additional] Scene #9 "1927 Vito's Revenge" shows
> Vito murdering the two men who 20 years prior carried out Don
> Ciccio's order to kill the Andolini family. We hear the *Love Theme*
> from *The Godfather* followed by the ocarina melody heard in De-
> leted [Additional] Scene #1. This episode concludes with *The God-
> father Waltz*. During the following cue, Vito kills the *mafioso* Don
> Ciccio.

65. REMEMBER VITO ANDOLINI PART II (19M2A&B)
    [00:37:56-00:40:07]
    It consists of *The Love Theme* from *The Godfather* (N. Rota)

    +

    Michael's Theme (N. Rota) [00:39:30] on close-up of baby Mi-
    chael

    +

    The Immigrant Theme (N. Rota) [00:39:46]
    From when preceding cue dissolves until the gates are closed af-
    ter a car enters.

    MM:

    C) *Remember Vito Andolini* scored for 2 Fl, 2 Ob, 2 Cl, 1 B. Cl,
    2 Bsn, 3 Hn, 3 Trbn, 1 Perc, 1 Hp, 1 Mandolin, 1 Gt, 1 Accor-
    dion, Strings (8-8-6-6-4). Recorded on 10/29/74.

66. THE BROTHERS MOURN PART III (20M1A) [00:43:04-
    00:43:53]
    It consists of *The Immigrant Theme* (N. Rota).

From when a man near Vito is shot until the camera dissolves to a train station.

MM:

C) *The Brothers Mourn Part III* consists of 37 measures from *The Immigrant Theme* scored for 2 Fl, 2 Ob, 2 Cl, 2 Bsn, 2 Hn, 1 Hp, Strings (8-8-6-6-4). Recorded on 10/29/74.

CD 2–Track 12 *The Brothers Mourn*

8. Mama Corleone's Funeral

67. CONNIE AND MICHAEL (20M1B) [00:48:31-00:49:57]

It consists of *The Immigrant Theme*

+

Michael's Theme [00:40:58]

+

The Immigrant Theme [00:49:11] and [00:49:33] with great passion

+

Michael's Theme [00:49:48]

From after Connie says "I want to take care of you now" until Tom walks towards the boathouse. Recorded on 10/29/74.

CD 2–Track 12 *The Brothers Mourn*

9. You Can Kill Anyone [no music]
10. Like the Roman Empire

68. REFLECTIONS ON ROMANS (21M1) [00:56:31-00:58:22]

It consists of *The Godfather Waltz* (N. Rota), Viola sola.

From after Pentangeli says: "... like the Roman Empire" until he says: "See ya, Tom."

MM:

C) *Lento–Triste* consisting of 39 measures from *The Godfather Waltz* scored for 2 Cl, 1 Vla, 2 Vlc. Recorded on 10/30/74.

11. Kay with Her Children [no music]
12. Hail Mary, Full of Grace

69. DEATH OF THREE (22M1) (N. Rota) [01:02:20-01:04:59]

+

The Immigrant Theme (N. Rota) [01:02:40]–French Horn solo.

From a medium long shot of the boat on the lake until cut to the boathouse interior.

MM:

C) Reuse of previously heard material consisting of 36 measures of non-thematic underscoring and *The Immigrant Theme* at the very end played by a French Horn scored for 1 Piccolo, 1 Fl, 1 Ob, 2 Cl, 1 Bsn, 1 Hn, 1 Perc, [1 Hp], [1 Pn], Strings (6-4-3-3-2). Recorded on 10/30/74.

13. Surprise Party

70. THE FORTIES (A23M1) (C. Coppola) [01:05:00-01:08:18]
From after the preceding cue and before the camera dissolves to dining room until end of scene.
MM:
C) *The Forties* consisting of 56 measures in Glenn Miller Style scored for 1 Cl, 5 Sax, 3 Tpt, 3 Trbn, 1 Perc, 1 Pn, 1 Gt, 1 Cb. Recorded on 10/30/74.

71. FOR HE'S A JOLLY GOOD FELLOW (Traditional) [01:09:13-01:09:31]
From after the group says: "Surprise," then sing.

72. MICHAEL ALONE AT THE TABLE [01:09:24-01:09:39]
It consists of *The Godfather Waltz* (N. Rota).
From when Michael remains alone at the table and a close-up of Michael in Lake Tahoe to the beginning of Cue #73 End Credits.

14. End Credits

73. END TITLES (23M2) [01:09:52-01:13:48]
It consists of *Michael's Theme* (N. Rota)
+
Kay's Theme (N. Rota) [01:10:21]
+
A New Carpet Part I (N. Rota) [01:11:39]
+
The Immigrant Theme (N. Rota) [01:11:54]
+
The Godfather Waltz (N. Rota) [01:12:48]

MM:

C) *End Titles* consisting of 114 measures scored for 2 Fl, 2 Ob, 2 Cl, 2 Bsn, 3 Hn, 2 Tpt, 3 Trbn, 1 Tb, 3 Perc, 1 Hp, 2 Pn, 2 Mandolins, 2 Gt, 1 Accordion, Strings (8-8-6-6-4). Recorded on 10/29/74.

CD 2–Track 14 *End Title*

Music Cues Recorded but Not Used

October 29, 1974

ENTRE' ACTE (INTERMEZZO) PARTS 1&2, 2 Fl, 2 Ob, 2 Cl, 2 Bsn, 3 Hn, 2 Tpt, 3 Trbn, 2 Perc, 1 Hp, 1 Pn, 1 Gt, Strings (8-8-6-6-4)

ENTRE'ACTE (INTERMEZZO) PART 3 consisting of 34 measures from *The Immigrant Theme* and *Love Theme* from *The Godfather*, 2 Fl, 2 Ob, 2 Cl, 2 Bsn, 2 Hn, 2 Tpt, 3 Trbn, 1 Tb, 1 Perc, 1 Hp, 1 Gt, 1 Cel, Strings (8-8-6-6-4)

ENTRE'ACTE (INTERMEZZO) consisting of 31 measures from *Kay's Theme* and *The Godfather Waltz*, 2 Fl, 2 Ob, 2 Cl, 2 Bsn, 2 Hn, [2 Tpt], 3 Trbn, 1 Tb, 1 Hp, 1 Pn, {2 Mandolins}, Strings (8-8-6-6-4)

FREDO BRINGS HOME THE BREAD–TEMPO DI RUMBA consisting of 19 measures, 2 Fl, 2 Cl, 1 Tpt, 4 Trbn, 1 Hp, 5 Perc, 1 Fender Gt, 1 Gt, Strings (8-8-6-6-4)

ENTRE'ACTE (INTERMEZZO) consisting of 37 measures to be connected to "Intermezzo Part 2" #29 recorded on October 30, 2 Fl, 1 Ob, 4 Sax, 3 Tpt, 3 Trbn, 1 Perc, 1 Gt, Strings (8-8-6-6-4)

END TITLES (ALTERNATE) consisting of 114 measures from *Michael's Theme, Kay's Theme, A New Carpet Part I, The Immigrant Theme, The Godfather Waltz*, 2 Fl, 2 Ob, 2 Cl, 2 Bsn, 3 Hn, 2 Tpt, 3 Trbn, 1 Tb, 1 Hp, 1 Tack Pn, Strings (8-8-6-6-4)

October 30, 1974

"I'M REALLY IN LOVE" (C. Coppola): 0:15
(5 Sax, 3 Tpt, 3 Trbn, 1 Pn, 1 Perc, 1 Cel, 1 Accordion, 6 Vl, 2 Vlc, 1 Cb)

TANGERINE (C. Coppola): 2:27
(5 Sax, 3 Tpt, 3 Trbn, 1 Pn, 1 Perc, 1 Cel, 1 Accordion, 6 Vl, 2 Vlc, 1 Cb)

[8M5] (C. Coppola): 2:54
(1 Vl, 1 Cb, 1 Perc, 2 Gt)

INTERMEZZO PART 2 (N. Rota) consisting of 39 measures from *Kay's Theme* and *The Godfather Waltz* (2 Fl, 3 Sax, 2 Tpt, 1 Pn, 5 Perc, 2 Gt, 1 Org, 1 Cb)

[14M3] (C. Coppola): 0:47
(1 Vl, 1 Cb, 1 Perc, 2 Gt)

BUSETTA'S DEATH (N. Rota) consisting of 3 measures ([1 E. Hn], {1 Cb}, 1 Pn, 2 Percussions)

THE FORTIES (N. Rota) consisting of 56 measures composed in Glenn Miller style, 1 [2] Fl, [1 Ob], 5 Sax, 4 Tpt, 4 Trbn, 1 Perc, 1 Pn, 1 Gt, Strings (8-8-6-6-4)

Cues recorded by Carmine Coppola at Kings Castle in Incline, Nevada:

"Let's Play House" Fox-Trot for Accordion and Violin

Cues recorded by Carmine Coppola at Paramount Studios, Hollywood:

Marcia Sinfonia (Military Band)
Marcia a la Italiana (Military Band)
"I've Got a Girl in Reno" (Country-Western)

Cues recorded by Carmine Coppola on location in Santo Domingo, Dominican Republic:

"A la Cubana"
"Rumba di [sic] Amor"
"Inno al Anno Nuevo" Small version

PART III

1. Michael's Letter

1. THE GODFATHER WALTZ (XM10) (N. Rota) [00:00:19-00:01:28]
   In on black screen as Main Titles begin.

   (b) Deleted [Additional] Scene #34. Alternate Opening.

2. MICHAEL'S LETTER [00:01:28-00:02:53] and CHANT
   (Traditional) [00:02:51-00:03:14]
   From preceding cue to Archbishop chanting, "Adjutorium nostrum ..."

3. LAKE MEMORY (XM11) [00:03:14-00:04:03]
   Consisting of *Lake Memories* (C. Coppola)
   +
   Finding the Man (N. Rota) [00:03:37]
   +
   The Immigrant Theme (N. Rota) [00:03:50]
   From after the Archbishop chants, "Oremus," to when he says:
   "Oh Almighty God, bless this insignia ..."

4. MARCIA RELIGIOSO (C. Coppola) [00:05:11-00:05:57]
   (Choral Version)
   From when the audience says: "Amen."

2. Party at Michael's Apartment

5. EH CUMPARI! (La Rosa & Bleyer) [00:05:55-00:07:49]
   From cut to Connie holding a microphone and singing until the
   end of the song as Michael sits down at a table.

6. EL CHA CHA CHA DI SANTO DOMINGO [00:07:54-00:08:32]
   Consisting of *Tu* (Fuentes Sanchez/C. Coppola).
   From cut to little girls sitting on the floor until the end of the
   song when Dominic says: "The Holy Father himself ..."

7. NOTTURNO from STRING QUARTET #2 (Borodin/Coppola)
   [00:08:38-00:09:59]

From when a girl says: "She loves you," until just before the camera cuts to trumpets.

8. FANFARE (C. Coppola) [00:10:06-00:10:15]
   From after guests applaud until before Michael says: "Carissimi amici ..."

9. VITTI 'NA CROZZA (G. Li Causi) [00:11:11-00:11:42]
   From after Mary Corleone says: "Don't spend it all in one place" until the Archbishop says: "Michael, you have done a wonderful thing for Sicily."

3. Anthony's Decision

10. TO EACH HIS OWN (Livingston & Evans) [00:12:35-00:16:05]
    From when Michael says: "I'll be back" until Kay says: "Well, that he got from you."

11. SOPHIA (C. Coppola) [00:16:05-00:18:36]
    From when Michael says: "You could have helped me ..." until Kay says: "Thank you" to Michael.

12. DIMMI, DIMMI, DIMMI (C. Coppola) [00:18:44-00:20:26]
    From after Kay exits the study until Vincent Mancini says: "He dips his bullets in cyanide."

13. ON SUCH A NIGHT (C. Coppola) [00:21:28-00:22:49]
    From when a man says: "Mr. Corleone, can I ..." until Michael says: "Vincent Mancini call about her?"

4. The Trouble with Vincent and Joey Zasa

14. LUCA BRASI (G1-5M1) (N. Rota) [00:22:55-00:23:29]
    From when Al Neri says: "Joey Zasa showed up" until Joey Zasa says: "The Meucci Association has elected you ..."

15. IN A PARIS CAFÉ (C. Coppola) [00:23:50-00:26:00]
    From when Michael says: "And this is the reason you've ..." until he says: "Out of the kindness of his heart ..."

16. BEYOND THE BLUE HORIZON (Harling, Robin & Whiting)
[00:29:40-00:30:26]
From when a photographer says: "It's just about ready."

17. THE GODFATHER WALTZ (4M2) (N. Rota) [00:30:26-00:32:19]
It continues from the preceding cue until a photographer says: "Smile."

5. Who Sent You?

18. TOUGH NEIGHBORHOOD (4M3) [00:32:19-00:32:53]
It consists of *Sollozzo the Turk* (N. Rota).
From cut to the exterior of Vincent's apartment until Vincent says: "I love you, I love you."

19. TOUGH NEIGHBORHOOD (4M3) [00:33:09-00:33:35]
It consists of *Sollozzo the Turk* (N. Rota).
From when Vincent says: "Go get us some water ..." until Grace Hamilton looks outside.

6. The Archbishop Asks for Michael's Help

20. CONNIE (XM12) (C. Coppola) [00:39:11-00:39:29]

7. Shareholders' Meeting

21. SHAREHOLDERS' MEETING [00:42:53-00:43:31]
It consists of *The Godfather Waltz* (N. Rota).
From cut to New York City's skyline until Michael says: "but the Eastern techniques ..."

22. ALTOBELLO
It consists of *Altobello* (C. Coppola) [00:47:16-00:49:23]
+
Autumn (N. Rota) [00:48:01]
+
Michael's Theme (alternating with above) (N. Rota) [00:48:21].
From when Don Altobello exits a Chinese restaurant, continues as Don Altobello and Michael talk in limousine, and concludes as screen fades to black.

8. The Vatican Bank, Rome

23. TO ROME (6M1-R) (Traditional/C. Coppola) [00:49:25-00:50:09]
From a long shot of Vatican City until Michael's car drives through the gate.

24. UNCLE MICHAEL (6M2-B) (C. Coppola) [00:53:05-00:53:23]
From cut to hallway inside the Vatican until screen fades to black.

9. Atlantic City Massacre

25. MIRACLE MAN (Elvis Costello) [00:53:24-00:53:54]
From cut to a Little Italy street scene until a woman says: "Now, I'm an older woman."

26. CAFÉ SCENE [00:54:56-00:55:57]
Consisting of *Vincent's Theme* (C. Coppola).
From after Vincent says: "He was the Prince of the City," continues as Vincent and Mary talk in a restaurant, and concludes on cut to helicopter over Atlantic City.

27. LUCKY (C. Coppola) [00:56:57-00:57:13]
From cut to the interior of a meeting room until Michael enters.

10. Just When I Thought I Was Out

28. ESCAPE (8M1) [01:03:42-01:04:00]
It consists of *The Immigrant Theme* (N. Rota)–B. Clarinet Solo.

29. ROTH IS NEXT PART III (G2-12M4) (N. Rota) [01:06:57-01:07:40]
From when Michael yells: "Altobello, you ..." continues as Michael has diabetic attack and is placed in ambulance, and concludes after Connie says: "I'll call Kay."

30. WE HAVE AN UNDERSTANDING [01:08:36-01:09:45]
It consists of *Finding the Man* (N. Rota).

From when B. J. Harrison walks to ward door, continues as Vincent, Neri, and Connie talk in the hospital chapel, and concludes on cut to the hospital exterior.

31. MICHAEL COMES HOME (G2-15M2) [01:09:50-01:11:53]
It consists of *Michael's Theme* (N. Rota)
+
Kay's Theme (N. Rota) [01:10:41]
From cut to Kay in Michael's hospital room, continues as Kay and Michael talk, and concludes when Michael says: "I won't miss that."

32. MICHAEL AND ANTHONY (G2-5M3) [01:12:06-01:12:30]
It consists of *Michael's Theme* (N. Rota).
From when Kay says: "Go see Dad" until Anthony hugs Michael and screen fades to black.

11. Mary Visits Vincent at the Club

33. VICIN A ME (C. Coppola) [01:15:40-01:16:23]–Accordion solo.
From when Vincent says: "Okay, let's cook."

12. Street Fair

34. SICILIANA (C. Coppola) [01:16:23-01:18:42]
From preceding cue to cut to Italian festival then the camera fades out as gunshots are heard.

13. Michael at the Hospital

35. VINCENT KILLS (C. Coppola) [01:19:24-01:19:40]
From when Zasa falls to the ground until before Michael says: "Not while I'm alive."

36. VINCENT HELPS MICHAEL [01:21:25-01:23:06]
It consists of *Vincent's Theme* (C. Coppola)–Cello solo, then with orchestra
+
The Godfather Waltz (N. Rota) [01:22:56]
+
Michael's Theme (N. Rota) [01:22:41]

From when Michael says: "You know, I always felt responsible
..." continues as Michael talks with Vincent and Vincent helps
Michael into bed. It concludes when Vincent puts his hand on
Michael's head.

14. Return to Sicily

37. LO STORNELLO SICILIANO (Folk Song/C. Coppola)
[01:24:43-01:25:09]
It fades in when Michael says: "In Sicily" until a little boy runs
waving an American flag.

38. VA PENSIERO from *NABUCCO* (Verdi/C. Coppola) [01:25:10-
01:26:09]
From when cars drive towards the palazzo's entrance.

39. SICILIAN PLOT (11M1) [01:26:09-01:26:28]
It consists of *Sicilian Plot* (C. Coppola)
+
Autumn (N. Rota) [01:26:19].
From when the camera dissolves to the palazzo's interior until
Don Tommasino says: "Un uomo di talento."

40. DANZA TARANTELLA (C. Coppola) [01:28:53-01:29:07]
From when the camera dissolves to the interior of Michael's palazzo until the song ends and guests applaud.

41. BRUCIA LA TERRA (N. Rota/G. Rinaldi) [01:30:02-01:31:35]
Voice and Guitar, then with orchestra.
From after Anthony says: "I learned it for you" and sings, continues as Michael remembers (via flashback) dancing with Apollonia.

42. LOVE THEME FROM *THE GODFATHER* (N. Rota)
[01:31:35-01:32:01]
It continues from the preceding cue as Anthony sings the line
"Brucia la luna" while the song fades out. It concludes when
Michael says: "... you're such a warmhearted girl."

15. Michael Tells Vincent His Plans

43. MIRACLE MAN (Elvis Costello) [01:32:58-01:33:52]
From cut to the exterior of Michael's palazzo, continues as Vincent and Mary kiss in bedroom and Vincent and Michael talk while Vincent shaves Michael.

44. SOLLOZZO THE TURK (G1-4M4) (N. Rota) [01:33:52-01:35:15]
It continues from the preceding cue from after Michael says: "To betray me" until Vincent says: "... indebted to you forever."

45. SOLLOZZO THE TURK (G1-4M4) (N. Rota) [01:35:47-01:36:43]
From after Michael says: "... that's his trap" until Vincent says: "... learning a lot from you."

46. AUTUMN (G2-15M1-X) (N. Rota) [01:36:45-01:37:10]
From when Don Altobello says: "... most powerful friends" until Don Altobello says: "... Joey Zasa in his grave."

16. Confession

47. DRIVE TO CONFESSION (6M4-R) (C. Coppola) [01:38:09-01:38:42]
From cut to the exterior of a cloister until Michael says: "I trusted him."

50. GREGORIAN CHANT (Traditional) [01:44:30-01:44:55]
From when the camera dissolves to the exterior of Vatican City, until it dissolves to Michael sitting on the porch.

51. THE NEW GODFATHER #1 (G1-15M2) [01:46:20-01:47:14]
It consists of Michael's Theme (N. Rota).
From when Connie says: "Michael, you know ..." until the camera cuts to the exterior of Mosca's villa.

52. ALTOBELLO TO MOSCA (C. Coppola) [01:47:14-01:47:44]
From when a car appears in Mosca's driveway until before Don Altobello says: "Eh! U picciriddu!"

17. Michael Shows Kay Sicily

53. A VISIT TO ROTH (G2-7M3) [01:51:07-01:52:00]
It consists of *Finding the Man* (N. Rota).
From when the light is flipped on in Mosca's house until the camera cuts to Vincent and the twin bodyguards shooting pool.

54. LOVE THEME FROM *THE GODFATHER* (N. Rota)
[01:53:53-01:54:23]
+
RUSTIC WEDDING PARTY FOLK MUSIC (Traditional)
[01:54:53-01:55:16]
From when Michael says: "... It's dangerous" to Kay, continues as Michael and Kay watch puppet show.

55. LA BARONESSA DI CARINI (Traditional) [01:55:16-01:56:53]
Pianola sola
+
SONO STATI I MIEI PECCATI (Traditional/C. Coppola)
It continues from the preceding cue as female puppet says: "Oh ... oh Dio ..." continues as Michael and Kay dance at wedding.

56. SANTA ROSALIA (Traditional) [01:56:53-01:57:32]
In continues from the preceding cue to the Sicilian countryside until Mosca and Spara dressed as priests fire shots at Don Tommasino sitting in his car.

57. KAY'S THEME (N. Rota) [02:01:26-02:02:40]
From after Michael says: "What do we do now?" continues as Michael and Kay talk, and concludes before Kay says: "You know, Michael ..."

18. Pope John Paul the First

58. WHITE SMOKE (12M2-R) (Traditional/C. Coppola) [02:03:53-02:04:25]
From when the cardinals applaud until a close-up of white smoke.

59. VATICAN CRIMES (XM16-C) (Traditional/C. Coppola)
[02:04:48-02:06:03]

From when Cardinal Lamberto says: "... spesso la parola," continues as the Archbishop speaks to Lucchesi on the phone and Lamberto gives a Vatican blessing. It concludes on fade to black screen.

19. Give Me a Chance To Redeem Myself

60. TOMMASINO COFFIN (Xm3-A-R) (C. Coppola) [02:06:04-02:07:08]
From when the camera cuts to Michael by coffin until after Michael says: "Why do I condemn myself so?"

61. CALL YOURSELF A CORLEONE (XM3-B-R) [02:11:07-02:12:12]
It consists of *The Godfather Waltz* (N. Rota).
From before Michael says: "Nephew, from this moment on ..." continues as Calo, Neri, and Lou kiss Vincent's hand, and concludes when screen fades to black.

20. Teatro Massimo

62. PRELUDIO from *CAVALLERIA RUSTICANA* (P. Mascagni) [02:12:15-02:14:28]
From when the camera dissolves to exterior street scene, continues as Corleone family arrives at opera house, Kay reads a letter out loud, and Connie and Don Altobello talk. It concludes as Connie says "Happy Birthday" to Don Altobello.

63. ORCHESTRA TUNING [02:16:10-02:16:26]
From after Vincent says: "Stop it ..." until he says: "It's over, Mary."

64. VINCENT–MARY BREAK-UP (XM1) [02:16:28-02:-02:16:34]
It consists of *Love Theme* from *The Godfather Part III* (C. Coppola).
From after Vincent says: "Don't hate your father," continues as Vincent and Mary talk and the family toast Anthony, it concludes as the crowd applauds the orchestra's conductor Anton Coppola.

21. *Cavalleria Rusticana*

65. SICILIANA from *CAVALLERIA RUSTICANA* (P. Mascagni)
[02:17:49-02:19:18]
From when the opera house lights dim, Anthony sings, Mosca enters the opera house with a group of priests until the camera cuts to train tracks.

66. SORTITA D'ALFIO from *CAVALLERIA RUSTICANA*
(P. Mascagni) [02:19:22-02:28:48]
From when the camera cuts to Neri on the train, continues as action on the opera stage continues, bodyguards patrol the theatre's lobby, and Mosca hides behind a curtain. It concludes when Vincent says: "They won't try it here."

22. Revenge

67. CALO ARRIVES (C. Coppola) [02:20:54-02:21:19]
From when the camera cuts to the exterior of Lucchesi's house until Calo enters the gate.

68. A CASA AMICHE from *CAVALLERIA RUSTICANA*
(P. Mascagni) [02:21:25-02:22:16]
From when the camera cuts to the opera house interior, continues as the opera continues while Mosca stabs a guard and unwraps a rifle. It concludes when the audience cheers and applauds.

69. FINALE from *CAVALLERIA RUSTICANA*
(P. Mascagni) [02:22:59-02:26:36]
From when the camera cuts to the interior of the opera house, continues as the opera continues, a guard searches Calo, Mosca mounts scope on a rifle, Neri checks a pistol in a cookie box on train, and Mosca kills both twin bodyguards. It concludes when the crowd applauds.

70. SPARA BACKSTAGE (XM18) [02:26:51-02:28:35]
It consists of *Fredo's Stay of Execution* (N. Rota)
+
Michael's Theme (N. Rota) [02:27:04]
+
The Godfather Waltz (N. Rota) [02:27:45] Bass Clarinet solo.

71. PREGHIERA from *CAVALLERIA RUSTICANA* (P. Mascagni). Superimposed over the preceding cue as the Archbishop lifts a cup to his lips.

72. THE GODFATHER WALTZ (N. Rota) [02:28:35-02:28:47] From when Spara peers through the curtain, continues as Spara exits the stage carrying a rifle and the Vatican accountant is smothered with a pillow.

73. PREGHIERA from *CAVALLERIA RUSTICANA* (P. Mascagni) [02:28:47-02:29:47]

74. SPARA BACKSTAGE (XM18) [02:29:47-02:30:47] *Fredo's Stay of Execution* (N. Rota) + *Michael's Theme* (N. Rota) [02:29:52] + *Fredo Stay of Execution* (N. Rota) [02:30:26] It continues from the preceding cue before Michael says: "This Pope has powerful enemies," continues as nun discovers deceased Pope.

74. PREGHIERA from *CAVALLERIA RUSTICANA* (P. Mascagni) [02:30:44-02:33:00] It continues from the preceding cue as a nun cries, "Eminenza!," through cuts to the nun screaming, action on the opera house stage, Connie with binocular, Don Altobello dying.

75. SPARA BACKSTAGE (XM18) [02:32:54-02:33:30] It consists of *Fredo's Stay of Execution* (N. Rota) + *Michael's Theme* (N. Rota) [02:32:59] It continues from the preceding cue as Lucchesi gestures to Calo to sit.

76. FINALE from *CAVALLERIA RUSTICANA* (P. Mascagni) [02:33:19-02:33:39] It continues from the preceding cue as the Archbishop walks up stairs.

77. CALO KILLS LUCCHESI (XM20) (C. Coppola) [02:33:39-02:35:05]
It continues from the preceding cue as Lucchesi says: "Parla, dimmi." It continues as Neri prepares to shoot the Archbishop.

78. FINALE from *CAVALLERIA RUSTICANA*
(P. Mascagni) [02:34:42-02:35:30]
It continues from the preceding cue before Neri fires a gun, continues as Calo stabs Lucchesi with eyeglasses, and it concludes when the audience applauds.

23. Finale on the Steps

79. POVERO SCECCU MEU (Sicilian Folk Song/C. Coppola)
[02:37:49-02:37:56]
From when Anthony kisses the mezzo-soprano until a bodyguard takes a rifle from Spara.

24. Death of Michael Corleone

80. INTERMEZZO from *CAVALLERIA RUSTICANA*
(P. Mascagni) [02:39:26-02:42:30]
From when Kay holds Mary and cries, continues as Michael screams, and as Michael dances (via flashback) with Mary, then with Apollonia, then with Kay, and as Michael, now an old man sitting outside in the sun, collapses and falls to the ground. It concludes when the camera fades to black screen.

25. End Credits

81. END CREDITS [02:42:32-02:45:24]
It consists of *The Godfather Waltz* (XM3-B-R) (N. Rota)
Vincent's Theme (XM3-B) (C. Coppola) [02:43:42]
+
Love Theme from The Godfather (N. Rota) [02:44:26]
+
Love Theme from The Godfather Part III (C. Coppola)
[02:44:58]
+
Promise You'll Remember (Love Theme from The Godfather Part III (C. Coppola/J. Bettis) [02:45:24-02:49:47]

Notes

Introduction

1. Joseph Kerman. *Opera as Drama* (Berkeley, CA: University of California Press, 1956): 132.

Chapter 1

1. See Pier Marco De Santi. *I disegni di Fellini* (Rome: Laterza, 1983).
2. Giovanni Rinaldi (1840–1895) was one among the few 19th-century composers who wrote only piano music. Although such a cultural undercurrent in a country dominated by the complex world of opera has been historically epitomized by the figures of Giovanni Sgambati (1841–1914) and Giuseppe Martucci (1856–1909), Giovanni Rinaldi could rightfully join them. The validity of Rinaldi's music has been pointed out from time to time. In 1941, Lidia Carbonatto presented a thesis at the Facoltà di Lettere–Università di Torino entitled *Giovanni Rinaldi, pianista, didatta e compositore*, and "Giovanni Rinaldi, un precursore dell'impressionismo musicale," *La Rassegna Musicale*, 1941: 453–462. Manlio La Morgia published a short but eloquent essay, "Giovanni Rinaldi: Indicazioni per lo studio di un musicista da 'riscoprire,' in *I grandi anniversari del 1960* (Siena: Accademia Musicale Chigiana, MCMLX): 200–220. Finally, Ernesta Rota-Rinaldi wrote *Mio padre e storia di Nino*, a cura di Francesco Lombardi (Comune di Reggiolo, 1999). Rota himself was very enthusiastic about his grandfather's music, as he stated on many occasions. At the dawn of his career he even signed his name as Nino Rota-Rinaldi, Nino being a diminutive of Giovanni.
3. The figure of Margherita Sarfatti (1880–1961) has been exhaustively analyzed by Philip V. Cannistraro and Brian R. Sullivan in their volume *Il Duce's Other Woman* (New York: William Morrow & Company, 1993).
4. Mario Sironi (1885–1961) was a modernist artist active as a painter, sculptor, illustrator, and designer. He was a strong supporter of Mussolini. Achille Funi (1890–1972) was a Futurist painter echoing the school of Umberto Boccioni (1882–1916).
5. It is intriguing to note how diverse charismatic personalities such as D'Annunzio (1863–1938) and Marinetti (1876–1944) were part of the same Fascist ideology.

6.   Mario Castelnuovo-Tedesco (1895–1968), Vittorio Rieti (1898–1994), Renzo Massarani (1898–1975), and Arturo Toscanini (1867–1957) died as expatriates in Beverly Hills, New York City, Brazil, and New York City respectively.

7.   Ildebrando Pizzetti (1880–1968), Gian Francesco Malipiero (1882–1973), Alfredo Casella (1883–1947), Ottorino Respighi (1879–1936).

8.   Pietro Mascagni (1863–1941). The opera *Cavalleria rusticana* was composed in 1890.

9.   Born in 1858, Puccini succumbed to cancer of the throat in 1924.

10.   See Franco Sciannameo. "The Duke's Children," review/essay of "Italian Music during the Fascist Period," edited by Roberto Illiano. *The Musical Times* (Summer 2006): 91–102.

11.   Ruggero Leoncavallo (1858–1919), whose masterpiece *I pagliacci* (1892) has remained a staging companion to *Cavalleria rusticana*, and Umberto Giordano (1867–1948), who achieved fame with his operas *Andrea Chénier* (1896) and *Fedora* (1898).

12.   Information on the Rinaldi and Rota families is taken from Ernesta Rota-Rinaldi's volume mentioned in note 2.

13.   Compare the Casella-influenced works like *Partita for Orchestra* (1932) and *Concerto for Orchestra* (1933–34) by Petrassi (1904–2003) and *Partita for Orchestra with soprano solo in the last movement* (1930–32) or *Musica (Inni)* per 3 pianoforti (1935) by Dallapiccola (1904–1975) with Rota's transparent *Sonata* for violin and piano or *Sinfonia No. 1*. Newly recorded performances of Rota's music of the 1930s include: 1. Dynamic 211. Luigi Alberto Bianchi, violin and viola, and Marco Vincenzi, piano [*Sonata* for violin and piano (1936–37) and *Sonata* for viola and piano (1934–35)]; 2. ASV 1072. Ex Novo Ensemble [*Quintetto* for flute, oboe, viola, cello, and harp (1935) and *Sonata* for flute and harp (1937)]; 3. Bis 970. Norrköping Symphony Orchestra, Ole Kristian Ruud, cond. [*Sinfonia No. 1* (1935–39)] and *Sinfonia No. 2* (1937–39–41/1975).

14.   Anna Maria Rota was not a relative of the composer. However, Maria Rota, also a noted vocalist, was Nino's cousin.

15.   *Il principe porcaro*'s orchestration was never finished, so the opera remained unperformed until September 27, 2003, when a new version, prepared by Nicola Scardicchio, was presented at the Teatro Goldoni in Venice.

16.   In the course of a radio interview entitled *Voi ed io* (RAI, 1978), Rota offered a vivid account of his meeting with Maurice Ravel. Apparently, the teenaged Rota was not too impressed by Ravel's statement that in order to be a good composer one should master, as a pianist, the works of Chopin and Liszt especially since he [Ravel] was, according to Rota, a pianist of modest means. See Ermanno Comuzio and Paolo Vecchi. *138 1/2: I film di Nino Rota* (Reggio Emilia: Assessorato alla Cultura, 1987): 16.

17.   Ravel acted more or less in the same fashion with George Gershwin (1898–1937), when the American composer wished to study with him in Paris. See David Ewen. *George Gershwin: His Journey to Greatness* (New York: Ungar Publishing Company, 1976; 2nd 1986): 132.

18.   Rota and Castelnuovo-Tedesco kept in touch until Mario Castel-nuovo-Tedesco's death in 1968. The latter told this writer during a conversation in Beverly Hills (March 1964) that Rota always sent him a *panettone* from Italy at Christmas time, a gesture which, in addition to the customary exchange of letters and postcards, was particularly dear to him. On Castelnuovo-Tedesco's Hollywood period see James Westby, "Uno scrittore fantasma: A Ghostwriter in Hollywood," *The Cue Sheet*, vol. 15, no. 2 (April 1999).

19.   Rota was close to Stravinsky from the time of their first meeting in Rome in the late 1920s when the young composer accompanied Stravinsky on a concert tour of France and Spain.

20.   Moreover, after private tutoring with Michele Cianciulli, Rota embarked upon obtaining a baccalaureate degree, which allowed him to enroll at the University of Milan, where in 1937 the composer earned a degree in the humanities. His thesis discussed the Renaissance theorist Gioseffo Zarlino (1517–1590). Rota and Cianciulli remained friends for many years. For more information on their relationship see Francesco Lombardi, "Pirati? Sirene? Una lettera di Federico Fellini" in *AAM–TAC (Arts and Artifacts in Movie–Technology, Aesthetics, Communication)*, no. 4 (2007): 145–151.

21.   Toscanini had made a similar suggestion to the Menotti family; in fact, Gian Carlo entered Curtis in the fall of 1928. See John Gruen. *Menotti: A Biography* (New York: Macmillan Publishing Company, 1978): 16.

22.   Rosario Scalero (Torino, 1870–1945) was a virtuoso violinist who studied with Camillo Sivori, the only pupil of Paganini, and August Wilhelmj. He was also a composer of renown; he studied composition in Vienna with Eusebius Mandyczewski who was a friend of Johannes Brahms. Many of Scalero's works were published by Breitkopf & Hartel. In 1919, Scalero came to the United States to head the composition department at the Mannes School of Music in New York. In 1928, he was appointed to Curtis. This singular musician was the teacher of Barber, Menotti, Rota, Foss, Rorem, and many more important composers.

23.   José Maria Latorre. *Nino Rota: La imagen de la Musica* (Barcelona: Montesinos, 1987): 30. Notwithstanding Toscanini's criticism, Casella had the great merit of pointing the way to young composers like Rota, Petrassi, and Dallapiccola among others toward the identification of a new national style which denounced excessive dependency on French Impressionism, Richard Strauss, orchestral descriptivism, Stravinsky's primitivism, and, ultimately, Schoenberg's atonality and dodecaphonic system.

24.   See a facsimile of these two brief works in Franco Sciannameo. *Nino Rota, Federico Fellini, and the Making of an Italian Cinematic Folk Opera: Amarcord* (Lewiston, NY: Edwin Mellen Press, 2005): 89–94. The balance of the Curtis Carillon Series consisted of *Suite for Carillon* by Samuel Barber (1910–1981) and *Six Compositions for Carillon (1. Prelude, 2. Arabesque, 3. Dialogue, 4. Pastorale, 5. Canzone, 6. Etude)* by Gian Carlo Menotti (1911–2007). Francesco Lombardi has in preparation an in-depth study examining Rota's Curtis period.

25.   Raffaello Matarazzo (1909–1966).

26.   For important views on Italian cinema of this period see Marcia Landy. *Fascism in Film: The Italian Commercial Cinema, 1931–1943* (Princeton, NJ: Princeton University Press, 1986), James Hay. *Popular Film Culture in Fascist Italy: The Passing of the Rex* (Bloomington: Indiana University Press, 1987), and Steven Ricci. *Cinema and Fascism: Italian Film and Society, 1922–1943* (Berkeley: University of California Press, 2008).

27.   Nevertheless, Rota managed to compose his *Sinfonia No. 2 "Tarantina–Anni di pellegrinaggio"* which can be heard on Bis 970, a CD mentioned in note 13.

28.   The city and the people of Bari and Torre a Mare, where the composer sojourned extensively, have paid homage to their honorary citizen. Furthermore, in the nearby city of Monopoli, a conservatory of music has been entitled to the composer's name. Symposia and concerts are periodically organized in honor of the musician who has been immortalized in streets and buildings named after him. See Dinko Fabris (ed.). *Nino Rota compositore del nostro tempo* (Bari: Orchestra Sinfonica di Bari, 1987) and *La Musica a Bari*, edited by Dinko Fabris and Marco Renzi (Bari: Levante Editori, 1993). The latter book expands considerably on Rota's activity at the *Conservatorio* and in Bari generally.

29.   Giorgio Strehler (1921–1997) was a highly influential director of operas and theater, favoring production bearing a heavy cultural significance such as Bertold Brecht's works. It is interesting that Strehler saw in Rota's opera cultural values discarded by others.

30.   Luigi Nono (1924–1990), Luciano Berio (1925–2003), Bruno Maderna (1920–1973). The Studio di Fonologia Musicale was created by Berio and Maderna in 1955 under the auspices of RAI in Milan.

31.   Dinko Fabris. Program notes to *Il cappello di paglia di Firenze*. Bari, Teatro Piccinni, March 7, 9, and 11, 2007.

32.   Recent recorded performances of these works include: 1. Chandos 7038. I Virtuosi Italiano. Marzio Conti, cond. (*Concerto* for Harp and Orchestra) [1943]; 2. Dynamic 211. Luigi Alberto Bianchi, violin and viola, and Marco Vincenzi, piano (*Sonata* for Viola and Piano) [1945]; 3. Nuova Era 7073. Orchestra Sinfonica Siciliana. Massimo De Bernart, cond. (*Sinfonia sopra una canzone d'amore*) [1947]; 4. Opera d'oro 1420. Chorus and Orchestra of the Théâtre de la Monnaie. Elio Boncompagni, cond. (*Il cappello di paglia di Firenze*) [1945–1955].

33.   Bernard Herrmann's activities as composer and conductor of radio music in the 1930s have been extensively analyzed by David Cooper in his *Bernard Herrmann's* The Ghost and Mrs. Muir (Lanham, MD: Scarecrow Press, 2005): 1–10.

34.   *Balli* (1932) is a 10-minute, 7-movement composition scored for piccolo, flute, oboe, English horn, 2 clarinets, 2 bassoons, 2 French horns, 1 trumpet, and strings. It can be heard on a CD labeled Naïve 1003. Orchestra Città di Ferrara. Giuseppe Grazioli, cond. The same recording contains also *Sonata* per orchestra da camera which is the orchestrated version of the *Sonata* for flute and harp listed in note 13. For details on the 1932 Radio Music compe-

tition including specific instrumental and harmonic requirements see "Documenti" in Veniero Rizzardi (a cura), *L'undicesima musa: Nino Rota e i suoi media* (Roma: RAI-ERI, 2001): 199–238.

35. These figures were substantially below Denmark's 303, Great Britain's 259, Switzerland's 238, Belgium's 212, and France's 198. See Franco Monteleone. *Storia della radio e della televisione in Italia* (Venezia: Marsilio, 1992): 245.

36. At the same time, Rota's Curtis fellow Gian Carlo Menotti was commissioned by NBC to compose the first opera specifically composed for television in America. In December 1951, *Amahl and the Night Visitors* was viewed on the small screen by an audience of millions across the United States.

37. Puccini's *Gianni Schicchi* (1918) embodied a genuine sense of shared Italianness as demonstrated by the praise it drew from unexpected quarters. Florentine critic/composer Giannotto Bastianelli portrayed *Gianni Schicchi* as "a work capable of inspiring the skeptical young, which signaled the fact that Italian culture was entering a new phase. . . . After the apathetic years of the Giolitti era, military struggle had finally led to artistic productivity, and Bastianelli urged the disaffected young to look to *Gianni Schicchi* as a model, because it expressed 'the purest word of the [Italian] race.' In the last work to be premiered during his life time, Puccini seemed finally to have produced what his supporters had boasted about all along: an authentically Italian work capable of creating a sense of shared Italian identity. *Gianni Schicchi* has united critics of almost all political colors." See Alexandra Wilson. *The Puccini Problem: Opera, Nationalism, and Modernity* (Cambridge: Cambridge University Press, 2007): 183–184. As for Rota's *I due timidi*, see the following recording: Bongiovanni 2367/68-2. Orchestra Filarmonia Veneta "G. F. Malipiero," Coro del Teatro Sociale di Rovigo. Flavio Emilio Scogna, cond. This double CD set also contains the 1959 one-act opera by Riccardo Bacchelli and Nino Rota entitled *La Notte di un nevrastenico* (A Neurasthenic Man's Night).

38. *Il Giornale*, June 23, 1977.

39. *Rinascita*, July 1, 1977.

40. Leonardo Pinzauti, "A Colloquio con Nino Rota." *NRMI* V, 1971: 74–83.

41. Puccini attended the Florence concert that took place in April 1924. He followed the performance with a score provided to him by Schoenberg.

42. From A. Casella, "Arnold Schoenberg ed il Pierrot lunaire," in concert program Sala Accademica di Santa Cecilia, March 28, 1924. See also A. Casella, "Schönberg in Italy," *League of Composers Review* [Modern Music] 1/2 (June 1924): 7–10.

43. Francesco Lombardi to author. Venice, May 2007.

44. See *Don Giovanni*'s dramatic finale at the words "non si pascia di cibo mortale che non si pascia di cibo celeste." ("He does not feed on mortal food who feeds on that of heaven.")

45. When in 1960 the Directorship of the Conservatorio di Musica "Santa Cecilia" in Rome became vacant, Rota's name was advanced as that of a

possible candidate, thus elevating the expectations of the entire student body, including this writer. Maestro Rota preferred to remain in his beloved school in Bari.

    46.   Vinci Verginelli (1903–1987) was a poet, teacher of classical philology at the Liceo Virgilio in Rome, and lexicographer for *Enciclopedia Treccani*.

    47.   See *Bibliotheca Hermetica. Catalogo alquanto ragionato della Raccolta Verginelli-Rota di Antichi Testi Ermetici (secoli XV–XVIII)*, (Firenze: Nardini Editore, 1986).

    48.   Translation in Sciannameo (2). See bibliography.

Chapter 2

    1.   From a letter Rota sent to Enzo Masetti in which he declared his inability to contribute to the volume listed in note 4. The letter can be found in the volume's pages 146–147.

    2.   Enzo Masetti (1893–1961) was a composer who followed Ottorino Respighi's colorful orchestral writing. A true pioneer in Italian film music, Masetti penned a theoretical treatise entitled *La musica nel film* (1950), which became the ultimate guide for Italian film music composers. Some of Masetti's outstanding film scores can be heard today on CD. See, for instance, *Hercules* (1957) and *Hercules Unchained* (1959), available on the DigitMovies label (CDDM057).

    3.   Riccardo Zandonai (1883–1944), the last important exponent of the *verismo* operatic school, composed the music for the French 1936 film *Tarakóanova* by Fedor Ozep.

    4.   See Enzo Masetti (a cura). *La musica nel film* (Roma: Bianco e Nero Editore, 1950). This collection of essays contributed by many Italian composers, directors, and technicians summarizes the state of film music in Italy and other parts of the world up to the late 1940s. See also Franco Sciannameo, "In black and white: Pizzetti, Mussolini and Scipio Africanus" in *The Musical Times* (Summer 2004): 25–50.

    5.   Guido M. (Maggiolino) Gatti (1892–1973) and Fedele D'Amico (1912–1990) were two very influential musicologists, lexicographers, and music operators. Their involvement with Lux Film and their relationships with many Italian composers have been analyzed by Alberto Farassino in *Lux Film: Rassegna Internazionale Retrospettiva* (Milano: Editrice Il Castoro, 2000).

    6.   Quoted in Comuzio and Vecchi (14), see bibliography.

    7.   Francesco Lombardi. *Fra cinema e musica del Novecento: Il caso Nino Rota dai documenti* (ANR–Studi II) (Firenze: Leo S. Olschki, 2000): 37.

    8.   Comuzio and Vecchi (96). It is interesting to note how Rota, from the remoteness of his beloved village of Torre a Mare in Apulia (see Chapter 1), was able to work on *Zazá*'s soundtrack while applying the finishing touches to his 19th-century-style opera *Ariodante* staged in 1942 at the Teatro delle novità di Bergamo, a festival dedicated to new theatrical works promoted by Giuseppe

Bottai, a very influential exponent of the moderate wing of the Italian Fascist party.

9. For an excellent study on Luchino Visconti (1906–1976) and cinema see Geoffrey Nowell-Smith, *Luchino Visconti* (London: BFI Publishing, 2003).

10. Camillo Boito (1836–1914), poet and playwright, was the younger brother of Arrigo, Verdi's librettist (*Otello, Falstaff*) and composer of the opera *Mefistofele*.

11. For a detailed analysis of the music soundtrack of *Senso* and Rota's adaptation of Anton Bruckner's *Seventh Symphony* (1881–1883), see Roberto Calabretto, "Luchino Visconti: *Senso*, musica di Nino Rota" in Veniero Rizzardi (a cura), *L'undicesima musa: Nino Rota e i suoi media* (Roma: RAI-ERI, 2001): 75–135.

12. Geoffrey Nowell-Smith (105).

13. Prince Giuseppe Tomasi di Lampedusa (1896–1957) was a Sicilian aristocrat whose novel *Il Gattopardo* (The Leopard), published posthumously in 1958, became a literary sensation. It won the coveted *Strega* prize in 1959.

14. Eduardo De Filippo (1900–1984), actor, playwright, author, and poet, was a pivotal figure in Italian theatre and cinema. Most of his plays were translated into English and, on his part, De Filippo published in 1982 a Neapolitan translation of Shakespeare's *The Tempest*.

15. Luigi Pirandello (1867–1936) remained skeptical about the narrative possibilities of cinema. Instead, he considered cinematography as a visual language to be integrated with abstract music, an intriguing proposition, which contributed greatly to the debate about music and cinema that took place in Italy in the 1930s. See Nina Da Vinci Nichols and Jana O'Keefe Bazzoni, eds. *Pirandello & Film* (Lincoln: University of Nebraska Press, 1995).

16. Lombardi (78).

17. Throughout his career, Rota presented his friends with the choice of thematic material he was planning to use for scoring films. It is not clear whether such a behavior was prompted by insecurity, plain modesty, or the desire (need) to share his findings and/or to communicate his ideas with others. Some noted composers like Italo Delle Cese, Gino Marinuzzi, Vieri Tosatti, and Luis Bacalov collaborated with Rota on various film soundtracks.

18. See Chapter 4 for a discussion on how this thematic material was transferred from *Fortunella* to *The Godfather Trilogy* Part I.

19. Gelsomina's theme has cunning "resemblance" to the *Larghetto* (second movement) of Antonin Dvorak's *Serenade for strings* Op. 22, a coincidence not lost on Rota's critics.

20. See Sergio Miceli. "Fellini e la musica come personaggio (1952–1963)" in *Musica e cinema nella cultura del Novecento* (Firenze: Sansoni, 2000): 405–447, as well as Claudia Gorbman, "Music as Salvation: Notes on Fellini and Rota," in *Film Quarterly* vol. 28, no. 3 (1974–75): 15–25; also in *Federico Fellini: Essays in Criticism*, ed. Peter E. Bondanella (New York: Oxford University Press, 1978). Following the same line of thought, I have pointed out the role of the accordion played diegetically by Cantarel in *Amar-*

cord (1974). See Sciannameo, *Nino Rota, Federico Fellini, and the Making of an Italian Cinematic Folk Opera: Amarcord* (2005).

21.   Giovanni Morelli, "Mackie? Messer? Nino Rota e la quarta persona singolare del soggetto lirico" in *Storia del Candore: Studi in memoria di Nino Rota nel ventesimo della scomparsa* (ANR–Studi III) (Firenze: Leo S. Olschki, 2001): 355–429 and same essay in Rizzardi (3–74).

22.   See "Lavorare con Federico . . . Conversazione con Nino Rota di Gideon Bachman" in Rizzardi (181–198).

23.   Rota categorically denied having intentionally plagiarized Weill's theme. Furthermore, the same motive (Rota's version) was used again by the composer in the evocation scene of *La dolce vita* in *Le tentazioni del dottor Antonio*, an episode of *Boccaccio '70* (1970).

24.   Comuzio and Vecchi (26). Also quoted in Miceli (410). Notice here Rota's and Fellini's difference of opinions concerning the role of music in cinema.

25.   Bachman in Rizzardi (181–198).

26.   See M. Thomas Van Order. *Listening to Fellini: Music and Meaning in Black and White* (Fairleigh Dickinson University Press, 2009).

27.   On Rota's non-Catholic religious mysticism there is an illuminating testimonial by Father Anselmo Susca, a professor of musicology at the Bari Conservatory. Susca engaged Rota on many a discussion concerning world religions and mysticism. See Anselmo Susca, "Il mio amico Nino Rota: Quel rapporto speciale fra un prete e un non cattolico" in *La repubblica*, 10 marzo 2009: XI.

28.   Rota composed a diabolical waltz which is heard every time Casanova has a sexual encounter. Indeed, one can hear several instrumental versions of this piece in the film's soundtrack. It was the second of *Due valzer sul nome di Bach* for piano composed in 1975. It brings to mind certain conflicting Faustian modes one hears in the music of Franz Liszt and Ferruccio Busoni.

29.   In *Otto e mezzo*. The Criterion Collection, 2001. This documentary contains also the sequence from the film *Fortunella* (1957), whose soundtrack showcases Rota's original theme which became *The Love Theme* from *The Godfather*.

30.   Rota and Fellini collaborated to the following films: *Lo sceicco bianco* (1952); *I vitelloni* (1953); *La strada* (1954); *Il bidone* (1955); *Le notti di Cabiria* (1957); *La dolce vita* (1960); *Le tentazioni del dottor Antonio* [second episode of *Boccaccio '70*] (1962); *Otto e mezzo* (1963); *Giulietta degli spiriti* (1965); *Toby Dammit* [third episode of *Tre passi nel delirio*] (1968); *Blocknotes di un regista* (1969); *Fellini-Satyricon* (1969); *I clowns* (1970); *Roma* (1972); *Amarcord* (1974); *Casanova* (1976); *Prova d'orchestra* (1979).

31.   The show was based on the novel *Il giornalino di Gian Burrasca* written in 1907 by Luigi Bertelli, a.k.a. Vamba (1858–1920). It took place in a Tuscan boarding school in 1900.

32.   Italian television music has always been much influenced by Hollywood. Nino Rota and Ennio Morricone (b. 1928) were the only Italian compos-

ers of talent who viewed the medium as an opportunity for innovative musical ideas.

33. See Nino Rota–Lina Wertmüller. *Gian Burrasca*. Riduzione per pianoforte a cura di Roberto Negri (San Giuliano Milanese [MI]: MBG Publications s.r.l., 2005).

34. Lombardi (120).

35. Franco Zeffirelli. *The Autobiography of Franco Zeffirelli* (New York: Weidenfeld & Nicolson, 1986): 223.

36. *Ibid.* (227).

37. *What Is a Youth* with lyrics by Eugene Walter. Portions of Rota's tune are quoted in Fred Karlin and Rayburn Wright's *On the Track: A Guide to Contemporary Film Scoring*, 2nd ed. (New York: Routledge, 2004): 230. For a detailed account of Rota's music in Zeffirelli's film see Stefano Toffolo, *Romeo e Giulietta e altri drammi shakespeariani–Musica, Cinema e Letteratura dalle origini a Franco Zeffirelli e Nino Rota* (Padova: Edizioni Armelin Musica, 2002): 95–155.

Chapter 3

1. Stephen Farber, "Coppola and *The Godfather*," *Sight and Sound* vol. 41, no. 4 (Autumn 1972): 223.

2. Harlan Lebo. *The Godfather Legacy* (New York: Fireside, 1997): 197.

3. Mario Puzo. *The Godfather: A Novel* (New York: G. P. Putnam's Sons, 1969): 113, 123, 140, 195, 212, 216, 259, 278, 326, 327.

4. Ironically, the Italian American Civil Rights League was founded by Mafia boss Joe Colombo, head of the Colombo crime family, one of the five New York *mafioso* families. The other four families were known as the Bonanno, Gambino, Genovese, and Lucchese. The Italian American Civil Rights League attracted the participation of 150,000 Italian-Americans at its inaugural Italian-American Unity Day rally in New York's Columbus Circle on June 29, 1970. The crowd displayed placards proclaiming ITALIANS ARE BEAUTIFUL; WE WANT EQUAL RIGHTS; THE FBI FRAMES ITALIAN-AMERICANS; ITALIANS UNITE! In the course of a second rally, which took place in the same location on June 28, 1971, Joe Colombo was shot in the head. He lingered in a coma until his death in 1978. Unfortunately this episode confirmed, in the minds of most Americans, that the majority of Italian-Americans had Mafia connections.

5. For "spinal soundtrack" I refer to the sounds and/or music we choose to accompany (underscore) consciously or subconsciously our everyday life.

6. Quoted in Richard Gambino. *Blood of My Blood: The Dilemma of the Italian-Americans* (New York: Doubleday & Company, 1974): 287.

7. See Pasquale Natella. *La parola "Mafia"* (Firenze: Leo S. Olschki Editore, 2002).

8. Gambino (308).

9.   Alessandro Camon. "The Godfather and the Mythology of Mafia" in *Francis Ford Coppola's The Godfather Trilogy*, ed. Nick Browne (Cambridge, UK: Cambridge University Press, 2000): 57–75.

10.   See Joseph Bonanno. *A Man of Honor: The Autobiography of Joseph Bonanno* (New York: Simon & Schuster, 1983).

11.   Gay Talese. *Unto the Sons* (New York: Alfred A. Knopf, 1992; Random House, 2006): 22.

12.   Puzo (161).

13.   Quoted in Joseph P. Cosco. *Imagining Italians: The Clash of Romance and Race in American Perceptions, 1880–1910* (Albany: State University of New York Press, 2003): 13.

14.   See *The Godfather Part II* DVD 1, Scene 8: "New York City 1917"; Scene 15: "Fanucci wants to wet his beak"; and Scene 16: "Murder of Fanucci."

15.   See especially Chapter 5 in Jacob A. Riis' *How the Other Half Lives* (New York: Charles Scribner's Sons, 1890).

16.   See Edward A. Steiner. *On the Trail of the Immigrant* (New York: Revell, 1906): 294.

17.   Cosco (104).

18.   Cosco (126).

19.   Filippo Corsi, Edward's father, was an Italian deputy, agrarian reformer, union organizer, editor, and disciple of Giuseppe Mazzini.

20.   Edward Corsi. *In the Shadow of Liberty: The Chronicle of Ellis Island* (New York: Macmillan Company, 1935).

21.   Cosco (155).

22.   See Samuel L. Baily. *Immigrants in the Land of Promise: Italians in Buenos Aires and New York City, 1870–1914* (Ithaca, NY: Cornell University Press, 1999): 87.

23.   Camon (72).

24.   The 2002 television documentary *Uncovering the Real Gangs of New York* was written and directed by Harry Hanbury.

25.   Gene D. Phillips. *Godfather: The Intimate Francis Ford Coppola* (Lexington: University Press of Kentucky, 2004): 112.

26.   For instance, in a flashback, Vito Corleone and his friend Genco Abbandando attended an Italian *vaudeville* in a neighborhood music hall. The "acted" song *Senza Mamma* was actually composed by Coppola's maternal grandfather Francesco Pennino, after whom he was named. The song, quite popular in Pennino's days, was about an immigrant who left his mother behind in Naples when he came to New York.

27.   Camon (74).

28.   In 1950–1951 Senator Estes Kefauver's Senate Committee to Investigate Crime in Interstate Commerce brought to justice Mafia bosses Willie Moretti, Joe Adonis, and Frank Costello.

29.   John McClellan's Subcommittee on Organized Crime hearings. The testimony of Joseph Valachi, September 25–October 1, 1963, had a fundamental role in inflicting a tremendous blow to organized crime. Apalachin was the

name of the village in upstate New York where a 150-acre hilltop estate belonging to Mafioso Joseph Barbara was located. A Mafia conclave in progress was disrupted by New York State Police on November 14, 1957.

30. See John H. Davis. *Mafia Dynasty: The Rise and Fall of the Gambino Crime Family* (New York: HarperCollins, 1993): 148. Also see Salvatore Lupo. *Quando la mafia trovò l'America: Storia di un intreccio intercontinentale, 1888–2008* (Torino: Einaudi, 2008), especially Chapter VI, Part 1 "Nel sentiero del padrino," 201–208.

31. "Mutilated Victory" was a term coined by Gabriele D'Annunzio. It was used as a critique of the 1919 Paris Peace Conference, which concluded territorial settlements among winners and losers of World War I. Italy, although among the victorious nations, did not gain certain territories it fought for.

32. For a concise, very accurate history of this period see Philip V. Cannistraro. *Blackshirts in Little Italy: Italian-Americans and Fascism, 1921–1929* (West Lafayette, IN: Bordighera Press, 1999).

33. See *Una storia segreta: The Secret History of Italian American Evacuation and Internment during World War II.* Edited with an introduction by Lawrence DiStasi (Berkeley, CA: Heyday Books, 2001).

34. Anticipations of the 1950s "Made in Italy" can be found in the works that Futurist painter, writer, sculptor, and graphic designer Fortunato Depero (1892–1960) did in New York in 1928–1930. Depero designed costumes for stage productions and covers for magazines, including *Movie Maker, The New Yorker, Vogue*, in addition to devising flashy advertising for the *New York Daily News* and *Macy's Department Store*. For a full bibliography on Depero see http://www.depero.it/bibl-ita3.htm.

35. See note 6.

36. Born in Brooklyn in 1939, Richard Gambino holds a Ph.D. in philosophy from New York University. He is also the author of *Vendetta* (Guernica, 1998), which was made in 1999 into a television movie by the same title; Nicholas Meyer directed it.

37. Fred L. Gardaphe. *Leaving Little Italy: Essaying Italian American Culture* (Albany: State University of New York Press, 2004): 18.

38. *Ibid.* (28).

39. *Ibid.* (34).

40. *Ibid.* (37).

41. See "Childhood and Education" in Gambino (245–273).

42. John Ellis. "The Literary Adaptation: An Introduction," *Screen* vol. 23 (May–June 1982): 3–4.

43. For further studies I suggest the following, which deal with literary adaptations of celebrated novels into milestone films: Millicent Marcus. *Filmmaking by the Book: Italian Cinema and Literary Adaptation* (Baltimore, MD: Johns Hopkins University Press, 1993); Carlo Testa. *Masters of Two Arts: Re-creation of European Literatures in Italian Cinema* (Toronto: University of Toronto Press, 2002).

44. See Mario Puzo. *The Godfather Papers and Other Confessions* (New York: G. P. Putnam's Sons, 1972): 32–69. After the success of *The God-*

father, Puzo and Coppola negotiated separate contracts for producing the screenplays of the trilogy Parts II and III.

45.   See, for instance, Mark Winegardner's two acclaimed novels *The Godfather Returns* (2004) and *The Godfather Revenge* (2007), and Puzo's own *Omertà* (2000).

Chapter 4

1.   Quoted in Pier Marco De Santi. *Nino Rota: Le Immagini and La Musica* (Firenze: Giunti, 1992): 56.

2.   *La musica della Mafia: Il canto di Malavita* (CD–PIAS 8 Recordings GmbH, Hamburg, 2002). Introduction by Goffredo Plastino.

3.   See appendix for details.

4.   See appendix for the complete recording schedules.

5.   Suso Cecchi D'Amico recalls accompanying Rota several times to a film studio to review portions of the film in a black-and-white copy. See her book *Storie di cinema (e d'altro)* (Milano: Bompiani, 2002): 175.

6.   The "Music of *The Godfather*" section in the bonus material, available in the 2001 and 2008 DVD Collections, contains fragments from taped conversations between Rota and Coppola discussing the film's soundtracks. In addition, Rota plays at the piano some of the newly composed cues.

7.   Quoted in Pier Marco De Santi. *La musica di Nino Rota* (Roma: Laterza, 1983): 95–96.

8.   For a scholarly discussion on the Arab influence on Sicilian music see Roberto Favacchio Catalano. *Mediterranean World-Music: Experiencing Sicilian-Arab Sound* (Ph.D. Dissertation, University of California–Los Angeles, 1999), especially pages 1–87. Furthermore, see Goffredo Plastino. "Open Textures: On Mediterranean Music" in David Cooper and Kevin Dawe (editors). *The Mediterranean in Music* (Lanham, MD: Scarecrow Press, 2005): 179–194.

9.   Mario Puzo's *The Godfather* was published in Italy by Dall'Oglio Editore, Milano, in 1970 under the title of *Il padrino*.

10.   A third-draft version of *The Godfather* screenplay credited to Mario Puzo and Francis Ford Coppola was available by March 29, 1971. See Sam Thomas. *Three Best American Screenplays* (New York: Crown Publishers, 1992): 7–61. I should add that Suso Cecchi D'Amico (see note 5) was familiar with Puzo's novel, thus she and Rota could have discussed it.

11.   John C. Hammell (1915–2002) was a much-in-demand Hollywood music editor. His work on *The Godfather* went unaccredited. William Reynolds (1910-1997) was an Oscar-winning film editor. His work on *The Godfather* earned him an Oscar nomination. Walter Murch (b. 1943) began his career with Francis Ford Coppola in *The Rain People* (1969). A formidable sound theorist and practitioner, Murch was credited with coining the title "Sound Designer." He wrote *In the Blink of an Eye: A Perspective on Film Editing* (Los Angeles: Silman-James Press, 2001) and was the subject of *The Conversations: Walter*

Murch and the Art of Editing Film by Michael Ondaatje (New York: Alfred A. Knopf, 2002).

12. *Giuseppe Mazzini's Philosophy of Music (1836): Envisioning a Social Opera.* English translation by E.A.V. (1867). Edited and annotated by Franco Sciannameo (Lewiston, NY: Edwin Mellen Press, 2004).

13. Anthony Arblaster. *Viva la Libertà! Politics in Opera* (London: Verso, 1992; 2nd ed., 2000): 99.

14. *Dallapiccola on Opera.* Translated and edited by Rudy Shackelford. (London: Toccata Press, 1987): 134.

15. The story was born out of the famous 1282 episode in Palermo during which the Sicilians slaughtered thousands of French soldiers who were then occupying their island under the rule of Charles of Anjou.

16. Timings are drawn from the 2001 edition of *The Godfather DVD Collection.*

17. See Marcia J. Citron. "Operatic Style and Structure in Coppola's Godfather Trilogy" in *The Musical Quarterly* 87 (Fall 2004): 423–467 (441).

18. Hereafter A indicates the appendix; Roman numerals I, II, III correspond to the trilogy's Part I, II, III, respectively, and the Arabic numbers 1, 2, etc., indicate the musical cue listed in the appendix.

19. Mario Puzo described the Corleone non-nuclear "Family" as one of the five New York fictionalized Mafia Families, which included the Barzinis, Corleones, Cuneos, Straccis, and Tattaglias. Puzo's description emulates the real New York Mafia five Families, which were named after their godfathers Vito Genovese, Carlo Gambino, Joseph Bonanno, Joseph Colombo, and Gaetano Lucchese.

20. The music for this choral scene was entirely composed/arranged by Carmine Coppola unless otherwise indicated.

21. The song's Sicilian verses translate into English as follows:
And the moon is in the middle of the sea: oh my mother I must get married
Oh my daughter who will we get?
My mother I leave it up to you
  (1) If I get you the butcher he will come and he will go, but he'll always hold the sausage in his hands . . . if he gets a bright idea he'll sausage you oh my daughter.
  (2) If I get you the fisherman he will come and he will go, but he'll always hold the fish in his hands . . . if he gets a bright idea he'll fish you oh my daughter.
  (3) If I get you the shoemaker he will come and he will go, but he'll always hold the shoe in his hands . . . if he gets a bright idea he'll shoe you oh my daughter.
  (4) If I get you the garden man he will come and he will go, but he'll always hold the cucumber in his hands . . . if he gets a bright idea he'll cucumber you oh my daughter . . .
and so forth, depending on the general euphoria of the moment, and . . . the power of homemade wine.

22. "Bobby socks" were ankle-length and frilly socks fashionable in the 1940s and 1950s. The adolescent girls who swooned at Frank Sinatra's singing wore them.

23.   A 1945 song adapted from the traditional Neapolitan song *O Mare-niarello*. It was very popular in the Italian-American community.

24.   The character of singer/actor Johnny Fontane was extensively developed in Mario Puzo's original novel. It was consistently patterned after the ups and downs of Frank Sinatra's career, notorious behavior, and association with underworld figures. Sinatra resented Puzo's allusions to his personality to the point of holding an irreparable lifelong grudge against the writer. However, upon learning about the casting of Coppola's Part I, Sinatra made himself available for the part of Don Corleone, which went to Brando instead. Coppola did propose to Sinatra a senior Mafia boss role in Part III, but the aging singer turned it down because of the film's demanding shooting schedule (Anthony Summers and Robbyn Swan. *Sinatra: The Life* [New York: Alfred A. Knopf, 2005]: 183–184). The Johnny Fontane role we see in Coppola's Part I is reduced to only four brief scenes. Nevertheless, the allusions to Sinatra's rifts with band leader Tommy Dorsey, his tumultuous love affair with Ava Gardner, and incident with Hollywood's most feared and hated producer, Harry Cohn, who, through the intervention of Mafia boss Willie Moretti, gave Sinatra the role he wanted in *From Here to Eternity*, are—some chronological details aside—well accounted for. See Peter J. Levinson. *Tommy Dorsey: Livin' in a Great Big Way, Biography* (New York: Da Capo Press, 2005): 160–164.

25.   Clever use of 11 seconds of Cherubino's *Aria* to underscore the coquettish behavior of bridesmaid Lucy Mancini. Sonny Corleone and Lucy Mancini's sexual relationship resulted in the birth of Vincent Mancini (Andy Garcia), who assumed control of the Corleone Family's affairs in Part III. Like Johnny Fontane, the character of Lucy Mancini, much developed in Mario Puzo's original novel, was reduced to a cameo role in Coppola's film version.

26.   Notice that this version of *The Godfather Waltz*'s original tempo marking is 6/4, thus the trumpet solo used in the Main Titles ends on the downbeat of measure nine. Mus. Ex. 4.2 is notated in 3/4 as is and has been reproduced by permission from *The Godfather Trilogy: Music Highlights from I, II & III* (see appendix).

27.   This tune was pre-recorded on location in Sicily by Carmine Coppola during the film's shooting; therefore, it was included in the rough cut Rota saw during the spotting session in Rome. In fact, the composer remained so impressed by the tune's potential that he jotted down in his notebook the first few measures of it perhaps thinking about using it in the future:

28. According to historian John H. Davis, the United States government entered into a virtual alliance with the underworld to ensure the safety of naval shipping in New York Harbor—and later to ensure the cooperation of the Mafia in Sicily at the time of the Allied invasion of the island in 1943. Lucky Luciano became, then, the main go-between for the United States and Sicily. See Davis, 61. For a detailed history of the Sicilian-American Mafia connections see the following texts: Salvatore Lupo. *Quando la mafia trovò l'America: Storia di un intreccio intercontinentale, 1888–2008* (Torino: Einaudi, 2008) and Tim Newark. *Mafia Allies: The True Story of America's Secret Alliance with the Mob in World War II* (St. Paul, MN: Zenith Press, 2007).

29. The four-masted steel ship *Moshulu* was launched in 1904 although the scene in the film takes place in 1901. This ship was also showcased in the film *Rocky* (1976). Today, this restored historical vessel functions as a renowned floating restaurant docked at Penn's Landing in Philadelphia.

30. See Nino Rota. *Quindici preludi per pianoforte* (Mainz: Schott, 2001): 10. Rota's biographer Pier Marco De Santi wrote that this theme, or part of it, was used by Rota in 1957 in the incidental music he wrote for Carlo Goldoni's play *L'Impresario delle Smirne*, directed by Luchino Visconti. However, the score written for the play has not re-emerged as yet (De Santi, 215).

31. Nino Rota was particularly attracted by the use of children's voices both in solo and choral settings; see, for instance the children's opera *Lo scoiattolo in gamba* (1959) and portions of his oratorio *Mysterium* (1962). Regarding young Vito Andolini's song, a note dated Oct. 5, 1974 (ANR) informs us that Rota composed a replacement song for voice and organ to be recorded in Rome (see A-II-6-C). Ultimately, Carmine Coppola's arrangement of *Lu me sceccu* remained on the soundtrack.

32. A very popular 1938 tune based on the most basic of chord progressions. Two people commonly play it side by side on a piano. This tune was used in various films.

33. 1955 title song of a Broadway musical starring Sammy Davis Jr.

34. *Stumble to the Loo*, a song with many ad hoc applications, including drunkenness and hangovers.

35. The so-called Paul Jones Tarantella was a nineteenth-century American barn dance.

36. See Deleted [Additional] Scene #27 "Fredo and Deanna."

37. See Deleted [Additional] Scene #28 "No Champagne Cocktails . . ."

38. Marino Niola. "La macchina del pianto" in *Sceneggiata: Rappresentazioni di un genere popolare*, ed. Pasquale Scialò (Napoli: Guida, 2001): 25–42. See also *Senza Mamma: The Songs of Francesco Pennino*. Sung by F. Rocco Ruggiero, accompanied at the piano by Bill Keck (CD Edizione Pennino, Coppola Estate, 2004). Furthermore, the song *Senza Mamma* as sung in the film by Livio Giorgi can be heard on Track 6 of Part II MCAD-10232.

39. The theme dealing with one's dead mother was a favorite operatic topos in the *verismo* repertoire. See, for instance, Umberto Giordano's celebrated aria *La mamma morta* from his 1896 opera *Andrea Cheniér*. Parenthetically, it is worth mentioning that Giordano's aria, sung by Maria Callas, as-

sumed a co-protagonist role in the film *Philadelphia* (1993), directed by Jonathan Demme.

40.   This episode can viewed in the Deleted [Additional] Scenes section of the DVD Collection (Deleted [Additional] Scene #4 "Boy Plays Flute").

41.   According to sound editors Walter Murch and William Brand's music suggestion annotations, Rota was supposed to compose a flute piece for the occasion. However, Carmine Coppola ended up playing a "Serenade" for unaccompanied flute of his own composition (see appendix).

42.   Written by Giuseppe Gabetti, arranged by Carmine Coppola.

43.   Written by John Stafford Smith and Francis Scott Key, arranged by Carmine Coppola.

44.   Citron (434).

45.   Julius La Rosa was born in 1930.

46.   This tune became popular thanks to its inclusion in the Broadway musical *Kismet* (1953) based on music by Alexander Borodin (1833–1887). The musical 1955 MGM Cinemascope film version starred Vic Damone (b. 1928), a favorite singer/actor within the Italian-American community. Rumors circulated in Hollywood at the time of Part I's casting that Vic Damone turned down the part of Johnny Fontane because of the role's reduced relevance in the film compared to its preeminence in the novel. Others said that the singer/actor rejected the role because he considered both novel and film offensive to Italian-Americans.

47.   This song was first recorded by Al Martino for inclusion in Part I but was never used. In the present scene the viewer may detect a little Italian-American ethnic joke exchanged between Johnny Fontane (Martino) and Michael about the song's title, which they refer to as "To each [his own] Sazeech" (sausage being a euphemism for penis). The song, apparently recorded in Rome, can be heard in its entirety (3:20) as Track #7 in CD Columbia 47078.

48.   A hit song introduced by Jeanette MacDonald in the 1944 film *Follow the Boys*.

49.   Citron (434).

50.   The entire Cuban episode was filmed in the Dominican Republic.

51.   Sebastian Yradier (1809–1865), Spanish composer who sojourned for a time in Havana, Cuba, where in 1855 he composed several art songs including the celebrated *La Paloma* (The Dove). See Cue #45 in Part II in the appendix.

52.   *Façade* (1922), an entertainment for reciter and instrumental ensemble on text by Edith Sitwell. Also, Walton re-elaborated it in other versions and as a ballet.

Chapter 5

1. While Rota's declaration that he found violence, murder, and crime stories contrary to his nature were sincere, his professional duties as a film composer obliged him to write an important score for Renato Castellani's 1961 Southern Italian crime film *Il brigante* (Italian Brigands), whose trumpet solo opening cue entitled *Risveglio notturno e attesa nei campi* (Nocturnal Awakening and Awaiting in the Fields) foreshadows the main titles of the trilogy. Furthermore, following the successes of *The Godfather* Parts I and II, Rota composed the music, in collaboration with Gino Marinuzzi, for the 1976 Italian television series *Alle origini della Mafia* (The Origins of the Mafia), directed by Enzo Muzii.

2. Rota refers to this harmonic sequence also as "Autumn."

3. See Deleted [Additional] Scene #14 "Michael and Kay in Bed" in the 2001 and 2008 DVD supplements.

4. *The Bells of St. Mary's* was a 1945 film starring Bing Crosby as Father Chuck O'Malley and Ingrid Bergman as Sister Benedict.

5. Rota's arrangement of *The Bells of St. Mary's*, although recorded, was not used.

6. Although this song was recorded by Peter King in New York on January 10, 1972, the singer heard on the music track resembles the voice of either Kitty Kallen or Kay Starr. [Information provided to the author by Adam Harvey in correspondence dated September 28, 2006.]

7. After using it in both Part I and Part II, the composer readapted this theme again for Fellini's *Il Casanova* (1976), this time as a sung version.

8. Puzo (392). Michael and Kay's wedding is never mentioned in the film script.

9. Nino Rota. *La Vita di Maria. Rappresentazione sacra per voci, coro e orchestra. Testi scelti e tradotti da Vinci Verginelli*. Prague Symphonic Orchestra and Chorus conducted by Nino Rota (2 Compact Discs CAM CVS 900-012).

10. See note 6.

11. The story surrounding the issue of plagiarism and self-plagiarism on Rota's part has been summarized in previous chapters.

12. In my opinion, Rota's original conception of this cue corresponds to Karl Jaspers' three mythical outlooks: Nature-Mythical, Psychic-Mythical, and Magical-Mythical (*Psychologie der Weltanschauungungen*, 1919). For various interpretations of Jaspers' precepts, see Roland Barthes' *Mythologies* (1957) and Eero Tarasti in his *Myth and Music* (1979) and *Signs of Music* (2002).

13. This is an ancient and celebrated Sicilian folk song that pays homage to the land's beautiful flowers growing all year round. It is often used with sarcasm when a male singer says that he is returning back to his female counterpart all the love she had given him. Rota's notes report that he discovered this old tune in a collection published by Ricordi in 1883, entitled *Eco della Sicilia. 50 Canti popolari siciliani raccolti da Francesco Paolo Frontini* (1860–

1939). Nino Rota had previously used this same folk song in the soundtrack of the 1961 film *Il brigante* (Italian Brigands). However, the tune was entered in *The Godfather*'s cue sheet as "Arranged and Adapted" by Carmine Coppola and copyrighted by Famous Music Corporation in 1971 and 1972.

14. The wedding night episode was the only instance in the trilogy showing nudity (Apollonia's naked breasts) as the bride and groom make love. Puzo, on the other hand, was even more graphic in describing this scene. He wrote: "That night and the weeks that followed Michael Corleone came to understand the premium put on virginity by socially primitive people. Apollonia in those first days became almost his slave. Given trust, given affection, a young full-blooded girl aroused from virginity to erotic awareness was as delicious as an exactly ripe fruit. . . . She had a wonderful fresh smell, a fleshly smell perfumed by her sex yet almost sweet and unbearably aphrodisiac" (343–345). For a contextual understanding of this scene, I suggest viewing Deleted [Additional] Scene #19 "Communist Demonstration 1947" during which, after a very brief echo of the just-heard *Love Theme*, Michael and his two bodyguards witness a marching horde of workers holding several red flags and singing *Bandiera rossa*, the Italian Communist anthem. Although pertinent to 1947 political sentiments, in 1972, the year Part I was released, this scene would have represented a different reality for the Italian Communist Party in the wake of the activities perpetrated by the terrorist group Red Brigade. Furthermore, the viewer should screen Deleted [Additional] Scene #20 "Seeking Vito's House." Here Michael and his two bodyguards explored the village of Corleone searching for the ancestral Andolini house. One hears again the *Love Theme* terminating with the disheartening descending chromatic sequence of fifths, which would have been heard for the second time (the first time would have been at the end of the deleted *Sicilian Pastorale*) in the film's music track had this scene not been deleted. A comparison between Nino Rota's use of this harmonic sequence denoting "emptiness" at this point and later when Michael and Kay reunite in New Hampshire would have been interesting.

15. An ancient Arab outpost located near Palermo, Sicily, Corleone became in the 15th and 16th centuries the rockfort of several religious orders. Today, notorious Mafia bosses including Navarra, Leggio, Bagarella, Riina, and the "Boss of Bosses" Bernardo Provenzano are known figures among Corleone's twelve thousand inhabitants. Mario Puzo and Francis Ford Coppola immortalized the town of Corleone in *The Godfather* novel and films. However, the films were not shot in Corleone but in the town of Forza D'Agro on the Sicilian east coast near the Taormina resort.

16. The woman screaming "Hanno ammazzato Paolo" (They have killed Paolo!) brings to mind a similarly dramatic utterance: "Hanno ammazzato compare Turiddu," which constitutes a key moment in Pietro Mascagni's opera *Cavalleria rusticana*. This nuance reasserts the operatic tone of the film previously established by *The Godfather* Part I, while anticipating by seventeen years the final scene of *The Godfather* Part III.

17. See Deleted [Additional] Scene #1.

18. The ocarina is a simple, small wind instrument made out of terra-cotta or wood.

19. Originally, this episode showed a four-minute scene (see Deleted [Additional] Scene #4 "Boy Plays Flute") that Francis Ford Coppola dedicated to his father Carmine and grandfather Augusto to balance perhaps the homage he had paid previously to his maternal grandfather Francesco Pennino. In this deleted scene, Augusto was a mechanic who repaired guns while his young son Carmine often displayed his talent as a flutist in his father's workshop for the clients' delight—Vito, Clemenza, and Tessio in this case. According to Murch and Brand's music suggestions list, Rota was supposed to compose a flute piece for the occasion. However, Carmine Coppola ended up playing himself a solo "Serenade" for unaccompanied flute. This scene concludes with a few measures taken from *A New Carpet* and *The Immigrant Theme*.
[Francis Ford Coppola's older brother, an academic and father of actor Nicholas Cage, was named Augusto after his grandfather portrayed in this scene.]

20. A favorite festival in the Mulberry district honoring St. Rocco, who, though born in France and canonized for miracles in Northern Italy, was widely revered among Southern Italians for his cures of the diseased and maimed. Paraders reevoked San Rocco's miracles by carrying wax arms, legs, hands, and, as one newspaper reported, "other portions of the body not normally exposed to view." See Jerre Mangione and Ben Morreale. *La Storia: Five Centuries of the Italian American Experience* (New York: HarperCollins, 1992): 170.

21. Oranges were used in the trilogy as the symbol of evil. They seem to be present in several crucial death scenes. Traditionally though, orange plantations were Sicily's main export products to be jealously guarded as precious possessions.

22. Marcia J. Citron, "Operatic Style and Structure in Coppola's Godfather Trilogy" in *The Musical Quarterly* (Fall 2004): 434. Also quoting Pauline Kael, "*The Godfather, Part II*: Fathers and Sons" in *For Keeps: Thirty Years at the Movies* (New York: Dutton, 1994): 599–600.

23. See my observation about the symbolism of this gesture in Chapter 3.

24. When viewed in chronological order, this 45-minute portion of the film, which is spoken in Sicilian with English subtitles, has all the characteristics of a one-act *verismo* opera.

25. See first choral scene described in Chapter 4.

26. De Santi (95–96).

27. Coppola and his young colleagues Scorsese, Polanski, Lucas, and Spielberg, among others, took the opportunity presented to them by similar episodes to attack the Hollywood old system regulated by greed, sex, and corruption at the hands of characters like the fictional character Jack Woltz.

28. I have reconstructed this episode's sequence of events as follows: *Saturday–August 25, 1945*. Connie's Wedding–Don Corleone receives Johnny Fontane's request for intervention–Tom Hagen is dispatched to Los Angeles that very night.

Sunday–August 26, 1945. Scenario 1: Hagen departs New York City for Los Angeles on a TWA Constellation flight leaving New York City at 1:00pm arriving in Los Angeles 11 hours later (9:00pm local time). Puzo writes that Hagen arrived in Los Angeles before dawn; however, the film shows the plane landing in daytime. Scenario 2: Hagen boards TWA Constellation, flying on special extra-fare nonstop from New York to Los Angeles which had begun service on April 17, 1944. Flying time was six hours and 58 minutes at 280 mph, altitude 20,000 feet. This plane had a 54-passenger capacity. So, if Hagen departed at 1:00am on Tuesday, the 28th, he could have landed at approximately 5:00am local time. Hagen was to meet with Woltz at 10:00am. The day before (Monday the 27th) Hagen had the chance to contact (via telephone from New York) Los Angeles labor union boss Robert Goff about planning to shut down Woltz Productions in case the producer did not cooperate.

Tuesday–August 28, 1945. Hagen arrives in Los Angeles at 5:00am–Meets Woltz at 10:00am–takes a 3-hour limousine drive to Woltz's mansion–Same evening returns by private plane to Los Angeles and flies back to New York City.

Wednesday–August 29, 1945. Hagen returns to New York City–Meets with Don Corleone–Reports on the infamous Janie episode–Hagen receives instruction about the Los Angeles job which he communicated via telephone to people on the ground in Los Angeles–The horse is decapitated on the night of Wednesday the 29th.

Thursday–August 30, 1945. Woltz discovers the horse's head in his bed as he wakes up in the morning. Afternoon New York City's local time–Hagen receives a phone call in his office from Woltz.

Friday–August 31, 1945. The Corleones meet with Sollozzo as planned.

Monday–September 3, 1945. Fontane reports to work on the movie set.

    29.   See Cues #14–16 in Part I in the appendix. *Manhattan Serenade* was written by Harold Adamson (lyrics) and Louis Alter (music). Other popular tunes considered for this cue were *Stella by Starlight*—lyrics by Ned Washington and music by Victor Young—and *Tangerine*, a 1941 song with lyrics by Johnny Mercer and music by Victor Schertzinger, both arranged by Peter King. Peter (Pete) King (1914–1982), a most reliable craftsman on the Hollywood studio system production line, was in charge of arranging piano reduction of all the musical source material to be used in Part I. King's arrangements were made for copyright purposes and ready-reference usage.

    30.   A 1971 film directed by George Lucas.

    31.   Michael Ondaatje. *The Conversations: Walter Murch and the Art of Editing Film* (New York: Alfred A. Knopf, 2002): 100–101.

    32.   See Deleted [Additional] Scenes #11 "A Gift from Woltz," #12 "Hagen Sees Janie," and #13 "A Family Fight" which shows Hagen reporting about the Hollywood trip to Don Corleone and Sonny.

    33.   Franz Kafka. *The Great Short Works of Franz Kafka: The Metamorphosis* (New York: Simon & Schuster, 1995): 117.

    34.   Ironically, the horse's name was Khartoum, a reference to Charles Gordon, the British commander of Khartoum in the Sudan of 1885, who, once

captured by the Sudanese Muslim, was beheaded—his head carried on a pole through the streets.

35. See note 28.

36. Although recorded on January 18, 1972, and synchronized to the picture, Rota's original score was ultimately discarded.

37. My analysis of this episode is based on theories discussed by Umberto Eco in his *Six Walks in the Fictional Woods* (Cambridge, MA: Harvard University Press, 1994).

38. A song by Hugh Martin and Ralph Blane written for the 1944 MGM musical *Meet Me in St. Louis* starring Judy Garland.

39. A favorite Christmas song written by J. Fred Coots and Haven Gillespie. Eddie Cantor first sang it on his radio show in 1934.

40. The comedy film *Analyze This* (Ramis, 1999), starring Robert De Niro, Billy Crystal, and Lisa Kudrow, offers a very entertaining parody of this scene, which pokes fun at those Mafia bosses who are psychologically too insecure to be in control of the mob, thus becoming afflicted by the "Fredo Syndrome."

41. Michael Ondaatje (120).

42. Marcia J. Citron (445).

43. CD 1, Track 11 contains an abbreviated version of Rota's *The Baptism and Godfather Waltz* recorded by organist Owen Brady on January 20, 1972.

44. For an exhaustive study of the various versions of *The Baptism* organ scores see Tobias Plebuch's *Die Musik J. S. Bachs im Film* (Habilitation Thesis at the Humboldt University in Berlin, 2009).

45. Anton Coppola (b. 1917), a well-known opera conductor, composer, and professor at the Manhattan School of Music in New York City, achieved much recognition for his opera *Sacco and Vanzetti*, premiered by Opera Tampa in 2001. See Eugene H. Cropsey, "Sacco and Vanzetti: An American World Premiere" in *The Opera Quarterly*, vol. 19, no. 4 (Autumn 2003): 754–780. Furthermore, Opera Tampa has created in his honor the coveted Anton Coppola "Excellence in the Arts" Award bestowed annually upon a great figure of the operatic world.

46. Sergio Miceli. *Musica per film: Storia, Estetica, Analisi, Tipologie* (Milano: Ricordi/LMI, 2009): 648–649.

47. See Carla Bianca's *Italian Folk Songs*, Folkways Records FE 4010 (New York: Folkways Records, 1965). Quoted in Silverman, "Coppola, *Cavalleria*, and Connick: Musical Contributions to Epic in *The Godfather, Part III*," *Mid-Atlantic Almanack* 1 (1992).

48. Naomi Greene, "Family Ceremonies: or Opera in The Godfather Trilogy" in *Francis Ford Coppola's The Godfather Trilogy*, edited by Nick Browne (Cambridge, UK: Cambridge University Press, 2000): 133–155.

49. Information gathered from a note in the musical suggestions sheet to *The Godfather Part II* prepared by Walter Murch and George Brand.

50. Citron (423–467).

51.   The Teatro Massimo in Palermo was closed from 1974 to 1997 for extensive renovation.

52.   Lars Franke, "*The Godfather Part III*: Film, Opera, and the Generation of Meaning" in *Changing Tunes: The Use of Pre-Existing Music in Film*, edited by Phil Powrie and Robynn Stilwell (Hants, UK: Ashgate Publishing, 2006): 31–45.

Bibliography

Arblaster, Anthony. *Viva la Libertà! Politics in Opera.* London: Verso, 1992; 2nd ed., 2000.

Bachman, Gideon. "Lavorare con Federico . . . Conversazione con Nino Rota" in Rizzardi: 181–198.

Baily, Samuel L. *Immigrants in the Land of Promise: Italians in Buenos Aires and New York City, 1870–1914.* Ithaca, NY: Cornell University Press, 1999.

Barthes, Roland. *Mythologies.* Editions du Seuil, Paris, 1957; New York: Hill & Wang, 1972.

Bonanno, Joseph. *A Man of Honor: The Autobiography of Joseph Bonanno.* New York: Simon & Schuster, 1983.

Browne, Nick (Ed.). *Francis Ford Coppola's The Godfather Trilogy.* Cambridge, UK: Cambridge University Press, 2000.

Calabretto, Roberto. "Luchino Visconti: *Senso,* musica di Nino Rota" in Rizzardi: 75–135.

Cannistraro, Philip V. *Blackshirts in Little Italy: Italian-Americans and Fascism, 1921–1929.* West Lafayette, IN: Bordighera Press, 1999.

Cannistraro, Philip V. and Brian R. Sullivan. *Il Duce's Other Woman.* New York: William Morrow & Company, 1993.

Carbonatto, Lidia. *Giovanni Rinaldi, pianista, didatta e compositore.* Thesis, Facoltà di Lettere, Università di Torino, 1941.

———. "Giovanni Rinaldi, un precursore dell'impressionismo musicale" in *La Rassegna Musicale,* 1941: 453–462.

Cecchi D'Amico, Suso. *Storie di cinema (e d'altro).* Milano: Bompiani, 2002.

Citron, Marcia J. "Operatic Style and Structure in Coppola's Godfather Trilogy" in *The Musical Quarterly,* 87 (Fall 2004): 423–467.

Comuzio, Ermanno and Paolo Vecchi. *138½: I film di Nino Rota.* Reggio Emilia: Assessorato alla Cultura, 1987.

Cooper, David. *Bernard Herrmann's The Ghost and Mrs. Muir.* Lanham, MD: Scarecrow Press, 2005.

Corsi, Edward. *In the Shadow of Liberty: The Chronicle of Ellis Island.* New York: Macmillan Co., 1935.

Cosco, Joseph P. *Imagining Italians: The Clash of Romance and Race in American Perceptions, 1880–1910.* Albany, NY: State University of New York Press, 2003.

Cropsey, Eugene H. "Sacco and Vanzetti: An American World Premiere" in *The Opera Quarterly*, 19:4 (Autumn 2003): 754–780.

Da Vinci Nichols, Nina and Jana O'Keefe Bazzoni (Eds.). *Pirandello and Film.* Lincoln: University of Nebraska Press, 1995.

Davis, John H. *Mafia Dynasty: The Rise and Fall of the Gambino Crime Family.* New York: HarperCollins, 1993.

De Santi, Pier Marco. *I disegni di Fellini.* Roma: Laterza, 1983.

———. *La musica di Nino Rota.* Roma: Laterza, 1983.

———. *Nino Rota: Le Immagini and La Musica.* Firenze: Giunti, 1992.

DiStasi, Lawrence (Ed.). *Una storia segreta: The Secret History of Italian American Evacuation and Internment during World War II.* Berkeley, CA: Heyday Books, 2001.

Eco, Umberto. *Six Walks in the Fictional Woods.* Cambridge, MA: Harvard University Press, 1994.

Ellis, John. "The Literary Adaptation: An Introduction" in *Screen*, 23 (May–June 1982): 3–4.

Ewen, David. *George Gershwin: His Journey to Greatness.* New York: Ungar Publishing Company, 1976; 2nd ed., 1986.

Fabris, Dinko (Ed.). *Nino Rota compositore del nostro tempo.* Bari: Orchestra Sinfonica di Bari, 1987.

———. *Il cappello di paglia di Firenze.* Program notes for the March 7, 9, and 11, 2007 performances in Bari.

Fabris, Dinko and Marco Renzi (Eds.). *La Musica a Bari.* Bari: Levante Editori, 1993.

Farassino, Alberto. *Lux Film: Rassegna Internazionale Retrospettiva.* Milano: Editrice Il Castoro, 2000.

Farber, Stephen. "Coppola and *The Godfather*" in *Sight and Sound*, 41:4 (Autumn 1972): 223.

Favacchio Catalano, Roberto. *Mediterranean World-Music: Experiencing Sicilian-Arab Sound.* Ph.D. Dissertation, University of California–Los Angeles, 1999.

Franke, Lars. "*The Godfather Part III*: Film, Opera, and the Generation of Meaning" in *Changing Tunes: The Use of Pre-Existing Music in Film*, ed. Phil Powrie and Robynn Stilwell. Hants, UK: Ashgate Publishing, 2006: 31–45.

Gambino, Richard. *Blood of My Blood: The Dilemma of the Italian-Americans.* New York: Doubleday & Company, 1974.

―――. *Vendetta*. New York: Guernica, 1998.

Gardaphe, Fred L. *Leaving Little Italy: Essaying Italian American Culture*. Albany: State University of New York Press, 2004.

Gorbman, Claudia. "Music as Salvation: Notes on Fellini and Rota" in *Film Quarterly*, 28:3 (1974–75): 15–25; also in *Federico Fellini: Essays in Criticism*, ed. Peter E. Bondanella. New York: Oxford University Press, 1978.

Gruen, John. *Menotti: A Biography*. New York: Macmillan Company. 1978.

Hay, James. *Popular Film Culture in Fascist Italy: The Passing of the Rex*. Bloomington: Indiana University Press, 1987.

Jaspers, Karl. *Psychology der Weltanschauungen*. Review in David K. Naugle, *Worldview: The History of a Concept*. Grand Rapids, MI: William B. Eerdmans Publishing Company, 2002: 129–132.

Kafka, Franz. *The Great Short Works of Franz Kafka: The Metamorphosis*. New York: Simon & Schuster, 1995.

La Morgia, Manlio. "Giovanni Rinaldi: Indicazioni per lo studio di un musicista da 'riscoprire'" in *I grandi anniversary del 1960*. Siena: Accademia Musicale Chigiana, 1960: 200–220.

Landy, Marcia. *Fascism in Film: The Italian Commercial Cinema, 1931–1943*. Princeton, NJ: Princeton University Press, 1986.

Latorre, José Maria. *Nino Rota: La imagen de la Musica*. Barcelona: Montesinos, 1987.

Lebo, Harlan. *The Godfather Legacy*. New York: Fireside, 1997.

Levinson, Peter J. *Tommy Dorsey: Livin' in a Great Big Way, Biography*. New York: Da Capo Press, 2005.

Lombardi, Francesco. *Fra cinema e musica del Novecento: Il caso Nino Rota dai documenti* (Archivio Nino Rota–Studi II, 2000). Firenze: Leo S. Olschki, 2000.

―――."Pirati? Sirene? Una lettera di Federico Fellini" in *AAM–TAC* (*Arts and Artifacts in Movie–Technology, Aesthetics, Communications*), 4 (2007): 145–151.

―――. *Catalogo critico delle composizioni da concerto, da camera e delle musiche per il teatro* (Archivio Nino Rota–Studi IV). Firenze: Leo S. Olschki, 2009.

Lupo, Salvatore. *Quando la mafia trovò l'America: Storia di un intreccio intercontinentale, 1880–2008*. Torino: Einaudi, 2008.

Mangione, Jerre and Ben Morreale. *La Storia: Five Centuries of the Italian American Experience*. New York: HarperCollins, 1992.

Marcus, Millicent. *Filmmaking by the Book: Italian Cinema and Literary Adaptation.* Baltimore, MD: Johns Hopkins University Press, 1993.

Masetti, Enzo (Ed.). *La musica nel film.* Roma: Bianco e Nero Editore, 1950.

Miceli, Sergio. "Fellini e la musica come personaggio (1952–1963)" in *Musica e cinema nella cultura del Novecento.* Firenze: Sansoni, 2000: 405–447.

———. *Musica per film: Storia, Estetica, Analisi, Tipologie.* Milano: Ricordi/LMI, 2009.

Monteleone, Franco. *Storia della radio e della televisione in Italia.* Venezia: Marsilio, 1992.

Morelli, Giovanni. "Mackie? Messer? Nino Rota e la quarta persona singolare del soggetto lirico" in *Storia del Candore: Studi in memoria di Nino Rota nel ventesimo della scomparsa* (Archivio Nino Rota–Studi III). Firenze: Leo S. Olschki, 2001: 355–429.

Murch, Walter. *In the Blink of an Eye: A Perspective on Film Editing.* Los Angeles: Silman-James Press, 2001.

Natella, Pasquale. *La parola "Mafia."* Firenze: Leo S. Olschki, 2002.

Niola, Marino. "La macchina del pianto" in *Sceneggiata: Rappresentazioni di un genere popolare,* ed. Pasquale Scialò. Napoli: Guida, 2001: 25–42.

Nowell-Smith, Geoffrey. *Luchino Visconti.* London: BFI Publishing, 2003.

Ondaatje, Michael. *The Conversations: Walter Murch and the Art of Editing Film.* New York: Alfred A. Knopf, 2002.

Phillips, Gene D. *Godfather: The Intimate Francis Ford Coppola.* Lexington: University Press of Kentucky, 2004.

Pinzauti, Leonardo. "A Colloquio con Nino Rota" in *Nuova Rivista Musicale Italiana,* V (1971): 74–83.

Plastino, Goffredo. "Open Textures: On Mediterranean Music" in *The Mediterranean in Music,* ed. David Cooper and Kevin Dawe. Lanham, MD: Scarecrow Press, 2005: 179–194.

Plebuch, Tobias. *Die Musik J. S. Bachs im Film.* Habilitation Thesis, Humboldt University–Berlin, 2009.

Puzo, Mario. *The Godfather: A Novel.* New York: G. P. Putnam's Sons, 1969.

———. *The Godfather Papers and Other Confessions.* New York: G. P. Putnam's Sons, 1972.

Ricci, Steven. *Cinema and Fascism: Italian Film and Society, 1922–1943.* Berkeley: University of California Press, 2008.

Riis, Jacob A. *How the Other Half Lives.* New York: Charles Scribner's Sons, 1890.

Rizzardi, Veniero (Ed.). *L'undicesima musa: Nino Rota e i suoi media.* Roma: RAI-ERI, 2001.

Rota-Rinaldi, Ernesta. *Mio padre e storia di Nino,* a cura di Francesco Lombardi. Comune di Reggiolo, 1999.

Sciannameo, Franco. "The Duke's Children" in *The Musical Times* (Summer 2006): 91–102.

———. *Nino Rota, Federico Fellini, and the Making of an Italian Cinematic Folk Opera: Amarcord.* Lewiston, NY: Edwin Mellen Press, 2005.

——— (Ed.). *Giuseppe Mazzini's Philosophy of Music (1836): Envisioning a Social Opera.* English translation by E.A.V. (1867). Edited and annotated by Franco Sciannameo. Lewiston, NY: Edwin Mellen Press, 2004.

———. "In Black and White: Pizzetti, Mussolini and Scipio Africanus" in *The Musical Times* (Summer 2004): 25–50.

Shackelford, Rudy (Ed.). *Dallapiccola on Opera.* London: Toccata Press, 1987.

Silverman, Deborah Anders. "Coppola, *Cavalleria,* and Connick: Musical Contributions to Epic in *The Godfather, Part III*" in *Mid-Atlantic Alamanack* 1 (1992).

Steiner, Edward A. *On the Trail of the Immigrant.* New York: Revell, 1906.

Summers, Anthony and Robbyn Swan. *Sinatra: The Life.* New York: Alfred A. Knopf, 2005.

Susca, Anselmo. "Il mio amico Nino Rota: Quel rapporto speciale fra un prete e un non cattolico" in *La repubblica* (10 marzo 2009): xi.

Talese, Gay. *Unto the Sons.* New York: Alfred A. Knopf, 1992.

Tarasti, Eero. *Myth and Music.* The Hague: Mouton Publishers, 1979.

———. *Signs of Music: A Guide to Musical Semiotics.* Berlin: Mouton de Gruyter, 2002.

Testa, Carlo. *Masters of Two Arts: Re-creation of European Literatures in Italian Cinema.* Toronto: University of Toronto Press, 2002.

Thomas, Sam. *Three Best American Screenplays.* New York: Crown Publishers, 1992.

Toffolo, Stefano. *Romeo e Giulietta e altri drammi Shakesperiani: Musica, Cinema e Letteratura dalle origini a Franco Zeffirelli e Nino Rota.* Padova: Edizioni Armelin Musica, 2002.

Van Order, M. Thomas. *Listening to Fellini: Music and Meaning in Black and White*. Fairleigh Dickinson University Press (Series in Italian Studies), 2009.

Verginelli, Vinci. *Bibliotheca Hermetica: Catalogo alquanto ragionato della Raccolta Verginelli–Rota di Antichi Testi Ermetici (secoli XV–XVIII)*. Firenze: Nardini Editore, 1986.

Westby, James. "Uno scrittore fantasma: A Ghostwriter in Hollywood" in *The Cue Sheet*, 15:2 (April 1999).

Wilson, Alexandra. *The Puccini Problem: Opera, Nationalism, and Modernity*. Cambridge: Cambridge University Press, 2007.

Zeffirelli, Franco. *The Autobiography of Franco Zeffirelli*. New York: Weidenfeld & Nicolson, 1986.

Index

About the Author

Franco Sciannameo is widely published in musicological and cultural studies from performance editions of classical and romantic music to issues concerning the role of artists in society. His most recent book is *Phil Trajetta (1777–1854): Patriot, Musician, Immigrant* (CMS Monographs and Bibliographies in American Music, Pendragon Press, 2010). Sciannameo is director and principal faculty of the BXA Intercollege Degree Programs at Carnegie Mellon University in Pittsburgh, Pennsylvania.

Breinigsville, PA USA
01 October 2010
246541BV00001B/2/P